@7.99

The Soviet–East German
military alliance

The Soviet–East German military alliance

DOUGLAS A. MACGREGOR

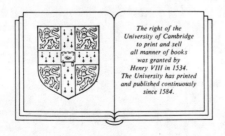

The right of the
University of Cambridge
to print and sell
all manner of books
was granted by
Henry VIII in 1534.
The University has printed
and published continuously
since 1584.

CAMBRIDGE UNIVERSITY PRESS

Cambridge
New York   Port Chester
Melbourne   Sydney

Published by the Press Sydnicate of the University of Cambridge
The Pitt Building, Trumpington Street, Cambridge CB2 1RP
40 West 20th Street, New York, NY 10011, USA
10 Stamford Road, Oakleigh, Melbourne 3166, Australia

First published 1989

Printed in Great Britain by Redwood Burn Ltd, Trowbridge, Wiltshire

British Library cataloguing in publication data
Macgregor, Douglas A.
The Soviet–East German military alliance.
1. Soviet Union. Military relations with East Germany.
2. East Germany. Military relations with the Soviet Union.
I. Title.
355′.033047.

Library of Congress cataloguing in publication data
Macgregor, Douglas A.
The Soviet–East German military alliance /
Douglas A. Macgregor.
     p.   cm'
Bibliography.
Includes index.
ISBN 0 521 36562 7
1. Soviet Union – Military policy. 2. Soviet Union – Military
relations – Germany (East). 3. Germany (East) – Military relations –
Soviet Union. 4. Germany (East) – Military policy. I. Title.
UA770.M24   1989.
355′.031′0947–dc19   89–7166 CIP

ISBN 0 521 36562 7

Contents

Foreword

S. N. MACFARLANE

The question of the role and reliability of non-Soviet forces in Warsaw Pact operations has enjoyed considerable attention recently. This is not surprising. The USSR's Eastern European allies make a sizable quantitative contribution to Warsaw Pact forces. Accurate threat assessment depends to some degree on an understanding of the significance of this contribution.

Western analysts have frequently dealt with the question of reliability in rather general terms. We are all familiar, for example, with the view that nationalism in Eastern Europe reduces considerably the reliability and hence utility of non-Soviet forces. But the Eastern European states are quite different one from another. Factors such as nationalism and resentment of the USSR impinge in different ways in each of the polities of the region. The USSR has over the years developed differentiated policies for dealing with each of its allies. For these reasons, it is difficult to generalize usefully about Soviet–East European relations.

There have been several notable efforts to deal with this problem through the preparation of anthologies, bringing analysts together to comment on the country of their expertise. Some of these have been very useful contributions to the literature on Soviet–East European military relations. But the limitations of the genre make it difficult to deal in a comprehensive fashion with each case. There is clearly room in the literature for monographs devoted to Soviet military relations with specific East European states. Condoleeza Rice's recent work on Soviet–Czech military relations provides an able and useful beginning to this effort.

Douglas MacGregor's *The Soviet–East German Military Alliance* continues it in a comprehensive and insightful analysis of the military relationship between the USSR and the German Democratic Republic. The book makes several important contributions to our understanding of the subject. His argument that in historical terms cooperation between Germany and Russia on regional security issues is as common as conflict is a useful corrective to the comfortable assumption that animosity between the two peoples runs so deep that there is no natural basis for cooperation between the two.

His stress on the critical role of the East German military both in Soviet force posture towards NATO and in Soviet efforts to maintain stability within the bloc – and particularly vis-à-vis Poland – demonstrates the centrality of the GDR in Soviet policy in Eastern Europe. This is particularly helpful since East Europeanists tend to focus on the Slavic states and Hungary in their analyses of the region while Germanists are predominantly West European in their orientation. As a result, the GDR has been insufficiently studied and its significance underappreciated. This is important in the security sphere, since Soviet–East German military relations are held up as a model for the rest of the bloc.

Two further attributes of this work should be highlighted. For those interested in civil–military relations in East European states, Dr MacGregor has provided a very useful characterization of relations between civilian and military elites and of the role of the military sector in the East German economy and society. Beyond this, the study breaks new ground in its analysis of the structure of Soviet–East German military integration. The latter aspect – and in particular the discussion of the structure of command – has important implications for assessing East German reliability.

In short, the work is a significant and overdue contribution to our understanding of relations between the USSR and what may be its most significant ally.

The University of Virginia

Preface

This book is about the nature and political consequences of institutionalized military cooperation between the East German and Soviet states in Central-East Europe. It was written not only for the specialist in Soviet and Warsaw Pact security studies but also for the student of European and international affairs in general.

In writing this work I relied on the patience and assistance of several people. Professor Neil MacFarlane of the University of Virginia guided me through the dissertation and the subsequent revisions that produced this book. Professors Vladimir Reisky, Paul Shoup, Audrey Kurth-Cronin, and Inis Claude provided useful criticism and constant encouragement. Colonel James Golden, Lieutenant Colonel John Reppert, Lieutenant Colonel Dick Norton, Major Jack Midgley and Major Jim Warner suggested many helpful revisions. I would also like to express my thanks to Dr Jeffrey R. Simon of the National Defense University, Mr Andrew Marshal, Director of the Office of Net Assessment, Office of the Secretary of Defense, my close friends in Germany, Werner Binder and Lore Freytag and, of course, my wife, Julie. I am, however, most deeply indebted to Lieutenant General William E. Odom, Director of the National Security Agency, and his wife Anne whose unrelenting confidence and support really made this work possible. None of these people or institutions should be held responsible for the views, arguments and deficiencies of this book.

Lastly, I would like to thank Colonel Lee Donne Olvey, Professor and Head of the Department of Social Sciences at West Point, who gave me the opportunity to write the study while I was teaching in the department. Colonel Olvey has been for many generations of army officers what George Kennan once said of Reinhold Niebuhr – "the intellectual father of us all."

Abbreviations

ADN	East German News Agency
CAF	Combined Armed Forces of the Warsaw Pact
CC	Central Committee
CDM	Council of Defense Ministers of the Warsaw Pact
CGSF	Central Group of Soviet Forces (in Czechoslovakia)
CMEA	Council of Mutual Economic Assistance
CPA	Czechoslovak People's Army
CPSU	Communist Party of the Soviet Union
CSCE	Conference on European Security and Cooperation
CSSR	Czechoslovak Socialist Republic
CST	Conventional Stability Talks
DM	Deutsche Mark; West Berlin and West German currency
FBIS	Foreign Broadcast Information Service
FDJ	Free Germany Youth Movement in East Germany
FRG	Federal Republic of Germany
GDR (DDR)	German Democratic Republic
GSFG	Group of Soviet Forces, Germany
HPA	Hungarian People's Army
INF	Intermediate Range Nuclear Forces
JPRS	*Joint Publications Research Service*
KGB	Soviet Committee for State Security
KPD	Communist Party of Germany
LRTNF	Long Range Theater Nuclear Forces
MBFR	Mutual and Balanced Force Reduction Talks
MC	Military Council of the Warsaw Pact
MD	Military District
MRD	Motorized Rifle Division
MVD	Soviet Ministry of Internal Affairs
NATO	North Atlantic Treaty Organization

NES	New Economic System
NGSF	Northern Group of Soviet Forces (in Poland)
NKFD	National Committee for a Free Germany
NKVD	Soviet People's Commissariat of Internal Affairs
NSWP	Non-Soviet Warsaw Pact
NVA	Nationale Volksarmee (National People's Army)
OMG	Operational Maneuver Group
PCC	Political Consultative Committee of the Warsaw Pact
PPA	Polish People's Army
PUWP	Polish United Worker's Party (ruling communist party in Poland)
RFE	Radio Free Europe
SAG	Sowjetische Aktiengesellschaft (Soviet limited company)
SBZ	Soviet Zone of Occupation
SED	Socialist Unity Party (ruling communist party in GDR)
SGSF	Southern Group of Soviet Forces (in Hungary)
SMAD	Soviet Military Administration
TASS	Telegraph Agency of the Soviet Union
TNK	Tank
TVD	Theater of Strategic Military Action or Theater of Military Operations
WTO	Warsaw Treaty Organization

Introduction

Since the founding of the Warsaw Pact in 1955, the Soviet Union has been both surprised and disappointed by the results of their efforts to forge a cohesive and responsive military alliance in the Warsaw Pact states. In fact, the periodic political convulsions that have become a regular occurrence in Poland and Eastern Europe have been an important source of insecurity for the Soviet imperium. For both Khrushchev and Brezhnev, the question of Eastern Europe eventually boiled down to "crisis management."[1]

The current conditions of economic stagnation and rising anti-Soviet nationalism in Poland, Czechoslovakia, Hungary and Romania are critical reminders that Gorbachev has inherited the traditional Soviet dilemma of how to cope with Eastern Europe: how to make this volatile and fervently nationalist region politically stable without tolerating genuine independence; how to permit movement toward some measure of autonomy without losing control;[2] and, how to elicit the active support of non-Soviet armed forces in the development of a reliable regional infrastructure for the westward movement of Soviet supplies and reinforcements along a 1,000 kilometer line of communications.

The major Warsaw Pact development over the past few years, however, has been the growing economic, political and, hence, military importance of the German Democratic Republic to the Soviet Union. Thanks to economic growth rates which the GDR's Pact neighbors can only envy, East German defense spending for military modernization has been sustained at a rate second only to that of the Soviet Union. Buttressed by a program of societal militarization and the most efficient suppression of internal political opposition and free speech in the Soviet Bloc, the GDR state seems capable of coping with any form of internal unrest.[3] At a time when Marshal Ogarkov is striving to develop the doctrine and force structure to support limited

1

theater conventional military operations, the Pact's Polish, Czecho-slovak and Hungarian ground forces often lack the equipment, training and motivation to perform their mission alongside their Soviet comrades. In contrast, today's East German forces are the best equipped, best led and the best trained of the Pact's non-Soviet forces. East German troops are kept in a state of continuous alert which "even Soviet troops – with the exception of the airborne forces – do not achieve."[4] This book seeks to explain this development.

Given East Germany's geographic position, it was probably inevitable that the GDR would serve as the bulwark of the Soviet military alliance system in Central-East Europe. In general strategic terms, the GDR's position in the Soviet Bloc today is analogous to that of Prussia in post-Napoleonic Europe. Just as Tsarist Russia relied on Prussia to help preserve Russian hegemony over Poland and to act as a Russian bridgehead against the West, the current Soviet Russian state counts on a politically and economically stable GDR to insulate its volatile European periphery from potentially destabilizing Western influences and to act as a glacis from which to project Soviet power and influence westward.

The GDR's emergence as the military linchpin of the Warsaw Pact has helped to sharpen the ongoing debate about the future of Eastern Europe. In many ways, the evolution of Soviet–East German military cooperation and the constant upgrading of their striking power have placed the GDR at the center of conflict among scholars and analysts over the changing contribution of the Pact's non-Soviet armed forces to the regional Soviet military effort. The question is whether the GDR's impressive military potential will compel Western scholars and analysts to look seriously at how armed forces allied with the Soviet Union may be structured to conduct joint military operations and how this capability may influence the outcome of a future crisis in the region.

Such an examination of the GDR's contribution to the Soviet military effort is long overdue. Neither the Soviets nor their Western counterparts appreciated the fact that like the Soviet political system, the GDR would be shaped by the historical conditions from which it emerged. Few observers in the postwar period appreciated the fact that East Germany's new communist leadership had inherited the remnants of a political system that was among the first in Europe to establish a standing army and to reorganize the modern state's administration in order to give it centralization, uniformity and a class of officials devoted to it.[5] In fact, for a quarter of a century, scholarship in the West ignored the GDR on the grounds that it was a transitory ·phenomenon that would "simply disappear from the European scene."[6]

This book examines the GDR's security role within the cooperative framework of the bilateral Soviet–East German military alliance. Chapter 1 looks at the forces for cohesion in Russo-Prussian relations before 1914, at military cooperation in the Weimar period, and at the military-political consequences of the Hitler-Stalin pact. The next three chapters examine the development of Soviet–East German military cooperation since the formation of the NVA in 1956, its value and limitations, and the utility of East German military power as an instrument of Soviet security policy in the 1980–81 Polish crisis. Chapter 5 discusses the importance of the GDR as a possible military model for the Pact's Northern Tier armies and concludes with some thoughts on the future of Soviet–East German military cooperation.

Although there has been general agreement on the quality of East German ground forces when compared with their Soviet and non-Soviet contemporaries,[7] it has been common in the West to treat the current Soviet–East German military alliance as a phenomenon unique in modern history, sharply distinguished not only from Nazi–Soviet military cooperation but also from earlier Soviet–German interwar collaboration and Russo–Prussian cooperation before World War I. This emphasis on the recent history of interstate hostility and conflict between Russians and Germans during World War II has led some analysts to discount the importance of Soviet–East German military cooperation on the basis of presumed German unreliability.[8]

And yet, the 1981 military coup which imposed martial law on Poland and crushed Solidarity initiated a period in the history and development of the Warsaw Pact that represented a departure from postwar Soviet history and experience. For the first time since 1939, thousands of Soviet and German troops were positioned to jointly invade and occupy Poland.[9] Still, very few Western political leaders and observers believed, even during the final chaotic months of Solidarity's struggle with Polish communism, in the possibility that an invasion of Poland would involve large-scale Soviet–East German military cooperation.

The slowness to recognize the GDR's important contribution to the stability of the Soviet Bloc reflects the widespread failure to appreciate the fact that the question of Soviet control over Eastern Europe is increasingly a matter of military power. For the Soviet Union, the GDR represents the military basis for Soviet hegemony over Central-East Europe and an important source of economic strength in the new round of Soviet military–industrial modernization efforts.[10] For the SED, Soviet support is vital in the GDR's political, economic and military competition with West Germany and the other states of the region. These points help to illustrate the degree to which Soviet–East German military cooperation currently depends on a set of political, economic and strategic relations that have changed little in the past 200 years of Russo-German relations.

The 1990s promise to be a period of considerable flux in East–West relations with Eastern Europe playing an important role in Europe's economic and security affairs. The Soviet Union has proposed a series of arms control measures in the context of CST, CSCE and START which could, if implemented, significantly reduce the Soviet military presence in the GDR, Poland and Czechoslovakia.[11] The interim agreements have already provided for the unprecedented exchange of military observers between the two Blocs and these may yield some valuable information concerning the execution of joint Soviet–East German military operations and the institutional framework surrounding them.[12] Although it is as yet unclear what the long-term implications of these proposals will be for the future of the Soviet–East German military alliance, any short-term reduction of Soviet conventional forces in the region will probably mean an increased role for East German forces in the Western TVD. The quality, readiness and forward area deployment of East German forces conform nicely to Marshal Ogarkov's emphasis on the need to launch offensive operations in the Western TVD in a state of peak readiness.[13] However, the single most important characteristic of the present situation is that the internal Soviet reform process overlaps with the need to address a lengthy agenda of economic and security issues that have accumulated in Eastern Europe over the last two decades.

If the Soviet Union is indeed entering an epoch of protracted systemic turmoil at home, it would seem to be only a matter of time until the East European populations seek to exploit this new domestic phase in Soviet "de-Stalinization" in order to achieve greater political and economic independence from Moscow. Several Western observers have already suggested that the 1990s may resemble the turbulent 1950s by noting that Gorbachev's reform and authority-building strategy echo many of the themes and points of style not seen since Khrushchev. (Like Khrushchev, Gorbachev is inexperienced in East European affairs.) Further, Gorbachev's approach "has the populism, the zest for change and experimentation and even some of the confrontational manner of Khrushchev."[14] All of these points suggest that whether or not Gorbachev retains his authority into the next decade and his reform efforts succeed, his legacy to the Soviet Bloc is likely to be one of political instability and socio-economic uncertainty.

To date, the reverberations of Gorbachev's campaign for more criticism and more information have been felt "unevenly" in Eastern Europe.[15] The impact of Glasnost' varies considerably from country to country. The SED under Honecker has responded skeptically at best to Gorbachev's reform initiatives or the adoption of Glasnost'.[16] Even more striking than the SED's disinterest in Gorbachev's programs is the absence of any Soviet pressure on the SED to change its social or economic policies to reflect the new emphasis in Moscow.[17]

It may be that Gorbachev understands better than anyone that economic weakness and rising anti-Soviet nationalism elsewhere in the region make the Warsaw Pact without East Germany irrelevant. Moreover, the reemergence of the "Polish problem" in the 1980s has reminded the Soviets that as long as the GDR remains economically and politically stable, the Soviet position in the region cannot be challenged and that the Soviet conventional military threat to Western Europe remains credible.

In sum, the consequences for the Soviet–East German military alliance of future Polish-type crises and greater Soviet assertiveness aimed at reinforcing its domination of Eastern Europe are likely to be profound. The military factor has become, and will continue to be, the critical element in Soviet–East German relations. This does not necessarily mean that military requirements have primacy over all other policy considerations, but rather that military requirements affecting the regional security interests of the two states will enjoy the highest priority. Thus, the possibility for resolving intra-Bloc conflicts in extreme ways will be maximised, and the Soviet tendency to rely on Soviet and East German military power to help preserve Soviet hegemony probably will grow.

United States Military Academy
West Point, New York

1 The legacy of success

Traditionally, Germany has played a major role not only in Russian foreign policy, but in the development of the Russian and Soviet military states. (See Tables 1a and 1b in the Appendix.) For the better part of three hundred years, neither the Prussian nor Russian states could have maintained their positions as leading European powers without the political, diplomatic, technological and military assistance of the other. After the Treaty of Versailles, the political isolation of the Soviet Union and Weimar Germany served as the catalyzing influence for a restoration of political–military cooperation on the pre-war model as well.

In this instance, the historical record reveals that Russo-German collaboration in military affairs is neither extraordinary nor new. Whenever the threats to German and Russian security interests appeared to be growing and the corresponding capacity to manage these threats independently seemed to be inadequate to the task, the leaders of the German and Russian states have readily turned to one another for support. Perhaps the important point to be noted here is that what distinguishes this illustration of interstate military cooperation from a simple function of the law of opposite boundaries or *Gesetz der Gegengrenzlichkeit* is the remarkable history of success which Russo-German military cooperation has achieved and the West's consistent failure to appreciate the recurring incidence of mutually reinforcing political interests which buttressed this success.

In this context, a German military relationship with Russia has not only offered Germany tangible economic benefits and material military assistance, but, equally important, military cooperation with the Germans has given Russia a channel of entry into European affairs and access to Western technology. Cooperation between the two states has also purchased a modicum of security for the two partners.

This was true for Peter the Great, Frederick the Great, Catherine the Great, Adolf Hitler and Joseph Stalin in their pursuit of independent, but complementary political objectives. Thus, the development of an active military relationship between the Germans and the Russians has always depended to a large extent on the two states' perception of common strategic interests, rather than on a cultural–political predisposition to assist each other in the sense of the Anglo-American experience. Nevertheless, a certain similarity of internal political development coupled with a mutuality of political needs has made it both desirable and possible for the Russians and Germans to establish surprisingly close and effective military ties.

The origins of cooperation

Russia's early contacts with the German-speaking world were largely a product of her quest for allies in the protracted war with Poland and Sweden. Predictably, the impact of the German factor and influence symbolized by the German physical presence in Moscow was felt most keenly in Russia's growing military establishment.[1] Under this foreign management, the Russian Army began the most dramatic expansion of its entire history, increasing from the more or less standard size of about 100,000 to roughly 300,000 troops in the late 1660s. Most of the officers and many of the ordinary soldiers continued to be imported from North European Protestant countries, "so that a good fourth of this swollen army was foreign."[2] As a result, when a dynamic Swedish state asserted itself in the Baltic and threatened the security interests of not only Russia, but Northern Germany's small but numerous principalities as well, the Russian predisposition to cooperate with the North Germans in order to guarantee the effectiveness of the Tsar's army was simply reinforced.

After the Swedes defeated the Russian Army at Narva in 1700 and frustrated Russian imperial aims in the Baltic littoral, Peter the Great turned anxiously to the West in search of scientific and educational assistance in order to effect the further modernization and reorganization of Russia's military forces. Peter I had already traveled through Riga and Königsberg to Central Germany, Holland and England. This earlier visit to Germany had offered Peter the opportunity to meet and to know North Germany's aristocratic leadership and to plan the marriages of Russia's leading aristocrats to North German Princesses. Eventually, Peter's prudent diplomacy produced important political results for Russia, and among the Germans, for Prussia. By 1715, Prussian troops were cooperating in the field with Russian armies against the Swedes. When the peace treaties of Stockholm and Nystad were finally agreed to in 1720–21, the Swedes ceded vast tracts of land around the Baltic to both Russia and Prussia. Prussia acquired Pomerania and Russia absorbed Eastern Karelia and part of the Baltic littoral.

Still, Peter's enthusiasm for the West and especially Prussia should not be exaggerated. Peter's efforts to accelerate Russia's modernization with mainly German assistance were almost completely focused on scientific, technical and linguistic matters of immediate military or diplomatic value to Russia.[3] Peter I did not significantly change Russia's traditional cultural–political insularity. His admiration and respect for Prussia seems to have been more a function of his own desire to create an effective military state apparatus at home rather than of his cultural affinity for the Germans. In addition, collaboration with the North German Princes, notably Brandenburg-Prussia, was, in a territorial sense, a mutually beneficial security arrangement. Eventually, Peter's admiration for the enlightened methods of German civil administration led him to guarantee his German subjects along the Baltic coast their religious freedom, existing class privileges and the continuation of their political–administrative status quo. This admiration for the German "administrative clock which functioned smoothly and with regularity"[4] extended to the military sphere as well. After all, Peter and the Prussian monarchs who became his allies and friends shared an interest in the achievement of maximum military power since both the early Prussian and Russian states relied heavily on their military establishments to acquire new territory and to play a domestic role in establishing social order.

The Prussian preference for former soldiers, officers and noncommissioned officers in civil administrative offices gave a distinctly military character to the Prussian bureaucracy since it was composed of men who were accustomed to obey. The reliance on military cadres to carry on the daily operations of the Prussian state placed virtual control of the country's economic life under the military commissariat – in modern terms the ministry of defense.[5] This militarization of Prussian society had important consequences for Prussia's rise to power in Central Europe.

Frederick William I completed the weapon that made the conquest of Silesia possible, established a financial administration so efficient that the income greatly exceeded the normal expectations of so small and poor a state, and molded the bourgeois–military elements of the civil service into a bureaucracy which with the army became the very backbone of the Prussian state.[6]

Small wonder that Peter adopted the Prussian–German system of an administrative rank structure in the form of the Table of Ranks, which required state service. Both Peter and Prussia's eighteenth-century rulers induced their noble classes to serve in a primarily military capacity. In support of this system, the toiling masses of agrarian peasants in both countries were also forced to supply the Prussian and Russian states with military manpower, as elaborate schemes for recruit mobilization and control were imposed on the countryside.[7] The fact that Prussia's first King had acted to destroy local self-government and to successfully center the administrative state in the cabinet of the King[8] inspired Peter to follow the Prussian prescription and forge a powerful standing army, reorganize the national administration to give it a centralized character and to create a class of elite officials who would be loyal servants of the crown.

In all the important branches of eighteenth-century Russian civil-military administration, the Germans made their influence felt. However, the adoption of German civil and military institutions and the influence of native Germans in Russian service was limited by the persisting cultural insularity, which also prevented Russia from participating in the broader political developments of eighteenth and nineteenth-century Western Europe.

While religious freedom flourished under Frederick the Great, Russians regarded the church as an arm of the state. Under Catherine the Great, who succeeded Peter III, the efforts to foster the development of an efficient German-style bureaucracy, which would be distinct from the nobility, failed and the Russian state bureaucracy remained welded to the Russian nobility. Furthermore, this alliance did not imply the crown's dependence on the nobility. On the contrary, the Tsar delegated to the nobility only "functions," not "power."[9]

As if to emphasize Russia's separate identity and resistance to German cultural influence, an eighteenth-century Russian officer remarked that while the Russian officers and soldiers dressed in Prussian-like uniforms, "their souls remained Russian."[10] In more important ways than language, Russian soldiers were culturally isolated from their enemies. Indeed, they were so accustomed to coercion whether they were serfs or soldiers, that desertion did not pose the problem in eighteenth-century Russian armies that it did in the Western European armies of the same period.[11]

In addition to the Russo-Prussian preoccupation with the amassing of military power and the common ancestral ties which united the Romanovs and the Hohenzollerns, Russo-Prussian military cooperation was also buttressed by external factors which positioned the two states in the world arena. Political instability in Poland and the later appearance of Jacobin France in 1789 produced a host of Russo-Prussian agreements based on a shared political conservatism (see Table 1b). These agreements contributed to the great power consensus which led to the partitioning of Poland between Prussia, Russia and Austria.

With the passage of time, it became increasingly clear to Russia's ruler, Catherine, that "Jacobinism" and limited enthusiasm for revolutionary political change had struck some roots in Poland. In Warsaw, hostility to Russian political influence and religious orthodoxy had always poisoned relations between the two peoples, but the impact of the French revolution combined the effects of war against the hated Russians with political instability at home. At the same time, the bulk of the Russian Army was stationed on the Turkish border in order to guard against the threat of war with the Turkish sultanate.[12] These conditions forced Russian reliance on the Prussians, who were eager to cooperate with the Russians in return for a share of Polish territory. By mid-July 1794, political revolution in Poland had sparked a general war in which 25,000 Prussian and 14,000 Russian troops under joint Russian and Prussian command were advancing on Warsaw. However, the Prussian Army's skillful and rapid advance into Poland (the Russians were still mobilizing and shifting forces for the final assault on Warsaw) made an agreement with Austria imperative in order to offset Prussia's territorial gains. According to her memoirs, Catherine reasoned that Russia was stronger than any of the German powers and could rely on the fact that they would never unite against Russia; one at least would always be allied with Russia.[13] This placed southern Poland under Austrian control and much of western Poland under Prussian administration. As a result of the last partition of Poland in 1795 in which Poland vanished from the map completely, Russia gained roughly the same territory that Stalin secured in a similar agreement with Hitler in 1939.

In the wars against Napoleon, conditions similar to those in revolutionary Poland served to unify Prussia and Russia. Between 1812 and 1815, Russo-Prussian military–political cooperation reached a zenith as Russians and Prussian regiments and officers fought shoulder to shoulder in a series of bloody campaigns to defeat the French armies.

Prussian ministers of war, finance and state served the Tsar, as well as the King of Prussia. Stein, Yorck, Boyen, Nesselrode and Diebitsch

– all Germans – played important roles in the political, diplomatic and military process of defeating Napoleon and restructuring the European state system after Napoleon. Finally, Russian military strength was used to reinvigorate the Prussian Army, which had been weakened through years of neglect under French occupation.[14]

The Prussian Army in this period owed its existence to Russian support. Russian and Prussian military equipment, tactics and organization were indistinguishable.[15] Prussian military cooperation with the Tsar after 1809 exacted a price, though not an especially high one. As a result of the Congress of Vienna, Russia's borders pushed farther West and the same Russian military assistance which had restored Prussia to health also turned out to be adequate to contain Prussian power in Eastern Europe.

From the standpoint of political circumstances in 1815, the extension of Russian influence and power into Central Europe at Prussia's expense may have seemed probable, if not inevitable. However, in the years after Napoleon's defeat, Russia's internal political weakness prevented the Tsar from aspiring to much more than was achieved at the Congress of Vienna and Prussia was able to retain her independence. In fact, the pattern of events that unfolded in the "liberated" atmosphere of post-Napoleonic Europe recast militant Prussia in a new role as a stable link in the chain of states on Russia's European periphery. Again, German capabilities matched Russian needs.

By 1848, revolutionary upheavals in Hungary, France and Poland had acted to further reinforce the already existing convergence of elite political interests in Berlin and St. Petersburg. Tsar Nicholas and his father-in-law, Frederick William III of Prussia, pledged to aid one another should revolution imperil their rule and authority. As it turned out, it was the Prussian Army which assisted the Russians in restoring Russian rule in Poland. Nicholas meanwhile stated publicly that he would not allow Prussia to "lose a single village"[16] if Russia were compelled to intervene in Prussia, as she later did in Austria, to put down subversive elements.

Not unexpectedly, Tsar Nicholas' preference for Prussian soldiers and statesmen became so pronounced that some Russian commanders began to resent the presence of German influence in the Tsar's General Staff and court. When Tsar Nicholas I asked Russia's famous field commander, General Mikhail Yermolov, what favor he would like in reward for his service to the empire in the Caucasus, Yermolov replied: "To be born a German, for then I shall be able to get all that I want in Russia."[17] Nicholas was only just beginning to feel the influence of a Russian nationalism which would inflame subsequent generations of Russians. In later years, Otto von Bismarck recalled the undercurrent of anti-German sentiment in the younger generations of Russians during his first tour as the German confederation's representative to St Petersburg in 1859[18] when Russia's leading ministers of state were often German and the one million man Russian Army resembled a Prussian Army writ large.[19]

Thanks to the good offices of Bismarck and the relationships which he forged with the Tsar and his ministers, Prussia enjoyed Russia's benevolent support for her ambitions during the nineteenth century. Ultimately, the Tsar's interest in disengaging the anti-Russian Austria from internal German affairs empowered Prussia to unite the German nation under Berlin's leadership. Unfortunately, Prussia–Germany repaid Russia for her assistance by opting for Austria–Hungary as the more reliable of the two allies. Despite this setback to Russo-German relations and even after Austro-Russian rivalry in the Balkans threatened the peace of Europe, Alexander III joined his friend and cousin, the Kaiser, and the Austrian Emperor in the 1887 Reinsurance Treaty, which assured Russia, Germany and Austria the neutrality of the others should one of them become involved in a war with a third power. More importantly, this treaty committed Germany to support Russian interests in Bulgaria and the straits.[20] For the German Chancellor, Otto von Bismarck, the alliance with Austria changed nothing in Germany's relations with Russia. The Russo-German alliance continued to take precedence and to remain the imperative of his foreign policy until his dismissal.[21]

Thus, in the 1880s, when the press in both Russia and Germany initiated campaigns of slander against one another's countries, Bismarck sought to defuse German fears by insisting that "Russia wishes to conquer no German land and we desire to conquer no Russian land." Helmuth von Moltke, chief of the German General Staff after 1871, in a rare public statement, had supported Bismarck's contention by describing Russia as a country "with absolutely nothing which could be taken from them even after the most victorious war. They have no gold and we have no need of land."[22]

However, the Tsars, who do not seem to have supported the anti-German sentiment in Russia's press, could not restrain their aspirations to gain control of a leaderless Pan-Slavic movement in order to exploit its potential for Russian expansion in the Balkans.[23] When the emotionally charged issues of imperial expansion were added to the demands for protection from foreign competition of Russian industrialists and German agrarians, the pro-German orientation of Russia's Tsars was placed under extreme pressure. In addition, domestic pressures on the German government to reduce German investment in Russia and reorient trade to other East European and overseas markets created new points of friction in relations between the two states.

With the closing of German financial markets to capital-starved Russia from midsummer 1887 on, the stage was set for a change in the course of Russo-German relations.[24] More important, Bismarck's dismissal from office in 1888 cleared the way for a new stream of consciousness in German foreign policy which was to struggle for dominance in Germany's foreign office against the conservative Prussian legacy of cooperation with Tsarist Russia. In contrast to Bismarck, who had consistently disabused the Austrians of their hopes for German support in a Balkan war with Russia, Wilhelm II allowed extreme nationalist elements in the political and military leadership of the German empire to encourage the Austrians to believe that an Austro-German assault on Russia was desired in Berlin.[25]

When the Reinsurance Treaty was allowed to lapse in 1890, Tsar Alexander III undertook to establish a new rapport with the French which would lead to the Franco-Russian alliance of 1894. This new alliance offered Russia a partial escape from the isolation and dependence that reliance on German military and diplomatic strength had fostered. In any relationship with a powerful, united Germany, Alexander III had come to realize that Russia's economic backwardness condemned her to be the junior partner. With France, as with Prussia before German unification, it was the Russians who were sought after most. Still, Germany continued to be Russia's number one trading partner, receiving 41 percent of Russia's exports and supplying 35 percent of her imports in 1902 – vastly more than France.[26]

Predictably, the mutually beneficial trade relations, which years of Russo-Prussian collaboration had fostered, declined precipitously in the last years preceding World War I. Germany began directing much of its trade away from Russia to the smaller trading states in the Danube valley.[27] At the same time, the rapid advance of German foreign trade created anxieties of a new type for Imperial Germany.

Always aware of the limited resources at home, Germany's leadership began to search for new ways to avoid increasing dependence on foreign countries for resources and markets. Russia's unanticipated advances in the areas of manufacturing and industrial production after 1900 alarmed the Germans, who preferred that Russia remain rural, underdeveloped and heavily dependent on German capital, business enterprises, managerial and scientific experts. Between 1870 and 1900, Russia's share of world steel output rose from 2 to 8 percent, putting Russia ahead of France – 4.8 versus 4.6 million tons. Though this improved industrial productivity seems impressive enough, Russia's output still represented only one-fifth the amount of steel produced by German mills on a per capita basis.[28]

There would appear, in all of this, to be a strong connection between the growth of modern nationalism and the decline in strength of the Russo-German connection in the late nineteenth century. Whereas German influence in the eighteenth century had been accepted because it seemed to advance Russian national pride and power, in the late nineteenth century German influence in Russia's cultural, scientific–industrial and military development stood for "a willingness to embrace the West in humble backwardness, as if it would be better to be the provincial backyard of Europe than to be independent and truly Russian."[29] In favor of the German orientation was, of course, the Tsars' own largely German background. All of the nineteenth-century Tsars had either married German Princesses or had been exposed at an early age to Western culture and civilization through the eyes of German educators, tutors, advisors and family members. Unfortunately, Russian suppression of Polish, Hungarian and Turkic Caucasian revolutionary armies conveyed the message to most West Europeans that Russia's true character was "Asiatic, despotic, and brutally aggressive when not subtly subversive."[30]

Eventually, the ascension to power of a Tsar and a Kaiser who lacked the intellect and the understanding to guide political and economic development caused the coincidence of strategic vision with decisive authority in both countries to vanish. In Russia, the gap between an immobile state and a dynamic society only worsened in the years just before and after 1900.[31] Russian citizens spoke more openly about the bureaucratic state and its headquarters in St Petersburg being an "alien and Germanic creation on Russian soil."[32] More significantly, Russian revolutionary expectations and aspirations survived the Tsar's attempts to eradicate them. While the Prussian–German state could temporarily contain the social–political discontent which simmered just beneath the surface it could not easily accommodate the dynamics of political and social change in a new industrial age either. Eventually, it would take the ruination of the Imperial German and Russian state systems as a result of World War I to partially recreate the conditions for cooperation which Peter I and Frederick I had discovered and carefully nurtured two hundred years earlier.

In sum, during the period 1701 to 1914, Russo-German relations appeared to demonstrate both stability and change. The two states' urge to collaborate for strategic and geopolitical reasons was ultimately balanced by the propensity of essentially incompatible nationalisms to come into conflict. Specific historical circumstances determined which tendency won out at any given point. While the two regimes appeared to consciously avoid contentious issues in the international arena before 1871, the substantial increase in German political, economic and military power *vis-à-vis* Russia after unification made conflict in certain areas unavoidable. With the gradual disappearance of a generation of ruling elites in both states who had shunned further territorial expansion in Central Europe in favor of stability, a new generation of leaders infused with the spirit of nationalism embarked on an expansionist course that made conflict a virtual certainty.

The resumption of cooperation after World War I

The postwar Russian and German states were shaped by the military, economic and political conditions in which they emerged from World War I. The war had been particularly devastating for Germany and Russia. Not only had the ancient regimes in both states been replaced, the successor regimes were in several important ways different from their predecessors.

Seven million Russian troops had perished in a catastrophic military defeat. Superior German military technology and manpower had exposed agrarian Russia's military and economic weakness. Millions more died in the struggle for power which ensued after the Bolshevik seizure of power in 1917. Out of this situation three critical features of the postwar Russian political order emerged. While the Bolshevik state itself constituted a new ruling class of sorts, the organizing imperative of the Soviet polity became industrialization and the modernization of the Russian military establishment. Second, the ideological orientation of the new ruling elite created conditions of hostility between Bolshevik Russia and her neighboring states, particularly Poland. And, third, Russia's relations with the rest of the world were conditioned by the need for Western technology.

Germany's imperial monarchy was succeeded by a republican structure of power that never won the allegiance of the German military elite or the trust of its population. In the series of domestic crises which gripped the new republic, the postwar pretence of professional military elite neutrality in social matters and diplomatic questions was abandoned in favor of more military intervention into the domestic and foreign affairs of the Weimar government. Domestically, the German military elite saw itself in a fight to the finish with socialists, communists and their paramilitary equivalents. In foreign affairs, the German military aims centered on the restoration of the 1914 borders and the reversal of Germany's defeat in World War I.

Such, in outline, were the political and military effects of World War I on Russia and Germany. For Western observers, these developments seemed to establish conclusively that cooperation between the two states was very unlikely.

When one of Germany's representatives to the negotiations at Versailles, Count Brockdorff-Rantzau, warned Woodrow Wilson and Lloyd George that the policy of the Western powers might give rise in Germany to an ideology which would combine nationalism with socialism or communism, neither of the Western statesmen took the warning seriously.[33] The prospect of cooperation between two inherently anti-status quo powers – anti-Versailles Germany and anti-capitalist Russia – seemed to European and American statesmen of the day highly unlikely. Yet, for both, the Western Entente was the common enemy. The fact that the Germans thought in terms of nations and the Bolshevik Russians in terms of classes shrank to insignificance next to their shared disdain for a despised, Western-imposed postwar status quo.[34]

Within two years of Germany's humiliation at Versailles, the more conservative Prussian elements of the German General Staff began to reassert themselves to seek political allies in the Weimar government who shared an interest in reviving the old patterns of cooperation with Russia. The Prussian core of the German Army, with its history of collaboration with the Russian military establishment, had survived the war in sufficient health to effect changes in German foreign policy. When the Treaty of Rapallo was signed by Germany and the Soviet Union in April 1922, it formally recognized a coincidence of interest which Lenin and the German generals had sought to restore in the months immediately following World War I.

Shortly after World War I, General Hans von Seeckt, chief of the postwar German Army, secretly dispatched a military mission to open direct negotiations with the Bolsheviks concerning possible military cooperation with the Soviet Union. Indeed, within two years of the war's end, von Seeckt had told his officers that a future understanding with Greater Russia should be the "permanent target of Germany's foreign policy."[35] Without official sanction, von Seeckt's agent in Russia, Enver Pasha, was already exploring the possibility of restoring the borders of 1914 as it appeared in August 1920 that Poland was doomed to be reannexed to Russia. Karl Radek, foreign policy advisor to Lenin, recalled that the German agents in Moscow were interested in striking a bargain "with the Communist Party and with Soviet Russia; they understand that we can not be conquered and that we are Germany's allies in the struggle with the Entente."[36]

With a renewed sense of confidence in the Bolshevik revolution's capacity to survive, Lenin turned his attention to the West and to the prospects of a land bridge through Poland to Central and Western Europe. In 1920, Lenin perceived political and economic events in Europe as developing along the lines which Marx had predicted in the nineteenth century. These perceptions buttressed the unquestioning confidence of Russia's ruling communist elites in the validity of the Russian revolutionary experience and its applicability to the rest of Europe.[37] Lenin's confidence supported the popular view that the westward expansion of Soviet Russia's borders would eventually join the revolutionary masses of Soviet Russia with the modern industrialized states of Western Europe. According to this analysis, events in postwar Germany paralleled those which had already occurred in Russia before 1917. Lenin constantly reassured his followers in Russia that the Germans were forming "Red Armies" of their own and were becoming "more and more inflamed" with each passing day.[38]

Proletarian socialist internationalism, Lenin claimed, would soon supplant nationalism as a unifying force to erase national distinctions and defeat international capital. The Red Army would then "plant its candidates in the respective European capitals."[39] Clearly, these beliefs imputed a cohesiveness and a consciousness to the working classes of Germany and the rest of Europe which were more imagined than real.

With the goal of reaching revolutionary Germany in mind, Lenin formulated his plans for the expansion of revolution through reactionary, "white" Poland on the bayonets of the Red Army to Germany. Lenin explained the conflict with Poland, which was then developing, in terms which revealed his continuing preoccupation with Germany. "We ought to recognize that [the creation of Poland] this has been done to strengthen the barrier and deepen that Gulf which separates us from the proletariat of Germany ... But they will only succeed in founding another Soviet state through which we will gain close relations with the proletariat of the West."[40]

For Lenin, Poland's destruction was an important intermediate objective in the campaign to erect a Soviet Socialist State on German soil in place of the new Weimar government. If Lenin's war with Poland achieved nothing else, it had to destroy Polish independence from Moscow in order for the Bolshevik revolution to reach its real, permanent target: Germany.

Despite Lenin's failure to create a German state on the Soviet model in 1920, the myth of a German revolution and the promise of eventual victory persisted in Lenin's thinking. Today, it is difficult to imagine the disappointment which the contradictory quality of the Bolshevik revolution in Russia must have caused in Bolshevik hearts in later years. Formulating excuses for the failure of revolution in the country where Marx had always predicted it – Germany – became a major enterprise for Lenin.

However, the Russian and German interest in removing a neighbor aligned with their mutual enemy – the Entente – insured that the peace agreements between Poland and Russia in 1921 would be tenuous and temporary in character. This did not alter the fact that from the Soviet perspective control of Germany remained the key to the rest of Europe. On the contrary, this condition guaranteed that some measure of cooperation between Germans and Russians would be restored.

After the Red Army's defeat in front of Warsaw, the Bolshevik leadership abandoned unilateral military action in Eastern Europe. Thus, the combined resentment in Germany against Versailles and the Soviet Union's failure to Sovietize Poland served in many ways to keep Germany at the center of Soviet long-term revolutionary aspirations. After all Marx had promised that revolution would come to Germany with the decline of capitalism and the collapse of world imperialism. And Lenin had not forgotten the benevolent neutrality of the German working classes during the Soviet Union's fight with Poland or, for that matter, the readiness of some elements in the German Army to intervene against Poland on the Soviet side. Hence, a relationship with the new German Republic offered many bright possibilities: (1) Germany could provide a channel of entry into the affairs of Europe which no other Western state would dare provide; (2) German technology could ultimately be harnessed to the task of reinvigorating the prostrate Soviet economy and military establishment; and (3) collaboration with the Germans could lead to the eventual liquidation of the independent, anti-Soviet Polish state on the Soviet Union's western frontier.

When the former World War I Allies met in 1922 at Genoa, Italy to consider the problems of German war debt and Soviet international status, the German and Russian representatives abandoned the conference and moved to Rapallo, where they quickly concluded a treaty specifying friendly relations and limited economic cooperation. Predictably, this event surprised the entire international diplomatic community, including several key members of the German foreign office![41] Again, little consideration had been given in the West to the geopolitical factors that positioned the two states in the world arena.

For the Germans who had despaired of any hope of building support in the West for a revival of German participation in a Europe on the pre-war model, the Soviet Union offered space and secrecy to develop and experiment with forbidden weapons and tactics, as well as an inexhaustible supply of cheap, natural resources.[42] However, *rapprochement* with Russia on a grand public scale beyond the terms of the 1922 Soviet–German Treaty of Rapallo was impossible since it might have led to the further isolation of Germany and to a potentially dangerous dependence on the Soviet Union. Germany's military relations with Russia in the period 1922–31 would of necessity be conducted in secret and on the basis of narrow, mutually advantageous arrangements in the field of avionics, mechanization and chemical warfare.[43] German industry was quick to seize the opportunity presented by the resumption of Russo–German economic cooperation. Krupp agricultural machines and technicians were sent in to plow up 65,000 acres in the Caspian steppe and the Soviet Union became the only foreign country to receive Krupp's new locomotives. Krupp technicians were also dispatched to Russia where they supervised the manufacture of artillery shells on assembly lines in the Urals and at the famous Putilov arms factory in Leningrad.[44] Although monetary difficulties in Germany and a Soviet interest in creating an indigenous military production capability eventually combined to limit the effectiveness of German industrial assistance,[45] the production lines in Russia did produce some 400,000 grenades for export to Germany and 300 aircraft, of which the Soviets kept 100, leaving 200 for the Germans.[46] Thanks to Soviet cooperation all of these deliveries went undetected by the 600 allied inspectors of German disarmament.

All of these developments were orchestrated under the auspices of the German military agency *Sondergruppe R* – the Reichswehr-directed company established in Berlin and Moscow under the innocent name "Society for the Promotion of Industrial Enterprises," and known from its German initials as "GEFU."[47] While economic cooperation diminished with the onset of the depression, the collaboration of Soviet and German officers in the field of military training was much more successful and from the standpoint of Soviet–German military relations, more significant.

As early as February 1922, Karl Radek had approached von Seeckt with the proposal that German officers should assist in the education and training of senior Soviet officers. After negotiations between members of the two armies' military leaderships, agreements were reached under which the Germans were granted military bases in the Soviet Union and the Soviets were given access to German military data and technology.[48] In this atmosphere of cooperation, particularly cordial, even warm relations developed between General Blomberg, German Defense Minister, and Marshal Voroshilov, Soviet Defense Minister. However, to what extent the two sides benefited from this cooperation is still open to debate.

From the Germans, the Soviets definitely acquired modern training techniques and witnessed the German methods of organization employed in a force dedicated to the idea of cadre and the exploitation of ultra-modern military technology.[49] One hundred and twenty senior Soviet officers also received training in German military schools including the clandestine War Academy in Berlin. According to German sources, these officers included some of the Red Army's finest commanders in World War II; among them Timoshenko and Zhukov. As a result, German military literature proliferated in the Red Army and von Seeckt's works on training, discipline and leadership were widely read. Not surprisingly, the Soviet officers in Berlin were considered some of the War Academy's best students. A former German General Staff officer of the period described those attending in very positive terms. According to this observer, while the Red Army officers longed for the glorious military past of Tsarist Russia and exhibited a strong affinity for German concepts of duty in their expressions of patriotism and duty to the fatherland, they were also visibly impressed and inspired by the quality and competence of the German officer corps.[50]

Some would suggest that this intimate exposure to the German Army infused the rough-hewn Red Army officers with some of the professional *savoir faire* of the ancient Prussian officer corps. Of course, some German officers of the period were less certain of this fact. Former General Helm Speidel, for instance, depicts cooperation as having been correct at best and fraught with the usual problems of Soviet secretiveness and xenophobia.[51] Naturally, Soviet sources credit the Germans with having done nothing to accelerate Soviet military modernization.

What is certain is that the presence of a German tank school in the vicinity of Kazan, a German air force training station at Lipetsk with 60 German instructors and 100 technicians and a German-operated poison gas school at Volsk had an effect on the modernization of the Red Army. During the period 1923 to 1932, the Soviet chief of the Mechanization and Motorization Administration was able to effect important exchanges of tank equipment between the Germans and the Russians and to retain control of key industrial components when the Germans withdrew. Tukhachevsky, Frunze and Voroshilov were all quick to point to the tremendous advances which Soviet military development was able to make in this crucial period of modernization thanks to German assistance.[52]

However, by 1932, Stalin was inching his way out of Rapallo and Soviet overtures to the West were receiving a new hearing in France and Britain. This created conditions which offered alternatives to exclusive cooperation with the Germans. And while Stalin continued to take all the military training and technical assistance that the Germans would provide, he quickly signed a non-aggression pact with the French which promised Soviet acquiescence in the anti-German territorial status quo. Meanwhile, the rise of Hitler in German politics made further military relations increasingly difficult. Hitler's public statements made no secret of his distaste for communism or the Slavic/Eurasian populations of the Soviet Union. Soviet–German political and military relations seemed to be taking another turn for the worse.

Nazi–Soviet collaboration

To the foreign observer in 1933, the spectacle of Nazi–Soviet polemics seemed to confirm the popular notion that Russian and German national interests would remain unalterably opposed as they had been during World War I. Above all, the West's best political analysts failed to note any mutually beneficial connection between Germany's fate and that of Russia. The idea that a community of interest between the two states could ever exist again after the installation of National Socialism does not seem to have been taken seriously.[53]

Of course, Western skepticism on this point was well-founded. Hitler's treatment of the Soviet Union in *Mein Kampf* suggested that German *rapprochement* with Russia was incomprehensible. Accord-

ing to Hitler's plans, Russia was to be the target of German coloni-
zation after its inhabitants had been deported or killed.

As for the Soviet Union's attitudes toward Germany, Stalin's
ruthless military–industrialization program for the Soviet Union and
his apparent orchestration of the international communist conspi-
racy through the Comintern convinced most observers that neither
state could realize any tactical or strategic political advantage from
collaboration.[54] Why then did the infamous Molotov–Ribbentrop
agreement make sense to the two ostensibly hostile states? What
military, economic and political benefits did the two sides think that
they would derive from cooperation which transcended the values
and preferences of the individual leaders involved?

Observing in 1933 that Germany and Russia were in fact linked by
strong, enduring mutual interests, Hitler's line of reasoning tended to
parallel Lenin's earlier postwar assessment of Soviet–German relations in that the two states shared essentially the same enemies and
interests.

The Soviets, for example, must be concerned about their eastern frontier,
while Germany must be concerned about her western frontier. Germany faces
a hard situation, but that of the Soviets is not easy. In both instances, as in
many others, one must remember all the time that the two countries can
complement one another and render mutual services.[55]

Unknown to Hitler, Stalin's antipathy for the German Social
Democrats and his distrust of the German communist party leadership predisposed Stalin to consider Nazi–Soviet cooperation long
before the thought had entered Hitler's mind.[56] Stalin had continued
to steer Soviet diplomacy with the goal of preventing those in the
Weimar German government who favoured cooperation with the
Anglo-American led West from disengaging Germany from Russia.
Stalin seems to have reasoned that a liberal democratic Germany
would ultimately be drawn into alignment with the West and join the
anti-Soviet camp. On the other hand, a nationalistic, revanchist,
illiberal, anti-democratic and anti-status quo National Socialist
Germany might turn on the West and fulfill Stalin's war and revolution scenario. This is not to suggest that either Hitler or Stalin
ceased to contemplate the possibility of war between them one day.

Stalin did appreciate the military threat which Hitler represented,
but he saw immediate overriding tactical and strategic advantages in
various types of mutually beneficial cooperation, especially after his
unsuccessful search for anti-Hitler allies in the West, first during
1932-33 and later between 1936 and 1939. Thus, Hitler's extreme

hatred for Russia and Soviet communism seem to have been viewed as secondary in importance to Hitler's threat to overturn the unpopular status quo of Versailles.[57]

Consequently, when the opportunity to aid and abet the Nazi seizure of power presented itself in 1933, Stalin had his reasons for restraining the German communists (KPD) from cooperating with the German Social Democrats in a united anti-fascist front to defeat Hitler. Whether or not such a front could have succeeded is an unanswerable question. But the potential influence which SPD/KPD collaboration represented was indisputable. In November 1932, the combined forces of the Social Democrats and the German Communists equalled 13 million registered voters. However, Stalin forced upon the KPD a policy of denouncing the SPD as a treasonable party of Versailles and of joining the National Socialists in a program of "national and social liberation." In this odd way, Stalin became Hitler's political benefactor – a fact of which Hitler probably was not aware. In Soviet circles, Stalin's tactical interests were masked by ideological justifications. In the attempt to explain this curious policy to the SPD leadership, the Soviet envoy in Berlin during 1932 remarked: "Moscow is convinced that the road to Soviet Germany leads through Hitler."[58]

Stalin was not unaware that Hitler had come to power in 1933 in a nation seriously affected by an economic depression and the fact of having lost World War I. Hitler was understandably capitalizing on rampant anti-Semitism and the fears of communism. In contrast to the vague and often failed promises of Hitler's political opposition on the right and the left, the Nazi party called for plentiful credit, insurance and welfare plans and especially for the establishment of selective training programs and mechanisms to restrict the competitive free market system.[59] As a former Bolshevik revolutionary, it was not difficult for Stalin to understand Hitler's intent within Germany to effect fundamental changes in the existing structure of society. In this way, the National Socialist revolution resembled the Bolshevik revolution since it called for the removal of the old elite from political power. Whether or not Stalin understood that the Nazis lacked the stamina, determination and intelligence of the Russian revolutionary elite to see the revolution through to its natural conclusion, even if they did not lack their ruthlessness, is impossible to know. What is more significant is that Stalin did grasp the coincidence of interest which Hitler's anti-status quo foreign policy was bound to create.

Externally, Hitler sought freedom of maneuver in the international arena to restore German preeminence on the European continent.

Consequently, he first set out to destroy the Versailles system which had been set up to contain a revanchist Germany and, in part, a potentially expansionist Bolshevik Russia. Hitler's search for an ally in the plan to regain German territory from Poland seemed to vindicate Lenin's prophetic vision: "Germany is one of the strongest advanced capitalist countries, it cannot put up with the Versailles Treaty, and Germany herself imperialist, must seek an ally against world imperialism."[60] Stalin, who had insisted in 1931 that Russia never had been and never would be Poland's guarantor, was ready to exploit the propitious turn of events in Hitler's foreign policy.[61]

As if to reinforce this view, Germany's military attaché in Moscow between 1931 and 1941 recounted the Soviet elite reaction to Hitler's occupation of the Rhineland:

Tukhachevsky, for example, went to the cabinet and brought out a bottle of champagne. After filling two huge goblets of champagne, he, Radek and the other Russians present congratulated me in grand style on this brilliant achievement. Tukhachevsky also suggested that according to his calculations in a few weeks the German Army could place enough troops in the Rhineland to attack France...I recalled this experience later in 1939 when Stalin responded surprisingly quickly to Hitler's request to send Ribbentrop to Moscow in order to confer with Stalin.[62]

The warmth and sincerity of this exchange is not surprising. Germany and the Soviet Union's leading military figures had undertaken their own efforts to reduce tensions and promote good will between their two countries since the early twenties. Germany's Minister of War, General Blomberg, continued to invite Soviet officials to Germany over the objections of the Nazis. In the Soviet Union, Germany's military representatives enjoyed the respect and esteem of their Soviet colleagues despite clumsy Nazi attempts to create friction. In a fascinating exchange between General Koestring and Marshal Yegerov in Moscow in 1936, Yegerov went so far as to reassure Koestring that "the forms of government come and go, but that the people remain." When Koestring agreed with Yegerov in principle but reminded him of how difficult his task of improving relations between the two countries had recently become because of the Nazis, Yegerov insisted that the abuse heaped on Russia in *Mein Kampf* could be attributed to Hitler's bitterness at being confined in the Landsberg prison and should not be taken too seriously.[63]

Consequently, when Hitler announced his intention to seek a *modus vivendi* with the Soviet state in 1939, his initiative enjoyed virtual unanimous support within the Seeckt-indoctrinated German General Staff and the Red Army leadership. When German and Soviet officers met along the Vistula in 1939, meetings and discussions concerning the dismemberment of Poland were conducted in an atmosphere of extreme cordiality. Borders were adjusted without incident and the disengagement of Soviet and German forces was capped by joint parades and exchanges of flags.[64] Within a few days of Poland's surrender, Stalin even contacted the German government's representative in Moscow to announce his desire to concede additional Polish territory to Germany on the grounds that "anything in the future which might create friction between Germany and the Soviet Union must be avoided."[65]

The restoration of Russo-German cooperation in the form of the 1939 mutual aid agreement had a number of unanticipated, as well as predictable consequences. In return for Russian foodstuffs and raw materials, the Germans, as in the past, promised to deliver machinery, weapons, and military technology to the Soviet Union. In 1940, Russian oil poured through Poland in support of the Wehrmacht's operations against France, the low countries and Britain.

In reflecting on this remarkable Russo-German or Nazi–Soviet agreement, it should be apparent that there is a deeper meaning within the text than that which is normally derived from the conventional interpretation of this event. Hitler had granted roughly the same territorial concessions to Stalin which Tsar Alexander I had sought from Napoleon in the peace of Tilsit. In addition, Stalin had gained much more. Not only did he receive a free hand in Central Asia and the Far East, but Russia was guaranteed the technical assistance which she badly needed. Having seen the value of Soviet–German military cooperation vindicated once again, it seemed unlikely that in so short a time Hitler would resurrect the imperial aims of World War I and hurl a million German soldiers at Germany's distant ally in the East. Still, Stalin's arrangements with Hitler did not in any way interrupt Soviet preparation for war. In fact, the pace of the effort to mobilize all human and material resources for war accelerated during the period of alliance with Nazi Germany.[66] Yet, Koestring's description of events in Moscow in June of 1941 and Erickson's depiction of Stalin's condition at the time of the invasion suggest no other plausible conclusion than that Stalin did not expect Hitler to attack just then.[67]

However, in the West, very few observers of the European scene expected the ostensibly hostile Soviet and Nazi states to collaborate in any extraordinary way beyond the partitioning of Poland. Nowhere did cooperation seem less likely to occur than on a military-security level. When both sides cheered the military achievements of the other and observed strict non-interference in one another's internal affairs, Western observers were dismayed to say the least. Russo-German collaboration assumed a new, and up to that time, unimaginable dimension.

At a time when the Nazis had not yet perfected the operational techniques of terror, the Soviet NKVD was easily able to add a few million Poles and West Ukrainians to their concentration camp populations in Arctic Russia, Siberia and Kazakhstan. Of the estimated 2 million Poles who were deported by the Soviets to these regions in 1939–40, at least one-half were dead within a year of their incarceration by the NKVD. The Gestapo cooperated further with the NKVD in the effort to trade sensitive intelligence information and exchange "German criminals" and Jews for communists and Ukrainians. While the Germans shot 20,000 civilian hostages in Bydgoszcz, the Russians massacred prisoners in the gaol of Vinnitsa, and 15,000 Polish Army officers in Katyn. Ultimately, Nazi–Soviet collaboration resulted in the reduction of the Polish people to "a leaderless, friendless nation."[68]

Despite these results, the political and economic interests which promoted cooperation in 1939 proved to be less resilient than either the Soviet or the German advocates of military cooperation had hoped. German economic recovery had already, before 1939, begun to rekindle in Hitler the old fears of being shut off from overseas food and raw material supply in wartime. The mistaken idea that German foreign trade would be threatened with collapse if predominantly agricultural Russia and Eastern Europe became industrialized was carried forward from the early 1900s by the Nazis and contributed to the eventual cessation of cooperation between the two armies. Indeed, the economic dimension of German National Socialist foreign policy indicates that preventing modern industrialization of Eastern Europe and the Soviet Union eventually became an integral part of German foreign economic policies.[69] The brief respite from the conflicting economic and political forces created by German National Socialism which the liquidation of Poland provided was not enough to restrain Hitler from seeking the complete destruction of Russian communism.

Under Nazi leadership, the objective geopolitical and strategic factors that led often to collaboration and stability in Russo-German relations were ultimately nullified by Hitler's radical policies.

However, even the Nazi–Soviet war could not succeed in eliminating all forms of Russo-German cooperation. Stalin actively pursued a separate peace arrangement with the Germans between 1942 and

1944[70] and Field Marshal Manstein's memoirs indicate that numerous German generals strongly favoured such an arrangement even before the Stalingrad débâcle.[71] For millions of Ukrainians and other non-Russians, hatred of Stalin and communism exceeded any fear of the Nazis.

Despite harsh Nazi occupation policies, at least 500,000 Soviet citizens did serve with the German armed forces during the war. From July 1941 onwards, the 134th Infantry Division of the German Army offered all of its Soviet prisoners the opportunity to become regular soldiers in the German Army. By the end of 1942, roughly half the enlisted strength of the division consisted of former Soviet troops.[72] In the course of the war, the rising number of German casualties and the subsequent shortage of eligible recruits compelled Hitler to authorize the formation of Army and Waffen SS division-size units which were composed almost entirely of non-German soldiers from occupied territories in the Soviet Union. Of course, many Soviet citizens were coerced into joining the Germans, but most appear to have volunteered for ideological reasons. How widespread and intense the distaste and hatred of the Soviet Communist Party must have been may be illustrated by the fact that after two years of German occupation, a call for Ukrainian volunteers to join the Waffen SS in the spring of 1943 resulted a week later in 100,000 volunteers, of which only 30,000 could be equipped and accepted for training.[73] Under the command of General Andrei Vlasov, a captured Red Army general, the Committee for the Liberation of the Peoples of Russia (KONR) managed to recruit entire divisions for the German military establishment from the large pool of Soviet prisoners of war.

Without overstating the significance of support inside the Soviet Union for the German military effort against the Soviet Communist Party, the point to be noted here is that the Germans enjoyed some success in their efforts to field Russian combat formations against the Soviet Army, whereas the Soviets experienced much less success with the thousands of German soldiers in Soviet captivity.

Summary

In retrospect, the degree to which the two states, Tsarist Russia and Prussia–Germany, cooperated militarily was influenced primarily by political factors. However, the values of the political elites, the goals and interests of political leaders, as well as the relative compatibility of socio-economic development in the two states all had a decisive impact on the patterns of cooperation before 1900 and after 1920.

Before 1815, the elite social structures in Russia and Prussia developed along similar lines in relative isolation from one another. Even as this parallel development abated with the accelerated scientific–industrial modernization of a united Germany in the final quarter of the nineteenth century, Prussia–Germany's Junker elite did not regard their Russian contemporaries as very different from themselves in terms of their political and cultural preferences. The proliferation of a Russo-German aristocratic elite throughout Tsarist Russia doubtlessly contributed to this situation.[74] However, this link was not adequate to deter the elites of either Russia or Germany from urging military action in 1914. Ultimately, the elimination of this elite from Russian politics in 1917 removed completely any meaningful cultural link between the two societies and placed relations on an even more sober and calculating basis then before.

After World War I, Soviet–German relations resumed on the German assumption that the Soviet Union's hostility toward the West did not necessarily make war inevitable between the two states, particularly when the importance of common geopolitical aspirations transcended ideological and social preferences. Weimar Germany and Soviet Russia shared the status of pariah states and viewed the alternatives to cooperation with equal trepidation. For the Soviets, reliance on the Germans for military technology and training assistance was not simply a case of opting for a friend of last resort. The recent world war had demonstrated the superiority of German arms even if German strategy had failed. It made sense to seek the advice and assistance of the world's best military establishment. Given that so many of the German military elite still reflected on the wisdom of Prussia's friendship with Russia in the past and sought relations with Russia on the old model again, it would have been senseless for the Bolsheviks to ignore the opportunity of cooperating with the Germans.

In addition, Poland's existence posed similar threats to both countries and clearly acted as a unifying force in the relationship. Poland represented the despised legacy of French victory and the Allied policy of containment which had been directed at both Germany and Russia. In view of the fact that neither state was strong enough during most of the interwar period to break the ring of pro-Western states in the East or the West without the help of the other, some measure of cooperation was probably unavoidable. As was the case with the Prussian–German victories against Austria and France in 1866 and 1871, Germany's dismemberment of Czechoslovakia and Poland and the conquest of Western Europe in 1939–40 would not have been possible without the cooperation of the Soviet Union. Similarly, German assistance contributed to the Soviet seizure of Finnish, Polish, Slovak, Lithuanian, Latvian, Estonian and Romanian territory after 1939.

However, the brutal subjugation of the German national state in 1945 to Allied control interrupted the historic pattern of Russo-German relations in a way that made an immediate *rapprochement* on the pre-war model impossible. It is at this point that cooperation, based on the shared security and foreign policy interests of ruling communist parties in Moscow and Berlin, began.

In the postwar era, many Europeans in the East and the West believed progress toward peace to be dependent not upon cooperation between the old national empires, but upon the creation of new, permanent supranational alliances that could contain the apparently destructive force of German nationalism. In the East, the Soviets sought to organize the belt of nationalities along their periphery within an alliance framework. In both NATO and the Warsaw Pact, the alliance structures were inextricably interwined with the unresolved German question and few, if any, political observers anticipated the important roles which German military strength would play again in either the East or the West.

In Eastern Europe, Stalin had learned the bitter lesson that the Tsars before him had not – that certain loyalty comes only through dependence. Offers of reunification in order to draw Germany away from the West, though tempting to the Germans, were highly impractical in the postwar period from the standpoint of the Soviets. A united national German state had proven twice in the twentieth century that it could not be depended upon to pursue a foreign policy which permanently coincided with Soviet–Russian national aims and interests. Consequently, the German social system in East Germany had to be developed after 1945 on political principles of hostility to the West and along lines which favored the strategic military and economic interests of the Soviet Union. Nevertheless, these events did not prevent the Soviet Union from successfully reviving the convergence of elite interests which animated Russo-Prusso-German relations in the past by installing in power a narrow ruling elite which owes its existence to Soviet political, military and, to a lesser extent today, economic support.

All of these points suggest an important distinction between prewar and postwar military cooperation. For the East German Communist Party (SED) leadership, independence in the conduct of foreign affairs and state sovereignty in the traditional Western context had to, of necessity, remain subordinate to the preservation of the prevailing elite's position. The resulting effect of these mutually reinforcing bilateral Soviet and East German political interests was the creation of new conditions for Soviet–East German military collaboration.

2 The East German rise to military prominence, 1956–1969

The most important military consequence of the Soviet-directed transplantation of Marxist–Leninist political and economic structures to East German soil has been the limited restoration of German military power and its integration into the Soviet regional force structure. Since 1956, the East German Army's integration with Soviet forces has been achieved through a number of cooperative measures.[1] Of these measures, the most important may have been the Soviet decision to develop the NVA in a cooperative framework with the Group of Soviet Forces in Germany (GSFG).

The significance of this development lies in the fact that the Soviets did not initially pursue the same type of relationships as they had with East Germany when pursuing military integration with the Warsaw Pact's northern tier military establishments in Czechoslovakia and Poland. As Thomas Wolfe has indicated, in the early sixties the Soviet military invested little effort in the attempt to weld the Warsaw Pact forces into an integrated military alliance.[2] However, when events in Hungary, Poland, Romania and Czechoslovakia demonstrated that changes in the relationships between the Soviet and East European military establishments would have to be made in order to render impossible any further East European efforts to treat seriously the façade of state sovereignty as expressed in the Warsaw Treaty, the Soviets turned to closer Pact integration under Soviet command. As a result, Soviet military control which had long been the pattern in East Germany increasingly became the focus of Soviet military policy in Eastern Europe's military establishments with the emergence of three additional Groups of Soviet Forces on the GSFG model.

By 1969 the political requirement to preserve social and economic stability in Eastern Europe coincided with a developing Soviet military interest in transforming the Warsaw Pact's doctrine for coalitional warfare into a rationale for tightly organized and Soviet-controlled multinational armed forces.[3] In many ways, East Germany appears to have provided the proving ground for this development.

With these points in mind, this chapter will discuss the Soviet approach to developing the NVA and the organizational evolution and integration of East German ground forces into the Soviet regional force structure. It can be argued that the special nature of the "German problem" in the fifties probably made impossible any alternative to Soviet subordination, however, the apparent success of GSFG–NVA cooperation within the Soviet coalition framework made the Soviet–East German military alliance a model which the Soviets eventually wanted their other, less enthusiastic allies in Eastern Europe to emulate.

The SED and policies of dependence

Toward the end of World War II, a small number of German officers concluded that a Soviet military victory over the Nazis could lead to a restoration of fruitful Soviet–German cooperation in the historic tradition of Prussia – a view which the Soviets naturally encouraged. This conviction among others led these officers to collaborate with the Soviet-sponsored Committee for the Liberation of Germany from Fascism (*Freies Deutschland*). While this collaborative effort produced no German military units which could fight under Soviet command, it did create a small cadre of officers who, after 1945, were employed by the Soviet military administration in the Soviet-occupied zone to train and organize German paramilitary forces.[4] Though initially underequipped and of questionable reliability, the so-called "People's Police" was intended to protect the new German Communist Party leadership which the Soviet Military Administration sought to resuscitate after the war.[5] This force was to provide the leadership cadres for the National People's Army (NVA) which would be formed in 1956.

In the summer of 1953, the Socialist Unity Party (SED) became briefly dependent on this paramilitary force for its survival. Stalin's death produced an outburst of hostility toward the East German communist regime. Eventually, unrest among the workers of Berlin and a number of other East German cities had to be put down by armed force. However, where East German paramilitary forces were deployed in fragmented formations, discipline quickly broke down and mutiny surfaced. When confronted with angry mobs of anti-communist workers, company commanders of the People's Police actually ordered their men to drop their weapons rather than fire on unarmed workers. Offending German officers were swiftly arrested and executed by Soviet Army units which had to intervene. But the experience was not forgotten by either the SED or the Soviet military leaderships.[6]

It should not have been surprising to the SED or the Soviet Military Administration that the young East Germans in the People's Police did not enthusiastically defend the SED. The brutality of the Soviet military occupation of German territory and the economic costs of Soviet reparation payments had alienated much of the population from communism. According to agreements among the victorious allies of World War II, Germany was to pay in kind for the losses caused by her to the Allied nations in the course of the war. Germany, the Soviets argued, would never again become a threat to the world, if "she not only disarmed militarily, but also industrially."[7] The consequences of this postwar Soviet attitude toward Germany included a significant decline in the East German standard of living through the removal of German industry and the forced transport of skilled German labor to the Soviet Union.

Soviet dismantling teams had arrived in the Soviet zone with the second echelon of occupying armies and were guided by the needs of the Soviet economy for all types of industrial equipment.[8] East Germany was ideally suited to their purpose. Before the war, East Germany had produced 23.3 percent of Germany's industrial output, 28 percent of the metal-working industrial output, and 33 percent of light industrial output.[9] Major targets of the Soviet dismantling programs were the heavy industries, particularly the machinery, ferrous metal and vehicle industries. In addition, transport and postal equipment, hydrogen processing plants, chemical factories, plywood factories and even university laboratories were removed.[10]

Even more significant from a psychological standpoint than the general decline in the standard of living brought on by Soviet economic exploitation was the fact that nearly every East German knew of friends or relatives imprisoned in the Soviet Union for many months or years.[11] In short, the impact of seemingly perpetual socio-economic insecurity and the precipitous decline in the standard of living was enormous.[12] Under these conditions, no one should have expected the East German People's Police to have behaved differently.

However justified Soviet actions may have been when looking at the war as a whole, Soviet policy was depriving the SED of the means to rebuild the economy of the new German Democratic Republic and gain acceptance at home and abroad. The incongruity of Soviet words and actions concerning the future of the German Democratic Republic between 1949 and 1956 became all too obvious with West Germany's rapid economic recovery and integration into the European Economic Community and NATO. More importantly, the United States, Great Britain and France could now point to the existence in the West of a sovereign German state with its own armed forces under supranational military command. A parallel development in the East was clearly impossible without similar concessions to the SED. The most important Soviet concessions would have to include conferring the trappings of national sovereignty – a "national" army – on the SED.

Various scholars have explored the possible reasons for the Soviet decision to rearm the Germans living in the Soviet zone of occupation. Based on a vague pronouncement by Joseph Stalin in 1942 relating to the eventual defeat of Germany's organized military power, Thomas Forster insists that Stalin had envisaged Germany's military–industrial might, in the context of the correlation of forces, as a potential asset to the Soviet Union early in the war.[13] On the other hand, David Childs and Robert Dean are less certain that the rationale for the decision to rearm East Germany had been formulated before the war ended. They have offered other considerations which may have influenced the Soviet decision-making process for national security.[14]

First, the Soviets may have seen the existence of some semblance of a German military establishment as offering bargaining power in negotiations with the West concerning Germany's postwar status. Second, if Germany had been reunited in the fifties, the presence of German communist officers in a postwar German army would also have preserved some measure of Soviet influence in an otherwise politically neutral state. Third, it is also extremely likely that the German communist party to which the Soviets had given titular governing authority under the auspices of the Soviet military administration supported the establishment of an army. In view of the SED's commitment to construct a new socialist society in the image of the Soviet Union, political power had to be concentrated in a Soviet-like party-police-state apparatus. For the state to be an effective weapon in the attempt to restructure East German society, it would have to be capable of mobilizing, developing and organizing power.[15] It followed logically that the state would have to have all the Leninist institutions of significance including the political police and the armed forces. Since Soviet pronouncements on the subject of East

German rearmament were of necessity often vague, contradictory and misleading in these years, it seems plausible to conclude that the Soviets and the East German communists simply shared an interest in creating the NVA for reasons of internal political development and Soviet foreign policy. However, the nature of the new Soviet–East German military relationship left no doubt as to who would control the German Democratic Republic's armed forces.

For the Soviets and the East German communists, the events of 1953 meant that a new more effective framework for Soviet–German military cooperation would have to be found in order to ensure the reliability of German communist military forces. Any new cooperative framework would have to assure the politicization of the East German military and its complete integration into the Soviet military force structure. The structure of this new framework became visible with the signing of the status of forces agreement between the GDR and the Soviet Union after the founding of the National People's Army (NVA) in 1956.

In contrast to the Soviet Union's bilateral arrangements with other Pact countries, the agreement which regulated the presence of Soviet forces in the GDR did not accord the East German communist leadership any decision-making power concerning the number, location and movement of Soviet forces on East German territory. More significantly, it implicitly granted authority to the Soviet forces commander to impose a state of emergency on the GDR in response to internal or external conditions.[16] During the Warsaw Conference in May 1955, at which the SED hoped to gain permission for East German rearmament, the Polish and Czechoslovak delegations demanded a series of treaties that would guarantee the post-war borders between them and the GDR before agreeing to the formal creation of an East German military establishment. After the SED's recognition of the GDR's new territorial limits and Soviet reassurances to the Polish and Czechoslovak party leaderships that the new East German force would be permanently assigned to the Joint Command of Warsaw Pact forces under Soviet command and control, the SED's paramilitary police forces were formally redesignated the National People's Army in January 1956.[17] Soviet officers participated in the planning and execution of East German political and military training down to and including the regimental level. Soviet political officers supervised political activities and added their recommendations concerning the promotion and advancement of the NVA's new officers to those of professional Soviet Army officers. In view of this pervasive Soviet presence, it is not surprising that the

NVA's command and control mechanisms were also carefully designed from the beginning to deny the GDR state an independent military capability.

The early practice of restricting local East German control of the NVA was reflected in the NVA's operational command structure. In addition to the NVA's permanent assignment to the Joint Command of the Warsaw Pact and the presence of large numbers of Soviet officers in the GDR's Ministry of Defense planning staffs, the activities of the NVA main staff were limited in scope to supply and procurement, recruitment, training, communications, intelligence dissemination, civil defense and planning. A G–3 operations cell was notably absent from the five principal subdivisions of the NVA staff.[18] Furthermore, the NVA's new Ministry of Defense supervised the training and logistical support of all field forces directly from the headquarters in Berlin. Subordinate headquarters were limited in their authority to matters of an administrative or logistical nature. This structured operational dependence of the NVA on the Soviet armed forces made independent German Army operations impossible.

On the one hand, the fact that the Soviet Union definitely regarded that part of Germany occupied by it as the "ideological spoils of war,"[19] made the decision to deny the GDR the essential feature of national sovereignty – control over the armed forces on its own soil – understandable. On the other hand, why would the East German communists submit to a relationship in which the East German state is tied as closely as possible to the Soviet Union? In this connection, it would be a mistake to assume that the SED leaders regarded the incorporation of their state into the Soviet Union's hegemonic state system as an unwelcome imposition. On the contrary, the destabilizing events of 1953 led them to view their position internally and externally as so exposed that close alignment with the superpower of the communist movement was regarded as an essential guarantee of continued existence and future prosperity.[20]

Thus, in the context of J. F. Brown's analytical framework for viability versus cohesion,[21] neither the East Germans nor the Soviets seem to have been as concerned with the independence of the fledgling German communist state as they were with the GDR's survival. Since the Soviet and East German objective was the same – retention of communist political control – viability had to be sacrificed for a cohesive relationship with the Soviets which alone could preserve the SED's position. While this condition has persisted largely unchanged up to the late 1980s and, thus, impeded national and

political integration in the GDR, it has allowed the East German
communist regime to "tread water in a category between full legitimacy and full repudiation."[22] From the Soviet Union's standpoint,
the GDR's problematic social equilibrium has underpinned Berlin's
continued dependence on Moscow and this helps explain, in part,
the Soviet Union's ability to extract full advantage from East
Germany's military potential.

Hand in hand with the Soviet decision to rebuild German military
strength went Soviet concessions to East German economic needs
which were inextricably intertwined with military–industrial recovery. While the SED pursued a new course to improve living standards, the CPSU waived reparation payments and reduced the cost to
East Germany of maintaining the Soviet forces stationed in the new
German Democratic Republic. Finally, most of the major chemical
and industrial works which the Soviets had appropriated during the
occupation were handed back to the East Germans without further
payment.[23] However, the broad pattern of Soviet controls was still
unaffected. Soviet occupation had ingrained the habit of obedience in
the East Germans which the gradual return to the form of state
independence in Eastern Europe as expressed in the text of the 1955
Warsaw Treaty did not change.[24]

However, the promise of greater political flexibility which the
foundation of common economic interests and ideological commitment in the WTO and CMEA were to symbolize meant that measures
to constrain East German military autonomy in the fifties and sixties
were not reflected in Soviet regional military policy. Within a year of
the founding of the WTO, Khrushchev announced the decision to
embrace "separate roads to socialism." This political response to the
progressive disintegration of Stalinist structures also subordinated
regional East European military forces to the nominal control of their
respective ruling parties.[25] Hence, Khrushchev's partial "renationalization" of East European forces at least implied, for the first time
since the end of World War II, that national distinctions would
persist in military form. As later events were to prove, this new
military policy represented a setback for the Soviet military establishment which, since 1945, had been organizing national territorial
formations of East European troops to fight under Soviet command.

As part of the effort to camouflage Soviet political hegemony,
Khrushchev catered to national sensitivities and signed status-of-
forces agreements with the ruling parties in Eastern Europe. He
acceded to a Romanian request and withdrew all Soviet forces from
Romanian territory in early 1958.[26] In Poland, Khrushchev agreed to

conditions for the stationing of Soviet forces on Polish territory which included a Soviet pledge to non-interference in Polish affairs and the removal of Marshal Rokossovsky – the Soviet Marshal who had commanded the postwar Polish Army. The ruling parties of Hungary and Romania signed status-of-forces agreements with the Soviet Union in 1957. The introduction of a permanent Soviet military presence in Czechoslovakia resulted in a similar treaty with that country in 1968.

Khrushchev's concessions resulted in the exodus of large numbers of highly visible Soviet officers and advisors from the East European armies (the East German forces remained small and highly penetrated by Soviet personnel). This permitted the re-emergence of strong nationalist sentiments within the military establishments of these countries[27] and provided the ruling communist parties with several opportunities to consolidate command of their national military forces in an environment of reduced Soviet penetration.[28] Only the East German forces escaped the partial "renationalization" of the Pact's non-Soviet forces, but excepting the NVA from this regional Pact military development entailed long-term benefits for the Soviet Union which the Soviet leadership was to appreciate much later.

Equally important for region-wide developments in this period was the transition from one-man dictatorship to collective dictatorship in the Soviet polity, during which, in Alfred Meyer's terms, the Soviet leadership lost some authority in accomplishing the task of shifting from system building to system management.[29] While the Soviet leadership endured this difficult transition, the SED's First Secretary struggled with the problem of creating a separate national identity for a part of the German-speaking world which had not had a separate existence since 1871. In view of the challenge to the GDR which the West German government's interest in national reunification represented, Ulbricht chose to view the new GDR state as the product of an inevitable process of historical development.[30] By the late fifties and early sixties, this meant that reunification could only occur on the basis of socialism. This helped to justify the SED's policies of political isolation from the West and, in particular, West Germany and led to the East German society's awareness of its own identity – at least as distinct from the country's Eastern neighbors as from the West Germans.[31] Self-imposed isolation from both the West and the problematic social and political developments in Poland and Czechoslovakia coupled with domestic economic growth helped East German society to evade some of the destabilizing socio-economic effects of de-Stalinization.

Interestingly, the SED's failure to "de-Stalinize" resulted in the insulation of the NVA and enabled it to avoid the consequences of reduced Soviet penetration – the struggle among local parties for greater political independence from Moscow and the development of a military doctrine with a national orientation. Thus, while the Soviets contended with anti-Soviet, nationalistic elements in the Pact's other military establishments, the creation of a new political and military order in the GDR on principles which favored Soviet strategic interests proceeded at a steady pace. By 1961 all the key sectors of the economy were in the hands of the state with nationalization and collectivization of the remaining private elements proceeding rapidly.[32]

Still, political subservience and general repressiveness at the expense of viability meant that the desired social, economic and political conditions conducive to effective East German cooperation with the Soviets in any sphere could not be rapidly forged without an additional Soviet concession to the SED's need to consolidate its political and economic position internally. In 1961, Soviet policy to support the consolidation of the SED regime meant hermetically sealing off the East Germans from the West Germans. Owing to the refugee movement, the GDR, which had no trouble in employing all workers in suitable jobs, up to 1961, experienced a serious skilled labor shortage.[33] As it turned out, this and other Soviet concessions to the SED's internal political needs coincided with important developments in Soviet strategic military thinking and planning in the postwar period.

Trends in Soviet foreign and security policy

At the end of World War II, the primary concern of Soviet military planners was to hold the ground which the Soviet Union had gained defeating the German armies on the Eastern Front while demobilizing a large portion of the Soviet armed forces. Implicitly or explicitly, the Western powers had given this territory to the Communist Party of the Soviet Union. Nevertheless, Soviet "worst case" military planning dictated the decision to embark on a rapid and extensive expansion of Soviet conventional and strategic military capabilities. These actions doubtlessly represented a response to the conditions of Soviet military inferiority *vis-à-vis* the United States and they also reflected an understanding of the demands of a new technological age in military affairs:

They (the Soviet leadership) appreciated the terrifying destructive power of the US nuclear strike forces, the creation and expansion of NATO, the development of British nuclear power, the relative invulnerability of the US homeland until the late 1950s, the growth of tactical nuclear forces in Europe, the revival of German military power and the complete encirclement of the USSR by a ring of US military bases and a series of hostile military alliances. There was even talk about roll back and the liberation of Eastern Europe. All this maintained the spectre of surprise nuclear attack on the Soviet Union as a possible if increasingly improbable scenario.[34]

However, Khrushchev's bellicosity in this early period actually obscured the Soviet Union's military weaknesses in Central-East Europe[35] and convinced many in the West that Khrushchev was no less dangerous than Stalin had been.[36] What made an analysis of postwar Soviet strategic interests in Germany difficult for many analysts was the fact that Khrushchev in particular proved willing to accept risks despite the relative military–strategic inferiority of the Soviet Union until the early seventies. This also created uncertainty on both sides of the inter-German border. The SED was often uncertain of Soviet intentions toward West Germany and the West Germans could not be certain of the Soviet interest in a permanently divided Germany.

For the Soviets, though, next to retaining control of East Germany, preventing a nuclear-capable, independent, rearmed West Germany was most likely the overriding concern of Khrushchev who was all too aware of the glaring weaknesses in the infant German Democratic Republic. While this goal was partially achieved in the West, the Soviet military had to struggle to reconstitute Soviet political and military control of Eastern Europe through the instrument of the WTO and to subdue those East European peoples who had sought greater political autonomy. However, by the late fifties and early sixties Khrushchev had consolidated his power at home and in Eastern Europe to a point where he could turn his attention to the Soviet armed forces and create the conditions for the consolidation of communist authority in what continued to be regarded in Soviet elite circles as the Soviet zone of occupation.

In the same period, Soviet military theorists were struggling to understand the nature of future war. This effort revolved around the desire to understand the immediate and future *military* implications for the use of nuclear weapons. Ultimately, Marshal Sokolovsky's work entitled *Soviet Military Strategy* summarized Soviet military thought on the subject of future war and signaled the initiation of a new phase in Soviet force development. Sokolovsky's blueprint for a new Soviet military force posture placed greater emphasis on the use of high speed conventional forces which could advance with nuclear fire support to break through an enemy's defense along an entire front and achieve dispersion into the enemy's rear. This development in Soviet military thought meant that the Soviet military leadership in the early 1960s concluded that nuclear war might break out and that Soviet forces must be designed, organized and trained to fight successfully under nuclear, chemical and biological battlefield conditions.[37]

Sokolovsky's pronouncement that a new world war would be a coalition war[38] refocused attention on the need for enhanced cooperation and training with non-Soviet forces in order to ensure that they could participate together in combined conventional and nuclear arms operations.[39] A combination of factors which included growing confidence in the capability of the expanding Soviet arsenal of nuclear weapons to defend the Soviet military position in Eastern Europe, domestic pressure on the Soviet economy, and the requirement to retrain and restructure the Soviet armed forces for the new conditions of the nuclear battlefield, also precipitated substantial reductions in Soviet ground forces.[40] According to Soviet sources between 1955 and 1958 the strength of the Soviet armed forces was reduced from 3,623,000 to 2,140,000 men.[41] Similar measures were adopted in 1960 with the result that there was pressure on non-Soviet forces in the Pact to be able to effectively compensate for the reductions in Soviet military strength.

Soviet military modernization led the Soviets to search for opportunities to begin restructuring and retraining Soviet and non-Soviet Pact forces. In view of the preponderance of Soviet military power already in East Germany and the high level of technical expertise in the more advanced scientific–industrial East German society, the NVA became the natural laboratory for developing effective non-Soviet conventional forces to augment Soviet military strength.[42] In addition, the setbacks of Soviet occupation had not prevented the East German economy from beginning to catch up with its neighbors, and the Soviet economy had begun at the same time to slow down.[43] Thus, the East German industrial capacity to sustain military modernization and the small numbers (six divisions) of East German forces under Soviet command made modernization inherently easier. The SED's new task was, however, far from easy.

Compulsory conscription had not yet been introduced in East Germany when the Berlin wall was erected in 1961, probably because of the SED's fears that implementing conscription might precipitate a mass exodus of draft-eligible men from the GDR. Also, the few joint exercises held had revealed glaring inadequacies in East German military training[44] and equipment,[45] as well as strong German resentment for the heavy-handed attitude of their Soviet comrades.[46] These problems had to be handled jointly by the East German party leadership and the Soviet military command if real success was to be achieved.

The GSFG and the NVA

In the early postwar years, the Soviet garrison in East Germany consisted of the sixteen Soviet armies which had occupied Germany after the war. In the fifties, this Soviet military presence was formalized and the remaining six-army occupation force was redesignated the Group of Soviet Forces in Germany. As the GSFG's commander between 1953 and 1957, Marshal Grechko initiated reforms which were designed to deal with the Western strategy of massive nuclear retaliation in response to any offensive Soviet military operations against the West. In anticipation of the destruction and heavy casualties which nuclear weapons would inflict, Grechko deployed the GSFG armies in successive echelons from the north to south with only two armies facing the West German border.[47] However, Grechko's innovative solutions were handicapped by a shortage of technically competent and trained personnel, Khrushchev's enthusiasm for the new rocket forces and a reduction in Soviet ground forces. As the GSFG's military manpower shortages became more acute, more attention was directed at the restoration of German military power as one means of compensating for temporary reductions in the strength of the GSFG. This was suggested by the fact that the NVA's new units were stationed in close proximity to GSFG units and that the East German military district organization mirrored the Soviet structure.

According to GDR historians, the SED entrusted the establishment and leadership of the NVA and border forces to "sons of the German people who had once worn the rags of fascist concentration camps or prisons, or the uniforms of the Spanish People's Army or Red Army."[48] While operational command of the new East German force was reserved to the Soviet General Staff and its representative, the post of GSFG commander, the top military administrative post, was given to Willi Stoph in 1956, to Heinz Hoffmann in 1960 and Heinz Kessler in 1985. In peacetime, the ground forces command center was located at Potsdam-Geltow.

Hoffmann and Stoph were both members of the prewar German Communist Party and Hoffmann had actually fought with the communist brigades against Franco in Spain during the Spanish civil war. Hitler's rise to power forced them to flee to the Soviet Union where

Hoffmann with the assistance of his Russian wife was able to gain the confidence of Stalin's military and political leadership. The conquest of East Germany by the Red Army in 1945 returned him and many other German communists to Berlin. Consequently, he was a natural choice for the job as the GDR's new Minister of Defense. His contemporaries and subordinates in East Germany's border and security forces had similar backgrounds.

Heinz Kessler, who ultimately succeeded to the position of Defense Minister on Hoffmann's death in 1985, had deserted to the Red Army in 1941 and helped found the "National Committee for a Free Germany." As former chief of the NVA air force and main political administrations he received extensive military education in the Soviet Union and played a role in the creation of the NVA after the war. Herbert Scheibe, an old line Jewish communist, had been held in Buchenwald concentration camp until the Soviet occupation authorities selected him to head the SED's security department of the central committee. Secret police chief Erich Mielke, also a veteran communist, spent the war in Moscow and rose to command of the East German secret police in the fifties. In every instance, these military–security elites were the vanguard of a small Stalinist elite which was committed to Soviet political goals and military methods.

Under their leadership and Soviet supervision, the NVA's organization, main political administration, tactical structure and security system were modeled on the Soviet armed forces. Since German rearmament was primarily designed to compensate for reductions in the size and strength of Soviet forces in the GDR, the NVA's six divisions were operationally and logistically configured for deployment within the GSFG's Soviet fronts. After all, as a completely new army in 1956, the NVA was not encumbered by any existing organizations.[49] In the NVA, the peacetime military administration of the NVA's ground forces was split between two military districts. District III with headquarters in Leipzig became responsible for the equipment and daily training of three divisions and their supporting elements:

    7th Armored Division in Dresden
    4th Motorized Rifle Division in Erfurt
    11th Motorized Rifle Division in Halle

Military District V with headquarters in Neubrandenburg became responsible for:

    9th Armored Division in Eggesin
    1st Motorized Rifle Division in Potsdam
    8th Motorized Rifle Division in Schwerin

Following the Soviet model, the six-division force was organized into five combat arms: motorized rifle units, armored forces, air defense, rocket and artillery forces. (In the seventies, the East German Army expanded to include an airborne infantry regiment as well.) Initially, all equipment was of Soviet origin, although some weapons of Czechoslovak manufacture were acquired in the early sixties.[50]

Since the GSFG headquarters would be transformed into a Soviet military "front" command center in time of war, it made excellent sense to configure the NVA's six divisions for deployment within the GSFG "fronts." This suggested that the three divisions of Military District V could be operationally commanded by the GSFG commander and the three divisions of Military District III by either the GSFG or the NGSF commander. However, it would be some time before the high probability of this arrangement could be confirmed in practice. However, the absence of an artillery division, intelligence, transport and logistical formations in the NVA which have been historically present in Soviet fronts since the end of World War II further confirmed the NVA's doctrinal employment as division-size components of the GSFG's armies.[51] The fact that Marshal Grechko supervised the transformation of the SED's People's Police into the NVA and witnessed the first large-scale Warsaw Pact exercise that involved non-Soviet troops – 11,000 soldiers of the NVA and an unspecified number of troops from the GSFG[52] – only confirms this view. Although these early joint efforts suffered from the fact that vivid memories of the recent war persisted in the minds of participants on both sides, joint Soviet–East German field training did mark the start of a regional trend which Grechko later continued as the supreme commander of the Warsaw Pact.

Structured dependence on Soviet support was reflected in the gradual development of the GDR's small defense industry. While Russian conquest of East Germany had provided the Soviets with many scientific–industrial pearls, these territories were almost devoid of armaments industries. However, with Soviet assistance, the GDR did develop defense industries in the sixties which eventually produced small arms, ammunition, spare parts, communications gear, optical instruments, wheeled vehicles and clothing. Nevertheless, the GDR remained totally reliant on the USSR for virtually all of its heavy weapons and aircraft.[53]

In the meantime, the SED began to systematically eliminate officers with a flawed ideological orientation and replace them with younger, more compliant officers who were willing to accept the condition of subordination to Soviet military control.[54] In the attempt to consolidate communist political control, the SED adopted a main political administration (MPA) on the Soviet model. Manned with former "anti-fascists" – German communists who had spent the war in Moscow – and Soviet army political officers, the MPA reported directly to the MPA of the GSFG. Technically, the two political administrations were simultaneously agencies of the respective Ministries of Defense and departments of the respective parties' central committee. In practice, however, the top leadership of the East German MPA was characteristically informed rather than consulted on questions of political training in the NVA.[55] However, a lost war and the brutality of Soviet military occupation had not promoted widespread interest in the GDR in military service under Soviet command. One means of fostering a popular image for the NVA was to reissue the soldiers Wehrmacht uniforms with Soviet-style helmets. This, however, was not a solution to the problem of recruiting capable young men to serve as officers and noncommissioned officers. Because of the large numbers of former Wehrmacht military personnel who were understandably thought to be inherently unreliable, some sacrifice in quality had to be made in favor of political reliability. This had a number of interesting effects.

One effect was the introduction of agents from the GDR's Ministry of State Security into the NVA's formations and subunits. With the arrival of the NKVD on German soil in 1945, the practice of enlisting elements of the German population as active or passive spies, especially when selecting individuals for administrative posts in the government or party, had formed part of the GDR's postwar social and political order.[56] It followed logically that the NVA would include among its ranks informants for the GDR Ministry of State Security and the Soviet KGB. A special liaison detachment was set up to exercise control of Soviet–East German military affairs. According to several sources, the KGB's third directorate monitored not only Soviet troops in the GDR, but German "comrades" in the SED's military cadres as well. The GDR's Ministry of State Security collaborated during operative actions inside and external to the GDR and assisted in the establishment of KGB contact offices in East Berlin, Potsdam, Neubrandenburg, Rostock, Schwerin, Magdeburg, Halle, Leipzig, Erfurt, Gera, Dresden, Karl-Marx Stadt (Chemnitz), Cottbus and Frankfurt an der Oder.[57] Naturally, the network of agents in the new NVA went a long way toward ensuring that the NVA would not represent a threat to the GSFG.

Meanwhile, with Soviet military assistance, the Friedrich Engels Military Academy was founded in 1959 and large numbers of working-class and peasant youths with little formal education were appointed to study a curriculum which placed a far greater premium on understanding Marxist–Leninist ideology than military technical expertise.[58] Of these men, roughly 5,000 were dispatched to the Soviet Union for instruction in a variety of military schools.[59] East German and Soviet military elites have stressed the fact that in 1956 sufficient officer cadres with the desired political orientation did not exist and have emphasized the Soviet military–political role in the process of educating the NVA's new officer corps. Colonel General Stechbarth, NVA Ground Forces commander, stated recently:

Everyone who was present during the first hours of our NVA remembers gratefully how we were able to draw on the rich political and military experiences of our Soviet brothers-in-arms, how the Soviet comrades taught us the military craft in a socialist manner. In those first years, the germs of a brotherhood-in-arms were incubated which are bearing fruit today so many thousand-fold.[60]

Army General Gribkov, Warsaw Pact chief of staff, alluded to the same process in his remarks concerning the important role of Soviet military power within the framework of the Warsaw Pact: "Essentially with the assistance of the Soviet Union, military training institutions were established in all the socialist countries. At the same time, the training of cadres for the national armies continued in Soviet military academies and schools."[61]

What may have been true for the small number of German communists who had arrived on the bayonets of the Red Army in 1945 was not necessarily true for East Germany's draft-age population. In an effort to rationalize military subordination to Soviet command and influence in the NVA, the SED fell back into dependence on the same ideology which had guided political development in the Soviet zone of occupation after 1945.

According to the SED, "proletarian socialist internationalism" provided the theoretical foundation for the defense of the new German socialist fatherland under Soviet leadership. This old Leninist concept presupposed the existence of an international working-class consciousness that the Bolsheviks claimed would supplant nationalism as a unifying force and defeat international capital. A succession of Soviet leaders have interpreted the doctrine to mean that the real test of communist party membership is first and foremost loyalty to the Soviet state – "the fatherland of all the workers."[62] In line with the SED's tendency to equate the internal consolidation of the GDR state with subordination to Soviet military command, the

The East German rise to military prominence

SED established "smooth cooperation by commanders, staffs and troops with those of the Soviet Army as a preeminent political and military duty" in the NVA.[63]

The SED's forceful insistence on cooperation coupled with the introduction of national service in January 1962 served to ameliorate the formerly unfavorable domestic conditions, and with the Berlin wall in place, the SED probably hoped that the majority of draftees in East Germany would simply come to terms with Soviet-style social-ism in the NVA. This goal of improving the NVA's cooperation with the GSFG was given an additional boost in September 1962 when the first graduates from the NVA's new Soviet-style Friedrich Engels Military Academy joined the East German forces.[64]

Concurrent with the NVA's military modernization and sociali-zation into a modern "socialist coalition army," the SED sought to expand the size and scope of its border forces and "workers' combat groups" (*Arbeiterkampfgruppen*).[65] Recruited mostly from the *Lumpenproletariat*, the *Arbeiterkampfgruppen*, who were originally designed to defend the SED's internal political order, were increas-ingly deployed in a paramilitary role under exclusively SED control in order to augment the NVA. In contrast, the border forces were originally subject to the control of the Ministry of the Interior which functioned in most ways as an extension of the Soviet KGB. However, whereas the worker's combat groups were issued used or obsolete equipment and were assigned to largely internal civil defense roles, the organization and training of the GDR's border forces correspon-ded completely to service and education in the regular armed forces. Just as Soviet KGB troops had been included with other armed contingents as competent members of the Soviet armed forces, the SED sought to include the GDR's border forces as integral parts of the East German ground forces.[66] This high ratio of security and pro-fessional military cadre to the NVA's conscript manpower suggested that these additional paramilitary and military–security forces could be employed to guarantee the reliability of the NVA in any new conflict; internal or external.

By 1963, a moderate expansion of the NVA after a period of relative contraction culminated in the participation of the NVA in the joint Soviet–East German–Polish–Czechoslovak exercise "Quartet" which had for the first time an East German general as its nominal comman-der.[67] On 13 November 1964, the start of the 1964/65 training year, the first long-range plan was reportedly developed for the "consoli-dation" of cooperation and "comradeship-in-arms" between the NVA and the GSFG.[68] In June 1964, the SED and the CPSU signed the first treaty of mutual assistance and cooperation since the cessation of Soviet–German hostilities and the related treaty on mutual relations in 1955. The 1964 treaty promised close consultation and coordination among the appropriate government and party institutions to ensure concerted action in areas of foreign, economic and security policy.[69] This and a similar agreement on 6 January 1965 prescribed all-around cooperation in military affairs and political work between the GSFG and the NVA and established the practice of NVA consultation with the GSFG staff to coordinate joint military planning and training.[70]

Having regularized Soviet intervention into the NVA's internal affairs, the SED's efforts to improve and modernize the NVA continued with "October Storm" in 1965 representing a milestone in this regard. Under the command of the GSFG commander[71] NVA soldiers operated in regimental and battalion formations under GSFG control. By 1967, the frequency and fluidity of Soviet–East German cooperation suggested that a new hierarchy was appearing in the northern tier "triangle" – the East Germans were competing with their Polish and Czechoslovak comrades for prominence in the Pact.[72]

One of the most important factors that contributed to the SED's willingness and capacity to keep pace with Soviet military modernization requirements was the East German population's acceptance of their political fate. This depended, in part, on the ability of the SED leadership to deliver sustained improvements in mass consumption and economic welfare. Despite some shortcomings in the level and quality of consumer goods and services, the sixties were marked by significant growth in this area.[73] The gains in the standard of living were also matched by rapid growth in the GDR's economic capacity to sustain military modernization. (See selected data on NVA military capabilities in Tables 3 and 6.) This was doubtlessly a reflection of the fact that whereas the other states of Eastern Europe had been compelled to construct socialism on an agrarian base, the SED had erected the GDR on a solid industrial foundation.

In retrospect, the SED doubtlessly perceived the Soviet commitment to coalitional warfare as an opportunity to demonstrate the GDR's military value and potential to the Soviets who were now eager to exploit it for their own purposes. In 1968, the SED had their first opportunity to demonstrate their militant opposition to the West and commitment to collective security under Soviet leadership. After discussions with Dubcek during August of 1968 in Karlovy Vary, Czechoslovakia, Ulbricht undertook to convince the coalition-ridden Soviet Politburo that Dubcek's experiment with pluralism could have unfavorable consequences for the stability of neighboring East Germany.[74] Consequently, the SED regime urged military action against Dubcek's government in order to forcefully reverse the process of Czechoslovak democratization. When Soviet military intervention began, the Soviet–East German condominium of interest found its best expression in the patterns of troop deployment to Czechoslovakia. Unlike the Poles, who operated as an independent army of three divisions during the occupation phase, two East German divisions invaded Czechoslovakia as component parts of two of the GSFG's Soviet tank armies. (See Table 8 in the Appendix.)

Contrary to Soviet expectations, collaborative efforts elsewhere in the Bloc encountered greater resistance. After the withdrawal of Soviet forces from Romania in 1958, the Romanian Communist Party leadership made the most of every opportunity to contradict Soviet foreign policy initiatives and to reject Soviet initiatives aimed at closer military coordination and doctrine. Openly nationalistic, senior Polish officers advocated the defense of national Polish territory and the wartime employment of Polish forces under Polish, rather than Soviet command.[75] However, the gradual retreat after 1956 of Wladyslaw Gomulka, PUWP First Secretary, from promised political and economic reforms pitted him against nationalist and reformist factions in the Polish party and made him increasingly dependent on Moscow for political support. Gomulka's dependence on Moscow seems to have induced the removal from the Polish armed forces of military elites having a nationalist orientation.

Furthermore, a number of Soviet officers had continued to serve in the Polish military's key command and staff positions even after Marshal Rokossovsky's departure. Soviet General Bordzilovsky served as Polish chief of staff from 1954 to 1965 and chief of training from 1965 until his retirement in February 1968. Lieutenant General Chaplevsky, a pre-war Soviet Army officer of Polish origin, served as a deputy chief of staff until 1968.[76] Soviet influence over Polish military promotions and appointments apparently persisted with Gomulka's assistance despite sporadic opposition to it within the post-1956 Polish military elite.

In Czechoslovakia between 1956 and 1968, de-Stalinization and Slovak isolation from the higher ranks in the Czechoslovak armed forces overlapped with issues of party military controls and national military doctrine. In mid April 1968, the rector and several faculty members of the Gottwald Academy wrote a memorandum which criticized the Czech national defense system as "Devoid of rational criteria resulting from a twenty-year distorted development of our army."[77]

All of these experiences had an understandably profound effect on regional Soviet military developments. In addition, the emerging Chinese threat in the early 1960s suddenly confronted the Soviet leaders with a new dilemma: how to augment their standing forces in Europe while enlarging the Soviet military presence on the Sino-Soviet border. This dilemma led the Soviets to impute a stronger integrative meaning to Sokolovsky's concept of coalition warfare.[78] It was clear that the coalitional framework of the early sixties would not work in an atmosphere of East European political unreliability.

When First Secretary Brezhnev sought to elevate Lenin's principles of socialist proletarian internationalism to the level of state-to-state relations in the aftermath of the "Prague Spring," the military significance was not lost on the Yugoslavs or the Romanians who labeled the Soviet proclamation a plan to destroy the sovereignty of the WTO's member states.[79] New integrative pressures resulting from the Soviet experience with the Czechoslovak Army and "socialism with a human face" in Prague were immediately evident in the increase in scope and frequency of joint Soviet–East German military activity. One East German analyst observed that "the development of the cooperative relations among the socialist states is greatly influenced by the fact that with the onset of the 1970s, the socialist community entered a new stage of its development."[80] In East Germany, this new stage began with measures stemming directly from the agreements reached by the PCC meeting in Budapest during March 1969. The Budapest meeting proposed several structural reforms which established fixed command relationships between Soviet and East European forces within the framework of the Soviet-led Combined Armed Forces (CAF). The resulting statute sought to coordinate training and logistical efforts and to assign all East German and Selected units of the Polish, Czech, Hungarian and Bulgarian forces to the Soviet-dominated combined command of the Warsaw Pact.[81]

While the SED's official rationale attributed these measures to new aggressive Western policies, they were clearly aimed at (1) preventing the Czech "bacillus" from infecting the NVA, and (2) imparting an increased emphasis on integration to the already strong coalitional character of Soviet–East German military cooperation.[82] One East German source explained the aims of the Budapest measures as follows:

The introduction of plans for the transition of East German and allied forces on the national level to long-term joint and coordinated planning for the development of armed forces within the coalition framework.

The systematic elevation of East German and allied forces to uniform levels of Soviet military development.

Strengthening of relations with Soviet forces to achieve higher results in political and tactical orientation of East German and allied forces.

The expansion in all areas of military cooperation with the object of promoting East German collaboration with Soviet and non-Soviet Pact forces.

Clearly, the tone and spirit of this guidance suggested that the "new" direction in East German military policy had simply codified and reaffirmed what the CPSU and SED leaderships had already introduced in East Germany in the early phases of NVA–GSFG cooperation. Nevertheless, East German party military policy also reflected a new Soviet interest in closer regional cooperation.[83] A point often overlooked is that Soviet military thought in the post-Khrushchev era stressed the operational importance of the traditional services and a corresponding increase in the role of non-Soviet Pact forces. These developments could only serve to enhance the already important strategic–political role of the NVA. "After 1969 the number of NVA officers seconded to the Warsaw Pact organization grew significantly, expanding in proportion to the six NVA divisions committed to the Pact."[84]

Summary

As a study in Soviet-controlled force development, the National People's Army of East Germany provides a valuable contrast to the Soviet management of the Czechoslovak and Polish military establishments after 1956. Clearly, the Soviet military played a much more significant role both in defining the rules of cooperation and delimiting the options available to the East German communists. First, the legacy of Soviet military occupation and Germany's unconditional surrender had a profound impact on Soviet-controlled force development in the GDR. After the pretense of a German-wide policy implying eventual unification had been dropped, the Soviets recognized that their plan to reduce a unified Germany to economic peonage was incompatible with the creation of a communist state on German soil.[85] More importantly, postwar Soviet occupation policy made any measure of military cooperation impossible. With an end to Soviet dismantling policies, the existing industrial base regained most of its pre-war strength. As mentioned earlier, the area now known as East Germany[86] constituted a technically advanced industrial region within the German empire. As a result, the SED was able to sustain the economic growth that underpins a stable social system.

Second, in contrast to the Soviet political experience in which utopian-motivated revolution eventually gave way to a normative theory of government that emphasized hierarchical military organization and discipline, the East German communists, who had spent the war in Moscow, were not inclined to experiment with social, political and economic programs that violated Stalin's formula for highly centralized economic planning and political control. In addition, internal and external hostility to the new regime made the SED's sense of dependence on Soviet military support more acute. Consequently, the social, economic and security strategies pursued under Ulbricht, after Stalin's death, conformed to a Stalinist preference for societal control through militarization and centralized political and economic decision-making,[87] and to the strategic interests of the Soviet Union.

Third, the absence of pre-existing institutions in the NVA meant that the East German forces would conform to the Soviet model and would support and augment the SED's larger political effort. Professional military development during the period was of a high order, but access to promotion and command were political.[88] When combined with the condition of structured dependence on the Soviet military, this situation tended to minimize the potentially detrimental impact of societal factors on the reliability of East German forces and conditioned a generation of East German military elites to permanent Soviet control and influence.

In view of the Soviet experience with Nazi Germany during World War II, any suggestion to reconstitute an autonomous German Army under the SED's exclusive control would have evoked a viscerally negative response in the postwar period. However, the fragility of German communist rule and the persistent inability of the SED regime in succeeding years to forge a viable legitimate political position with the East German populace made East German subordination to Soviet military dominance both unavoidable and desirable. When Soviet strategic interests reduced the probability of German reunification, Soviet military doctrinal developments dictated an East German contribution to Soviet military strategy. As the SED undertook to erect the Leninist "dictatorship of the proletariat" in

East Germany, it followed that the party's insistence on conformity to Soviet military doctrine, organization and command simply meant that the NVA, like the GDR, would become a faithful replica of the existing Soviet model. The SED's military policy understandably reflected the SED's extreme dependence on Soviet military power in the effort to consolidate the ruling communist elite's position within the GDR between 1956 and 1969.[89] Since the SED resisted the temptation to "de-Stalinize" the GDR's political–economic structures or pursue any measure of "renationalization,"[90] in the end the SED turned out to be the CPSU's most reliable partner in the bloc.

No less significant is the fact that whereas the Polish, Hungarian, Bulgarian, Romanian, and, to a lesser extent, Czechoslovak Communist Parties had been compelled to construct Soviet-style socialism on a largely agrarian base, the SED began the same process with the advantage of a relatively developed industrial base. Consequently, the eventual emergence of the German component of the Warsaw Pact as the leading military–industrial power next to the Soviet Union was probably inevitable. No other state in the Soviet Bloc could support the military–industrial requirements which continuous military modernization entailed.

Whether or not either Stalin or Khrushchev had systematically calculated the military, political and economic strength which the East Germans under Soviet-sponsored communist leadership could contribute to the correlation of forces in the Marxist–Leninist ideological context is difficult to say. Aside from appreciating the scientific–industrial advantage that control of even part of Germany offered the Soviet Union, it is uncertain whether Stalin's successors comprehended the fact that German "imperialism" had coexisted with a culture of organization, discipline and cooperation which Russia had always needed, but seldom had.[91] Nowhere was this notion of discipline and organization more culturally ingrained than in the German populations of the East.

In any case, there is no doubt that after events in Romania, Hungary, Poland and Czechoslovakia demonstrated the inherently anti-Soviet nature of national military establishments, the Soviet leadership began to appreciate the politically pragmatic and socially industrious Prussian–Saxon mentality which isolation from the rest of the German nation had only served to refine and exaggerate.[92] Evidence of this appreciation could be detected in the observations of a Soviet Colonel General during his 1971 visit with the Group of Soviet Forces in Germany:

Speaking frankly, our soldiers have a lot to learn from their German friends. In recent years, workers in the German Democratic Republic have accomplished a great deal: they have built plants and factories and new homes and their agriculture is progressing very well. Our German friends are accomplishing all of this in a very firm and efficient manner. Thus, a Soviet soldier returns home, discusses all that he has seen, and will himself put certain new practices into operation.[93]

While the Soviet officer's hopes that Soviet soldiers would learn the German lessons of industry and exactitude may have been somewhat overly optimistic, the message in his comment is clear: from the Soviet standpoint, East German military–industrial achievements within a structure of collaboration based on Soviet, rather than national German strategic interests, were a success.

For the East Germans, unlike other East European forces, the requirement to integrate themselves into the Soviet force structure did not present a major problem. East German acquiescence in the Soviet domination of the Pact was a well-established behavior pattern within the SED and, hence, the NVA. In many ways, the often slow and painful process of military Gleichschaltung which the Soviets began to implement on a regional basis during the late sixties and then intensified after the unhappy 1968 experience in Czechoslovakia represented an already long-established pattern of Soviet command and control in East German military affairs. The 1969 measures to consolidate Soviet military control in and cooperation with non-Soviet Pact forces were merely a reaffirmation and intensification of already existing agreements between the NVA and the GSFG.[94]

This raises the question of why the Soviets waited so long to embark on a military program with the object of tightly integrating the Pact's best non-Soviet forces with the Soviet military force structure? One answer may be that, in sharp contrast to the Germans, the Soviets expected their East European allies to simply endorse this process without the "benefit" of experience with postwar Soviet occupation which understandably fostered habits of servility in the East German military.

The experiment with national East European forces after 1956 suggests that enthusiastic East European cooperation may have been a real expectation in the minds of many Soviet military and political elites. After all, from the Soviet perspective the survival of the Polish and Czech peoples after 1941 was due entirely to Soviet liberation of those countries from a Nazi occupation that had had the aim of ejecting the Slavs from Central-East Europe. In fact, Marshal Konev's visit to the Czechoslovak Ministry of Defense in the spring of 1968 led him to advise the Soviet leadership against military intervention on the grounds that the political developments in Prague posed no immediate danger to Moscow's security relationship with Prague.[95]

This conclusion also suggests that the integrative pressures of late are not exclusively a function of the Soviet need to combine the Pact's combined armed forces into a more responsive and reliable group of offensive forces. Marshal Sokolovsky's original notion of coalitional forces on a battlefield dominated by nuclear weapons probably anticipated the use of relatively autonomous Czech and Polish armies rather than the highly integrated and Soviet-controlled Pact military structure which Marshal Ogarkov's emphasis on fluid, non-nuclear and "high technology" offensive ground operations clearly necessitates.[96]

In reality, the installation of the Groups of Soviet Forces in Poland, Hungary and Czechoslovakia and the 1969 Budapest measures to promote East European military cooperation with Soviet Army units on the model of the GSFG–NVA relationship were actually thinly disguised admissions of communism's abject failure to accommodate the forces of political change and modernization in Eastern Europe. Only in East Germany, where the Soviets hardly expected Soviet-style communism to achieve any success, were measures originally taken to create an armed force with an entirely fabricated military tradition reflecting the SED's ideological ties to the CPSU and one which was completely subject to Soviet military control. From the Soviet perspective, the unanticipated effect of this arrangement has been that in contrast to other East European military elites who have on occasion responded negatively to party controls and Soviet military dominance of the Pact under conditions of a reduced Soviet military presence, mutually reinforcing Soviet and East German military policies have resulted in continuous and uninterrupted improvements in the East German increment to the regional Soviet military capability.

In the stronger integrative military concomitant of the Brezhnev doctrine, the East Germans continued to be distinguished by their degree of operational integration with the Soviet forces and its apparent success. However, new internal and foreign policy challenges associated with the CPSU's interest in detente with the West would confront the SED in the seventies. Could the SED leadership preserve the GDR's socio-economic stability in a new era of rapidly changing Soviet foreign policy interests? Would the GDR's economy

register sufficient growth to sustain a new wave of force modernization and still satisfy the rising consumer demands of East German
workers? What new roles would the CPSU and the SED find for the
GDR's growing military–industrial potential in the seventies?

3 Soviet–East German military collaboration in the post-1968 Pact

From its inception, ties linking the NVA to the Soviet military establishment were based on pervasive Soviet influence and penetration of the SED's party and state apparatuses, structural integration with the GSFG and the theory and practice of socialist internationalism – after 1968 reconstrued as the Brezhnev doctrine. On the positive side, this condition of dependence on Soviet military support had always afforded protection to the GDR's ruling communist elites. On the negative side, the NVA's unambiguous subordination to Soviet military command symbolized the SED's inability to forge a distinctive position for itself within the Soviet Bloc. However, after 1969 changes in Soviet foreign policy toward Western Europe and the SED's interest in gaining greater internal stability by establishing stronger links within the East German population coincided to turn the NVA's role in Soviet military strategy into an advantage for the SED.

The Soviet leadership, which after 1969 recognized the need to seek technical and economic cooperation with the West, was also prepared to accept the SED's limited independent policy toward the Federal Republic of Germany. After all, in addition to exerting diplomatic and social pressure on Bonn, the GDR in the seventies derived considerable economic and financial benefits from its evolving relationship with the West. In seeking to extend the frontiers of Soviet influence, the SED's new role in Soviet foreign policy toward Germany and the West under the leadership of Erich Honecker was underpinned by a unity of view with the CPSU in the field of security policy. East Germany's capacity to endure the costs of military modernization, and the SED's interest in the NVA as a domestic instrument of socialization and control, kept pace with a Soviet interest in eradicating or, at least, neutralizing anti-Soviet tendencies in the Pact's non-Soviet military establishments and augmenting the

Soviet armed forces' offensive combat power with more reliable non-Soviet participation. In this process, the continuous integration and cooptation of East German military power into the Soviet regional force structure, controlled by the Soviet military, appeared to be the Warsaw Pact's most effective mechanism for making available additional conventional combat power and a stable military mobilization base to the Soviet High Command (VGK) without the loss of Soviet political control.

New directions in foreign and security policy

Under the leadership of First Secretary Ulbricht, the SED had sought to orient the East German communist polity to a state of perpetual animosity toward the West and West Germany in particular. In part, this was a function of the way the East German communists perceived their future in the context of German national unity. Early German communist attitudes toward the concept of a German nation held that reunification of the German nation would inevitably occur on the basis of socialism. Of course, the passage of time and the remarkable economic and political success of the Federal Republic made this eventuality increasingly unlikely. Since West German inroads in Eastern Europe were regarded as inherently antithetical to Soviet security interests, the antagonistic relationship which this attitude fostered between the two German states coincided with a Soviet interest, in the sixties, in the maintenance of cohesion and discipline in the bloc. In this environment, the SED's strong support for Moscow's intervention in Czechoslovakia had helped to facilitate Soviet efforts to reestablish stability and control. However, when the Soviet Union compelled the SED regime to yield to the process of detente with the West, the regime had to come to grips with the possibility that Moscow would pursue its goals with the West Germans at the possible expense of the GDR's internal order.

The SED was not only displeased with the prospect of Moscow ever formally accepting West German assurances on the renunciation of force and respect for the existing European borders, but was also uneasy about a relaxation in tension that could undermine the official "revanchist" and "imperialist" image of the Federal Republic of Germany in the East.[1] In the final Soviet–West German Treaty of 1970, the Soviets went so far as to characterize the agreement as an important step along the path to detente and a normalization of the situation in Europe.[2] For the SED, the fear that the GDR's internal order would not be able to survive a *rapprochement* between West

Germany and the Soviet bloc militated against any conciliatory attitude toward Bonn.

However, the East German state still lacked the political and military means to assert its demands in the face of the Soviet Union's overwhelming power. Brezhnev's statements intimated that in the final analysis, the SED would have to give up its inflexible position on the status of Berlin and relations with the West. When Ulbricht resisted, Brezhnev replaced him with Erich Honecker. For an East German leadership obsessed with internal and external security in the set of triangular relations between Moscow, Bonn and East Berlin, the consequences of their military and economic inferiority to West Germany could not be long endured. From this point forward, East Berlin realigned itself with Moscow and began to coordinate the CPSU's policy toward the West Germans with the SED's internal security concerns, and this allowed the SED to manage significant details of the complex inner-German relationship to the GDR's advantage. As a result of the weaker East German position in this Soviet foreign policy development, East German concessions to a renewed Soviet interest in a relationship with the West Germans necessitated a further strengthening of the Soviet–East German military relationship and some reexamination of the East German state's military–political mission.

As already mentioned, the SED viewed detente and any exposure to West Germany as threatening to the enemy image of imperialism which it considered indispensable for the political cohesion of the GDR state and the National People's Army. Closer East German military cooperation with the Soviet armed forces was the most important way of sustaining the credibility of the Western threat. In order to meet the challenge posed by international developments beyond its control, the SED's new defensive strategy *vis-à-vis* NATO and West Germany was to seek especially close ties with the socialist world system and its leading power, the Soviet Union.[3] At the SED's Eighth Party Congress in 1971, the military prescription for integrating the GDR into the Soviet hegemonic state system in order to shield against inroads from West Germany were expressed in the following terms:

First, mobilization of the forces of the socialist community of states is a most effective and efficient way of bringing to bear the advantages of socialism for the benefit of each socialist country. Second, the construction of socialism is most reliably safeguarded within the union of the Warsaw Pact, particularly by the superior military might of the USSR. Third, socialism is internationalist in its nature ... The Soviet Army sets the scope for the solution of problems and bears the main burden for the defense of socialism. The brotherhood-in-arms with the Soviet Army is for us the criterion of socialist internationalism in the military area and a firm foundation for our security.[4]

In Central Europe, the SED's prescription resulted in still stronger collaborative measures congruent with the structural reforms announced in March 1969 by Marshal Yakubovsky. Within the NVA, these measures were buttressed by a reinvigoration of political training and stronger disciplinary measures. Externally, the SED embarked upon an ambitious foreign policy which included the execution of security-related missions within the framework of the Soviet Union's global network of military assistance programs. Interestingly, the SED's more active role in relations between the two German states and the undiminished East German commitment to expanding regional Soviet military power combined to forge a new, stronger position for the GDR in its relations with the Soviet Union and within the Warsaw Pact. Moreover, while the SED's readiness to support closer military integration in the Pact and to assist in the projection of Soviet military power overseas was calculated to enhance the GDR's strategic military value to Moscow, the East German initiatives also paralleled important developments in regional and global Soviet military strategy.

Because of the Soviet emphasis on the probability of a war in Central Europe becoming nuclear, the Soviet military leadership in the sixties had viewed a conflict with the West as being a politically and militarily decisive clash between the two social systems, with strategic nuclear weapons being the major weapons used. According to this line of thought, the use of nuclear weapons created opportunities for new higher rates of advance and an earlier end to the conflict. However, NATO's adoption of a flexible response doctrine in 1967 and obvious NATO nuclear release problems may have led the Soviets to question whether a future war would be conventional or tactical nuclear in nature.[5] In addition, there was evidence that the Soviet military and political leadership questioned whether the use of nuclear weapons was compatible with the military objective of seizing what Clausewitz called the "center of gravity" in enemy territory. More and more, military analysts on both sides began to wonder what viable purpose a military campaign could have that culminated in the destruction of the scientific–industrial base for which the war was originally fought.[6]

In 1969, a new Soviet categorization of non-global wars included: (1) limited nuclear war; (2) war limited to conventional weapons; and (3) wars limited in geographical area and number of participants.[7]

Later, in 1971, Grechko declared that "under certain conditions conventional weapons will be the main weapons utilized."[8] In 1973, former GSFG commander, Marshal Kulikov, now commander-in-chief of Warsaw Pact forces, announced that conventional means of attack represented what he termed a new element in the "surprise attack inventory" of imperialist states and argued for improvements in Pact readiness to combat the threat.[9] A Soviet conventional option did not, however, come entirely out of the blue! James McConnell has described the evolution of Soviet military thinking about the use of nuclear weapons in the following passage:

In the mid-60s Moscow began to accept the possibility of a conventional phase that would, however, inevitably escalate. For about a decade, planning for this phase was evidently in terms of a "front operation" [8–20 days in World War II]. In the last half of the '70s such planning was apparently in terms of a "strategic operation" [up to 30 days in World War II]. Then, in 1981, a full-fledged conventional option for a whole war avowedly became part of Soviet doctrine.[10]

Along with this apparent evolution in Soviet military thought went the conviction that it would be possible for the Soviet armed forces to fight and win a war against the West without resorting to nuclear weapons and the Soviet Union's eventual declaration of no "first use" of nuclear weapons in June 1982.[11] In sum, there were cogent reasons to suggest that the Soviets were interested in avoiding the use of nuclear weapons in Central Europe.

In the course of this new emerging Soviet strategy for conventional arms-only conflict, developments in Soviet-East German military cooperation suggested that East Germany's growing military–industrial potential was being assigned a significant role in Soviet planning for a conventional conflict with NATO in Central Europe and in wars of "liberation" in other areas of strategic interest to the Soviet Union. The SED appears to have reasoned that a more significant role for the GDR in Soviet military affairs would further postpone the reopening of the German question and create greater leverage for the GDR in other areas of interest to them in Soviet–East German relations.[12] Again, apparent changes in the Soviet emphasis on the conventional phase of military operations against the West placed East Germany at the center of Soviet strategic military interests *vis-à-vis* the West. Still, the SED's efforts to make an important contribution to Soviet interests in military affairs entailed several demands on their own internal social and military policies.

The SED had to some extent to meet the social and economic expectations of the East German populace in order to counteract the attractiveness of the West German state in an era of detente. The social disturbances in Poland which culminated in the removal of the Polish Communist Party's (PUWP) First Secretary in 1971 only served to refocus the SED's attention on the importance of satisfying consumer demands for a higher standard of living. Implicit in this recognition was the need to sustain stable economic growth rates in order to meet Soviet demands for continuing military modernization.

During this time of expanding contacts with the West the SED pursued a more utilitarian approach to the problem of legitimacy. In contrast to Ulbricht's economic policies of limited decentralized reform and of sacrificing consumption to the demands of investment in order to overtake the West German economy, the SED embarked on a course that was calculated to court East German consumption needs. The effects of this change in economic strategy were evident as the East German economy achieved significant growth with the material product increasing 5.5 percent per annum in 1971–75 and some 4.2 percent annually during the period 1976–80.[13] Domestically, Honecker pursued economic policies that included greater centralization of party control over the economy and a distinctly egalitarian flavor. Minimum wage levels were raised in 1972 and again in 1976. Pensioners in 1976 received on the average 100 marks more a month than in 1970.[14] Honecker also launched the SED on an ambitious housing program with the self-proclaimed goal of eliminating housing as a social problem by 1990.[15] Foreign investment, mainly West German, poured into the GDR[16] and assisted greatly in sustaining the highest level of industrialization in the Soviet Bloc. In the GDR, per capita income rose to a level twice as high as in any other Pact country.[17]

To these internally propelled social and economic developments was added the probability that the Soviet-directed policy of limited cooperation with the Federal Republic would result in greater exposure of the East German armed forces to West German cultural, economic and political penetration. This set the stage for the SED's simultaneous policy of maintaining increasingly close Soviet–East German military cooperation within the framework of the Soviet-led combined armed forces and forging a stronger political base for the legitimacy of Soviet–East German cooperation.

Improving Soviet–East German combat collaboration

Between 1969 and 1977, the 73.5 percent increase in the size of the
GDR's defense budget confirmed that detente and peaceful coexistence had not persuaded anyone in East Berlin to reduce or simply
stabilize the GDR's defense expenditures.[18] In fact, East German
defense spending grew at a much faster rate from 1970 to 1975 than in
the 1965–70 period. Moreover, the higher annual percentage rates of
growth in nonpersonnel costs in the GDR during the early seventies
indicated rapid progress in the mechanization and modernization of
the East German armed forces.[19] This was evidenced by the fact that
while the nominal order of battle of both GSFG and NVA did not
change substantially after 1969, there were significant infusions of
newer T-62 (and later T-72) tanks and artillery, heavy folding bridges
and engineer equipment, MI-24 helicopters and MiG-23 fighters.
Although East German ground force strength in the NVA and border
troops grew only slightly until 1979, the personnel strengths of the
NVA air and naval forces did rise in response to the introduction of
newer equipment. As in the past, all NVA and GSFG units remained
Category I units. In addition, the East German Army fielded its first
airborne unit, the "Willi Sanger" parachute battalion (see selected
data and defense expenditure tables in the Appendix).[20]

These qualitative improvements in armaments were necessary to
support East German participation in a new wave of exercises involving command elements, staffs and troops of the GSFG and the NVA.
This activity followed on the heels of Soviet intervention in Czechoslovakia and continued through the seventies.[21] To some extent, the
GDR's military environment after the 1968 Soviet intervention in
Czechoslovakia and the Soviet interest in gaining international recognition for existing European borders was based on its geographical
location. However, the number and frequency of exercises do reflect
the already prominent East German role in the Pact's largest combined exercises even before the events in Poland during 1981 and
confirm the strong East German military commitment to Soviet
regional strategy. (See list of major Pact exercise activity involving
East German participation in Table 8 in the Appendix.)

In the words of one analyst, these exercises were designed to merge
the NVA and the GSFG into "a homogeneous and functional combat
machine."[22] In this regard, the problems of coordination and control
were clearly the focus of Soviet and East German attention in most of
these exercises. For instance, "Comrades-in-Arms 70," which took
place in the vicinity of Magdeburg in October 1970, engaged 100,000

troops from every country in the Pact (Romania limited its participation to 300 troops). During the exercise, Soviet and East German
troops operated jointly under the nominal command of the GDR
Defense Minister and were featured in combined air-sea landings
involving East German, Polish and Soviet airborne troops. Although
the exercise demonstrated problems in communications between
Soviet and East German staffs and headquarters,[23] "Comrades-in-
Arms," "Shield 72," "Visla-Elbe" and "Shield 76" confirmed the
new seriousness with which the Soviet and East German military
elites approached the challenge of military cooperation. This is not to
say that the previous emphasis on offensive operations was in any
way diminished by the focus on command and control. On the
contrary, the new initial phase of conventional operations in Pact
exercises suggested that the primacy of offensive action remained
intact.

Joint GSFG–NVA training now focused on dealing more
thoroughly with the problems of offensive conventional military
operations. During the seventies training tasks for the NVA called for
improvements in:[24]

(1) the time to mobilize reserve units to a state of combat readiness;
(2) combat training performance under conditions which closely
     approximate combat;
(3) the ability and skill of commanders and staffs to exercise con-
     tinuous troop control during combat and in organizing logistics;
(4) reinvigorated political work.

The emphasis on the East German role in military mobilization and
preparation for offensive operations against the West involved the
prepositioning of larger war stocks and the construction of logistical
pipelines across Poland to supply points in the GDR. In the seventies,
the GDR's well-organized administrative infrastructure began to
provide a substantial advantage to the Soviets in their quest for high
readiness combat power on the ground in a forward deployed
posture. By the mid seventies, over 1,200,000 Soviet and East German
men-at-arms were distributed over the territory of a nation the area of
which is smaller than the state of Ohio. This amounted to eleven
soldiers and armed security forces per square kilometer of East
German territory.[25] Stefan Heym, East German author and critic,
noted sarcastically that "everywhere you spit there is a Soviet
tank!"[26] In order to enhance the East German capability to mobilize
all military industrial assets for NVA–GSFG use, the SED increasingly subordinated the mission of civil defense and mobilization to
the NVA's control.[27]

At the Ninth SED party Congress on 22 May 1976, the forces of civil defense were officially included among the armed organs of the GDR state and for the first time placed under NVA command rather than control of the Ministry of State Security.[28] Included in this process were the former garrison Air Defense Battalions (roughly 15,000 men), special reconnaissance forces and armament enterprises and facilities. This shift of control doubtlessly occurred in response to similar measures that were then being implemented in the Soviet Union.[29] This point notwithstanding, the impact on the GDR state's military mobilization capability was quite significant.

Ten years earlier, training in the worker's combat groups suggested an essentially tertiary role for these units as home defense forces.[30] However, the introduction of new equipment and closer integration with the NVA and the GSFG during large-scale pact exercises indicate a more prominent role for the roughly 15,000 combat groups across the country. During the 1970s and 1980 exercises, "Comrades-in-Arms," East German civil defense forces in cooperation with mobilized workers' combat groups functioned under NVA command to practice plans for civil defense mobilization.[31] According too official statements these exercises acted to enhance, "combat, operational and mobilizational readiness and cooperation between the armed forces as well as with party and state organs."[32] In sum, the GDR's workers' combat groups were converted during the seventies into a military instrument to which the other pact states had nothing comparable. Most of the combat groups appeared to be capable of acting as reserve units for the NVA in the event of war and were sufficiently well equipped with artillery and armored vehicles in the eighties to conduct "limited, independent combat operations."[33]

The NVA's higher profile in matters pertaining to civil defense was also accompanied by growing military and security representation in the political and economic institutions of the GDR state. On the whole, the number of representatives on the SED Central Committee and Politburo from the areas of internal and external security steadily increased from the beginning of Erich Honecker's term in office as SED First Secretary.[34] A survey of leading positions within the party and state which are held by representatives of the security forces, in particular the NVA minus the main political administration, has shown a consistently strong presence.[35] While some of this may be attributed to Honecker's own experience in the Ministry of State Security, the proliferation of uniformed officers in key positions of civil administration is not without precedent in Russian or German history. As Ivan Sylvain notes in the following passage, the SED's reliance on military cadres to carry on the daily operations of the East German state bares a resemblance to the Prussian state of Frederick I that is too striking to ignore:

Besides occupying numerous directly related paramilitary positions, general rank officers are deputies in the Ministries of Foreign Trade, Construction and Transportation, the State Planning Commission and the General State Procuracy. In addition, a military officer is the state secretary of the Main Administration of the Council of Ministers. Those of lower rank, such as retired field grade officers, are likely to find a place in a parallel economic or party position.[36]

Subordination of defense-related activities in the civil sector to NVA control was also matched by similar developments in the armament, training and control of the GDR's 50,000 man border forces. Although the border forces had originally been assigned to the command and control of the GDR's ministry of state security, new infusions of modern combat equipment and restructuring on the model of the NVA's motorized rifle formations suggested that the GDR Ministry of Defense planned to integrate the border forces into the NVA in the event of a conflict.[37] According to former NVA and border force officers who now live in the West, with the approval of the VGK, NVA–GSFG war planning in the seventies began to assign to the border forces the mission to seize bridges, strategic road crossings and installations suitable for telephone points on West German territory along the roughly 1,400 kilometer line of demarcation between the two German states.[38] As part of the distribution of tasks, border units were also assigned the critical mission of protecting important areas from breakthrough attacks by the enemy into GDR territory.

This significantly expanded the cooperation of the border forces in the GDR's zone of military security with the GSFG. Of the thirty-two major installations which were erected along the inter-German border as part of the East German zonal complex for air space surveillance and early warning, the majority were placed under the permanent control of the GSFG for use in electronic disruption and deception measures.[39] This movement forward of Soviet-controlled installations and the inclusion of the border forces in war planning had important implications for the way in which the Soviets would initiate hostilities with the West.

The plan to turn the GDR into the advance fortress and logistical turntable for the Soviet Central European Front seemed to support NVA–GSFG deployment by exercise/maneuver along the lines witnessed in the 1973 Israeli–Egyptian war. In the field, NVA–GSFG training began to concentrate on the difficulties associated with traversing the impediments of West German rivers, and mounting movements to contact directly from military installations in the GDR.[40] This meant that Soviet and East German divisions were being trained to attack across the inter-German border from the march column without assembling prior to deployment. Though the problems of military interoperability still left open to debate just how closely Russians and Germans could cooperate in a conflict with NATO, Soviet coverage of these exercises did suggest that the East Germans were fully admitted to the offensive designs under consideration by the Soviet High Command.[41]

Exercise coverage after 1971 always featured the NVA ground forces in a mixed configuration with similar GSFG formations. The exercises were further characterized in the press as being conducted under conditions which were "maximally close to combat."[42] The following excerpt from an East German soldier's letter to his friends and family that was later published in Der Spiegel would seem to confirm the accuracy of this assertion:

When I returned to the Barracks, they told me to pick up my little satchel (combat pack). We were off on a battalion combat exercise. Our whole battalion launched an attack and kept it up for three days. We got no rest at all. They constantly kept us going with "charge!" or "dig in!" Night and day. And they fired live ammunition. The enemy positions were indicated with camouflaged targets which we had to shoot down ... My unit got through the maneuvers alright except for one soldier who died in the hospital after having an accident ... They had many accidents in the tank units but very little ever gets out into the open.[43]

In retrospect, it would appear that various forms and methods were utilized extensively by the SED to realize the aim of improving Soviet–East German military cooperation. At the alliance level, East German participation in joint Pact-wide exercises with the GSFG in the field allowed the command and staff elements of both forces to focus on the main tactical military tasks to be accomplished. On bilateral levels, the plans for cooperation which were developed by the GDR Ministry of National Defense and the command element of the GSFG seemed to have figured most prominently.[44] In 1972, the SED Central Committee announced plans to extend the uniformity of equipment and tactical battle drill to the areas of troop leading techniques and political training in order to reinforce Soviet–East German military interdependence.[45] Army General Heinz Hoffmann reiterated these plans to the NVA rank and file.

Relations among the brothers-in-arms must include all units and formations. The soldiers and noncommissioned officers should have more opportunity for direct meetings with the brothers-in-arms – including shop talk, athletic competition and cultural recreation. It is also necessary to increase the knowledge of the army members about the socialist fraternal countries and their armed forces.[46]

Below the division level in the East German Army, the vehicle for achieving these aims became a program known as *Waffenbrüderschaftsbeziehungen* or brotherhood-in-arms.[47] This program entailed East German subunits at common training centers and contacts between units in the course of "socialist competition," "combat cooperation weeks" and "regiment next door" meetings.[48]

Given the close proximity of all East German military installations to Soviet Army posts, organizing these programs did not present a major problem (see table in the Appendix). East German unit commanders were socialized to regular contact with the GSFG in the formative stages of the NVA's development. However, the emphasis on more frequent and regular contact after 1969 enabled the Soviets to train on what has amounted in some units to a weekly or monthly basis with East German units which may, in fact, go to war with them. Needless to say, in the volatile region of Central Europe which is characterized by strong anti-Soviet sentiment, these programs also allow the Soviets to keep the East Germans under constant surveillance.[49]

In this joint setting with the Soviets, East German and Soviet units from neighboring regiments compete in firing, cooperate in the utilization and maintenance of equipment and participate together in simulated combat exercises.[50] To support this kind of rigorous collaboration the East German soldier's time has been devoted to three general areas of activity: (1) the introduction into the NVA of newer equipment of Soviet manufacture; (2) the reduction in time to mobilize NVA units to augment the GSFG for war; and (3) an increase in the emphasis on uniform political–military training and socialization of East German and Soviet troops. From the standpoint of the SED, these areas of political and military cooperation between the Soviet and East German forces are designed to ease the "progressive integration" of East German forces with the Soviet-dominated combined armed forces of the Warsaw Pact.[51]

Breaching the limits of military integration

In an article which outlines the partnership experience between an armored regiment of the NVA and an armored regiment of the GSFG, the author begins by stating that the modernization of the NVA's equipment served as the chief catalyst for intensified collaboration with the Soviet forces.[52] Since in the view of the author it is virtually impossible for the NVA to accomplish its assigned tactical mission without the assistance and guidance of the GSFG, the political unity and resolve of the two socialist armies must find tangible, concrete expression in joint military activity. While casting the Soviet tank regiment in the role of tutor, the author proceeds to examine the areas in which partnership with the GSFG has produced qualitative improvements in the performance of an NVA tank formation with the GSFG. Predictably, these improvements have occurred in the areas of Russian language proficiency, conduct of operations in a nuclear environment, creative tactical initiative and general technical proficiency. Most interesting is the observation that NVA soldiers habitually overestimate the role and importance of technology in combat – something which the authors insist the Soviet "comrades" do not. In addition, the article contains descriptions of Soviet and East German tank companies operating jointly under Soviet and East German command.[53]

It is speculative to make any statements concerning the effectiveness and utility of these partnership associations. However, certain conclusions may be drawn from the open literature and discussions with former NVA officers and soldiers who now live in the West. First, the degree of Soviet–East German integration is a function of how well the units' officers and senior noncommissioned officers have mastered Russian. It stands to reason then that cooperation would be most effective in those units where the leader-to-led ratio is highest. This appears to be the case in tank units where every third tank has an officer as its vehicle commander. The fact that virtually all of the NVA's officers are party members simply reinforces this. On the other hand, man-intensive infantry or engineer battalions may have greater difficulty in their attempts to cooperate with the Soviet Army.[54]

Moreover, the actual extent of Soviet–East German military cooperation would seem to vary from branch to branch in the NVA. In the East German Army, effective cooperation is generally limited to the battalion level where there are sufficient numbers of officers who speak Russian well enough to collaborate with the Soviets. In the

Soviet and East German Air Force where there are greater numbers of officers, joint air activity and airspace control is more easily coordinated.[55] This is, however, no mean accomplishment for the East Germans who unlike their Polish or Czech counterparts speak a language which is radically different from Russian. No amount of common equipment, common training standards or simple "good will" is an adequate substitute for effective communication. This is one reason the NVA has stressed the importance of Russian language training and military education in the Soviet Union. East Germany reportedly sends more officers for schooling in the Soviet Union than any other Pact country.[56] On average, this amounts to roughly 120 officers a year.[57]

Although many of the factors which have affected the growth and development of Soviet–East German military cooperation have already been discussed, the key to the success or failure of these activities has always rested on the officer-to-officer relations between the two military establishments. To facilitate the cooperation of the Soviet and East German forces, major attention in the NVA has been directed to the training and education of East German officer cadres in the Soviet Union. By 1975, 1,000 NVA officers had reportedly graduated from several Soviet military institutions including Frunze and Voroshilov General Staff College.[58] This fact has been a source of growing satisfaction to the NVA leadership. In 1975, Horst Stechbarth, NVA ground forces commander, took the opportunity to comment on the achievement: "Presently regimental and division commanders of the NVA and GSFG have known each other from their student days at Soviet military academies."[59] In a speech celebrating the thirtieth anniversary of the National People's Army, the GDR Deputy Defense Minister, Lieutenant General Horst Brünner alluded to the important role which the graduates of Soviet military academies play in the NVA.

Today's Army has a highly qualified officers corps. Seventy-three percent are university graduates and 25 percent college graduates. The 2,400 graduates from Soviet military academies and 170 generals, admirals and officers who studied at the Academy of the General Staff of the USSR Armed Forces helped greatly to ensure that the findings of Soviet military science were applied broadly and creatively.[60]

The significance that the SED and the Soviet military establishment attach to extensive training in the Soviet military educational system cannot be overstated. Admission to the Soviet mid and late career academies guarantees advancement beyond the rank of major to the

East German officers and an opportunity to serve in the NVA's key command and staff positions. The price of admission to higher responsibility is demonstrated professional competence and acquiescence in the Soviet domination of the Pact military structure.[61]

Since Soviet political culture and the Russian language permeate the Pact command structure, a conformity of thought and action with Soviet norms seems unavoidable. If this is not present before training in the Soviet Union, the years spent in the Soviet Union and continued association with Soviet military elites attempt to foster it. In public gatherings and receptions for Soviet and East German graduates of Soviet military academies who serve in the NVA and the GSFG, the officer corps of the two military establishments are treated officially as part of one army.[62] Perhaps more important from the standpoint of SED and Soviet control of the NVA is the Soviet practice of asking candidates to sign what amounts to an oath of loyalty to the Soviet state under the pretext of having been given access to privileged Soviet military information.[63] Refusal to either attend Soviet education courses or to sign such statements immediately places an NVA officer's career in serious jeopardy. This policy appears to be another way in which the Soviets identify trusted loyalists who could be extremely valuable, particularly in a crisis. One Pact officer explained this point during an interview with A. Ross Johnson: "Graduates of the Soviet military academies who have signed a cooperation agreement should not be thought of as regular agents who cooperate with the Soviets on a daily basis. Rather they form a network which the Soviets may tap when the need arises."[64]

At the very least, the image of the loyal East German officer who can be trusted by the Soviet military is forcefully promoted in the Soviet and East German military presses.[65] An example helps illustrate this point. "I am a graduate of the Military Academy imeni M. V. Frunze," related NPA Major Horn, "I have many good friends in Moscow. Here too I have become acquainted with many Soviet officers. Our subunit maintains close ties with one of the battalions of the GSFG. We hold joint exercises and exchange know-how."[66]

In the process of consolidating the NVA's functional military ties with the GSFG that are formed in joint training, the NVA's leadership seemed to be projecting a military image which mirrored the policy stances of the SED itself. While the Czechoslovak Army underwent "resovietization" and the Soviet-sponsored political and social order in Gierek's Poland deteriorated further and further, the NVA's political organs exhorted East Germany's officer corps to strive for "the standards set by the Soviet Army" and to "educate the troops, train them and lead them in battle in accordance with this yardstick."[67] In this connection, cooperation with the Soviet Army has been consistently depicted in terms of emulating what the NVA's leadership continues to insist is the world's best military establishment. The historical lesson for members of the army means to "learn from the Soviet Army how one fights and wins."[68]

However, to those East German officers who have grown accustomed to the relatively efficient and technically competent approach to military training within the NVA, these assertions of military superiority must seem incredible. Regular contact with the GSFG cannot have inspired much admiration for the Soviet Army. The GSFG is not without its problems. Persistent training deficiencies have received attention in the Soviet military press in the hope of mitigating the tendency to laxity and complacency in GSFG units. The fact that these descriptions have appeared at all suggests that the problems are even more substantial than has been reported. In many cases, Soviet units fail to either achieve the standards of training which are established at higher headquarters[69] or to train at all.[70] In reviewing the training results in a motorized rifle battalion of the GSFG, one inspecting officer noted: "Let us say directly: the picture did not cause joy now either. The companies and other subunits which we had the occasion to visit were not distinguished by either the teamwork or the ability of the personnel ... It turns out that the reason for the failures was not nervousness, as someone asserted, but the irresponsible attitude of some leaders."[71] Under these circumstances, a "look over the fence at the Soviet comrades-in-arms" hardly "sharpens the eye for one's own level of performance."[72]

Notwithstanding these observations, joint training and education of the GDR's military elite with the Soviet military elite has probably assisted in the identification of those who resent Soviet military dominance and those who acquiesce in it. The evidence suggests that the functional integration between the East German and Soviet military elites in the GSFG has produced greater conformity of thought and action with Soviet norms than elsewhere in Eastern Europe.[73] As a result, a common feature of the Soviet and East German military elites in the GDR appears to be that they are both committed to a set of military habits and practices which are directed toward the realization of common political goals: defense of the socio-political status quo and advancing militarily the interests of the Soviet–East German regional political order. In some cases, however, the fact that the NVA's military elites seem more "Russian" in their attitudes than the Russians themselves has reportedly provoked revulsion among the East German conscripts.[74]

The view from below is never flattering to an officer in any army and the NVA is no exception. However, there is evidence that the existing morale problems associated with detente and latent German nationalism in the GDR have only been compounded by the unfortunate consequence of having adopted more than the organizational and political structure of the Soviet Army. The callous disregard of Russian officers for their men and the ensuing distaste of the enlisted ranks for their officers which has long been an historical characteristic of Russian military establishments seemed to find their way into some of the NVA's units in the seventies. In the Red Army this resulted in a level of enlisted hostility toward officers which far exceeded similar tensions in West European armies.[75] This would appear to be the case in today's Soviet Army and may have become a problem for the East Germans for the first time since the closing days of World War I. Naturally, the official picture of the East German officer suggests a much different image: "A socialist army officer distinguishes himself through unconditional devotion to party and people."[76] The real picture that emerged in the 1970s, however, would seem to contradict this image.

In contrast to the method and mentality of the officers in the Reichswehr and its offspring the Wehrmacht, NVA officers appear to be far less sensitive to the needs of their soldiers. While the bond between officers and enlisted men is emphasized publicly in the context of socialism, in reality, today's NVA officers are not as highly regarded by their soldiers as were their German predecessors. In the last war German soldiers described their officers as "brave, efficient and considerate."[77] In view of the fact that NVA officers are virtually all party members and their conscript soldiers are not, the existing gap between popular and official political culture would have to be reflected to some extent in the relations between the NVA's enlisted men and their officers.

It is therefore not surprising that the NVA has experienced some discipline problems since the onset of detente. Like all European armies, the NVA has had its share of deserters – in spite of almost insurmountable obstacles to flight and intensive political indoctrination.[78] Reports in 1972 indicated that the results of intrabattalion competition in all subjects had actually declined and the conduct of the NVA's enlisted ranks in public had deteriorated. In the Berlin garrison area alone more than 100 severe penalties were imposed in one month for enlisted soldiers' refusal to obey orders, violent assaults on superior officers, sloppy uniforms and alcohol abuse.[79] East German border troops were reported as listening to Western broadcasts, alternating sleep between sentries and simply skipping border patrols![80] Officer treatment of NVA and border force enlisted ranks may have only exacerbated the problems which an unconvincing Western threat to the GDR created. A conscript described his own experiences in the following terms:

We had to dig foxholes for ourselves and lie there, in position, 4 hours, at several degrees below zero. We were not allowed to start any fires – for tactical reasons. But the officers of course warmed their asses in the heater tent and drank brandy. This is where you find out that you are lower than dirt when you are a common soldier.[81]

In response to this state of affairs, the senior military leadership urged a greater sense of "comradeship" among all army members by stressing the essential class unity between officers and enlisted men. "All members of the NVA and the GDR Border Guard, regardless of their rank and assignment, are sons of the working population. They are unfamiliar with class barriers and misanthropy arising from private ownership of the means of production."[82] Of course, these assertions presuppose the existence of mutual esteem which apparently was not automatic between the officers and their enlisted men. Nevertheless, there was a growing recognition that working and living conditions were important factors in the NVA's efforts to increase combat strength and combat readiness. NVA soldiers, like their Soviet contemporaries in the GSFG, have not been above rioting over bad food and poor living conditions.[83]

As a result, the NVA's military leadership began efforts to upgrade living conditions for conscripts and to employ political officers in much the same way Western armies use chaplains.[84] However, the desire to sustain military performance at nearly any cost has led the NVA military elite to rely more heavily on coercion than on sound principles of leadership which the political contradictions in the NVA may make difficult to implement anyway. "To be a disciplined soldier, to render unconditional obedience to a military superior, to fulfill orders resolutely," these were and are the NVA's stated priorities for its enlisted men.[85] As of 1 October 1982, a new disciplinary regulation went into effect in the NVA. In this executive decree, service in disciplinary units modeled on Soviet penal divisions for serious infractions can last from one to three months. NVA sources termed this law "decisive for the fighting power and combat readiness of the National People's Army, that is, tightening up of military discipline."[86] This new regulation gave regimental commanders and above the authority to reassign NVA enlisted men for punishment to these units provided that "certain conditions" are met. These conditions remain vague, however, and open to command interpretation.

The evidence suggests that the SED's efforts to maintain a very high standard of discipline and to improve the working and living conditions of NVA soldiers could not remove all of the political and social contradictions which underpin enlisted discontent in the NVA. However, the combination of tighter control, more intensive training and improved working conditions have reportedly had a beneficial impact. According to former members of the US military liaison mission at Potsdam, East Germany, East German units are model formations when compared to their Soviet counterparts and overt expressions of contempt for officer authority are really quite rare.[87] One reason for the attention that is devoted to discipline in the East German military press may be that the standard of performance of East German conscripts is not only greater than that expected of their Soviet contemporaries, but greater than that of their opposites in the Bundewehr as well![88]

Still, the NVA's attention to these issues gives substantial reason to suppose that where meaningful cooperation breaks down or is almost non-existent is at the level of the individual soldier. Here the cultural and linguistic barriers which have traditionally inhibited more than an elite political consensus from emerging in the Russian and German-speaking worlds have coincided with the unconvincing Western threat to create significant obstacles to cooperation.

As mentioned, from the SED's perspective, detente was as much a Western strategy to subvert the socialist order in the GDR as it was a Soviet attempt to relax international tensions.[89] This helps to explain, in part, why the NVA leadership felt compelled to redouble the normal political effort in the NVA to disabuse East German conscripts of the notion that an apparent relaxation of tensions between the superpowers did not equate to a new era of international peace and stability.[90]

Part of the answer also lies in the SED's decision in the seventies to abandon Ulbricht's claim that a social order had been created in the GDR which was superior to that in West Germany. The alternative to Ulbricht's stance was simply to exaggerate the distinctions between the two German states in order to convey the message to GDR citizens that the differences were unbridgeable in political and social terms.

This change in official attitude necessitated a permanent friend–

foe polarization between East and West Germany. Thus, political training in the detente setting was designed to equip commanders and political cadres with the necessary arguments to counteract what NVA officers called "ideological softening" among soldiers and NCOs in the face of detente,[91] and to explain the new *modus vivendi* with the West as a consequence of the GDR's security relationship with the Soviet Union:

The results achieved are reflected in correctly understanding the fact that the policy of peaceful coexistence and the struggle for great fighting strength and combat readiness form an inseparable whole, that our time of class confrontation between socialism and imperialism requires great political and military vigilance and that the sights must be set constantly on the class enemy.[92]

Whereas before 1969 the SED emphasized the primary imperialist threat from the Federal Republic, after 1969 political work in the NVA stressed the aggressive nature of social democracy in the FRG and the multinational character of NATO's imperialist threat. With Honecker's accession to power, cultivating the enemy image in the minds of the GDR's youth, in the process of socialist defense education, became integrated into the GDR's education system at all levels.[93] In 1978, when deteriorating superpower relations were Europeanizing detente, Honecker elevated socialist military education to the status of a new independent central committee activity.[94] This reform introduced military science as a mandatory subject for East German children in the 9th through 12th grades. The stress of this educational approach became two-fold.

First, GDR educators sought to instill hatred for the traditional class enemy in the West and to strengthen resistance to supposedly imminent West German military aggression.[95] Secondly, the GDR's youth was pressured to accept and internalize the value of Soviet–East German military cooperation. To this end the SED assigned more than 52,000 specially trained SED members as propagandists in the Free German Youth (FDJ) educational circles during the 1977–78 school year.[96] "Under the direction of experienced educators, supported by comrades from the NVA and the Soviet Army, these Young Pioneers learn how to march by the map and the compass and to orient themselves in the terrain, to cross brooks and lakes, to send out radio messages and to render first aid."[97]

The SED party leadership evidently understood that without adequate preparation, new generations of East German soldiers might succumb to the ingrained cultural pressures which had often operated in the past to thwart cooperative efforts between East Germans and Russians:

A young soldier's readiness to seek conversation with his Soviet comrade-in-arms depends to a large extent on how his parents and teachers and his friends in the youth associations have trained him in respect to German–Soviet friendship. This also depends on the extent to which he has learned Russian, the language of his comrades-in-arms, in which commands are given in the joint defense forces.[98]

Without knowing precisely how effective these programs have been since their implementation in the seventies, their institutionalization in GDR society and the NVA probably did buttress the credibility of a Western threat and helped to justify closer integration with the Soviet armed forces within the NVA.[99] East German officers who are now in the West have always emphasized the effectiveness of the so-called "hate campaigns" in the NVA against the West. Since the young conscripts live in what amounts to a news blackout and total isolation (referred to as a "redlight period"), many former NVA officers refuse to believe that East German conscripts would be reluctant to engage NATO or West German troops in combat. A former battalion commander in the GDR's border forces made the following remark: "I warned officer cadets in the Federal Republic against believing that GDR soldiers would desert in droves in case of war. Despite all difficulties, the leadership is keeping a firm grip on the army, and it would be unconditionally deployed!"[100]

These observations suggest that when the impact of West German influence has been greatest the structure of NVA–GSFG cooperation with its emphasis on regular joint training, socialization and coercive discipline has helped to ensure the responsiveness of East German units to directives that may originate in higher Soviet headquarters.

Officially, the relaxation in tensions resulted in a justification for cooperation with the Soviet armed forces which was no longer based exclusively on the unity of class consciousness in the context of socialist internationalism or vague references to historical incidents of Soviet–German military cooperation. With the SALT accords in draft and the mutual balanced force reduction talks in Vienna about to begin, NVA political work took a more sophisticated approach. It reflected the Soviet line of thinking that the correlation of forces had shifted in favor of the Soviet Bloc:

The Soviet army is the nucleus of the allied armies, and it is their high state of combat readiness that is an essential prerequisite to the attainment of political results in the negotiations between the socialist community countries and the capitalist countries of Western Europe and the United States. In this sense the socialist defense forces produce security.[101]

At the same time, East German soldiers were supposedly encouraged to mix with their Soviet contemporaries on a new more intimate level:

Our army's leadership lays great store on having all units intensify their cooperation with the Soviet partner regiments so that enlisted men and noncommissioned officers can have even more contact with their comrades-in-arms at competitions both in simple professional matters and athletics and enjoy cultural events . . . [102]

In reality, the interaction of Soviet and East German soldiers remained constrained.[103] Soviet conscripts remained deliberately isolated from the German populace and contacts between Germans and Russians in other than a professional military setting were carefully staged and kept to a minimum. It may be hypothesized that the Soviet authorities were not really interested in closer relations at the soldier level since any intimacies which developed could complicate the requirement, under conditions of social disorder in the GDR, to shoot down local German inhabitants. Another reason may be that Soviet soldiers will discover how much better NVA soldiers live than Soviet soldiers.[104] One East German citizen summed it up differently: "These are people from the East and we are Central Europeans; it just does not go together."[105] After all, Germans have traditionally regarded the Eastern Slavs as economically backward and culturally inferior. Perhaps the Soviet authorities were concerned that greater East German exposure to the Soviet soldiers would only confirm rather than refute these German stereotypes. Former East German soldiers have remarked that the "Russian barracks always stank. The stench was really pervasive. They don't seem to hold much for hygiene. This creates a very bad impression."[106]

The East German willingness to break with the unhappy past in military terms has not been matched by similar Soviet efforts. Many Soviet officers reportedly still refer openly to the East German forces as the "fascist army" and the mention of Germans still conjures up images of bloodthirsty Nazis in the minds of Soviet youth.[107] At the same time, the disciplined ranks and professional performance of the East German Army have become a source of pride to the East Germans while the sloppy looking and ill-disciplined Soviet troops in the GDR have become objects of derision for the East German populace.[108]

East German pride in the NVA soldiers by the end of the 1970s should not be surprising. It should be remembered that by 1976 more than 57 percent of the GDR's population was under the age of forty. Consequently, in the seventies, the SED could claim that the GDR's postwar generation had become a product and part of the developing socialist system.[109] Since only very few East Germans could recall the vivid scenes of Soviet brutality and barbarism during the occupation period, most of the serious war wounds had been healed. This has been reflected in the comments of some of the more recent East German émigrés to the West:

I must state quite clearly that there is no feeling of hatred against Soviet people or Soviet troops, but there is clear resentment for the presence of these troops and the ensuant overpopulation. One might say that nearly all forest areas are occupied by troops. Wherever you go you find barracks. The main problem among the people, which troubles particularly the housewives, is the fact that the Soviet troops are supplied from GDR stocks. And this is what the people fail to understand. They say that the USSR is so big and rich in natural resources that it should really not need to be fed by the small GDR.[110]

This suggests then that while there have been reasons to doubt the accuracy of the official picture of Soviet–East German brotherhood-in-arms at the soldier level, the combination of time, joint socialization, education, training and control after 1969 did remove some of the most significant barriers to cooperation. However, the political consensus which sustained military cooperation between the two peoples was still limited before and after 1969 to the ruling military–political elites in both states.

Summary

Given the degree of integration which the East German forces had already achieved with the Soviet establishment in the formative stages of their military development, Soviet military planning continued to position the NVA in the forefront of the Pact forces deployed against the West. After 1969, the combination of already existing integrative mechanisms for Soviet–East German military collaboration and ever-rising East German defense expenditures left no doubt who the Soviet Union's junior military partner in the Pact really was (see defense expenditure, Table 6). The growth in East German trade with West Germany and the rapidly growing East German economy only confirmed that the GDR was regaining Prussia–Germany's central importance to Soviet Russia's European strategy. The same domestic economic strength which had helped finance military modernization in the sixties was used to support an ambitious military policy.[111]

External to the GDR, the factors which positioned the Soviet Union
and East Germany in the world arena changed with the departure of
Ulbricht as SED First Secretary. When West Germany abandoned the
trenches of the cold war and embarked upon a policy of East–West
reconciliation of its own, "Moscow shifted its interests in Eastern
Europe under a serious threat."[112] In a resumption of what appeared
to be the Rapallo strategy, Moscow focused its attention on enticing
the West Germans into a more cooperative economic and political
relationship with the Pact which the Soviet Union could manage.

Internally, the changes in Soviet foreign policy were matched by
changes in East Germany's relationship with West Germany. In order
to offset the potentially contaminating influences that an increasingly
porous border with the West might inflict on GDR society, the SED
turned to broader policies of societal militarization and control in
which the NVA played an important role. Beyond its ostensibly
external defense role, the NVA assumed greater responsibility for
civil defense and cooperated more regularly with the GDR's paramilitary forces.

Within the East German forces, the SED employed new methods in
order to augment the policy of ideological indoctrination for the
tighter integration of East German with Soviet forces and to enhance
NVA cohesion, discipline and morale. While the SED persisted in the
modernization of its armed forces and in the joint Soviet–East
German training and schooling efforts which had started in the
sixties, new programs such as the "regiment next door,"
"brotherhood-in-arms" and "combat collaboration" events and
"socialist competition" were introduced to make the structure of
Soviet–East German military collaboration as commonplace and
frictionless as possible.[113]

Despite the existing limits of integration imposed by language and
culture, by the end of the seventies, this structure appeared to ensure
that East German military resources were readily available for Soviet
use and that they would contribute effectively to a Soviet-led offensive against the West or any other opponent which the General Staff in
Moscow might be ordered to attack.[114] As the Soviet leadership began
to impute a new integrative meaning to the Pact's doctrine of
coalitional warfare, First Secretary Honecker lost no time in advertis-
ing the NVA as the archetypal "coalition army" or in pointing out
East Germany's thorough integration into the Warsaw Pact's emerging system for Soviet regional command, control and mobilization:

Cooperation between the staffs, divisions and units of both armies has
achieved a qualitatively new stage especially in recent years. More and more

directly does it affect the improvement of combat strength and readiness in the National People's Army. Our collaboration in the Alert System, common training bases, help in the mastering of new weapons and equipment, the fruitful exchange of experiences and performance comparisons have become everyday reality... [115]

Within the Soviet bloc, the Soviet Union's bilateral military relationship with the SED became even more prominent after events in Czechoslovakia and Poland raised questions in the minds of Soviet military planners about the reliability of the armed forces and party leaderships in those states. By the end of the seventies, there was reason to believe that the Soviet–East German structure of collaboration which stressed unquestioning subordination to Soviet command and cooperation with the Soviet military at the division level and below had become a model that the Soviets would like to replicate regionally. In light of the relatively new theater of military operations (TVD) orientation in the Soviet armed forces, reforming the Pact's military establishments along the GSFG–NVA lines would be vital if the Soviet design for combined and integrated Pact forces in war were to work.

The GSFG–NVA pattern of integration and control clearly offered the Soviets ideal conditions for control and influence with which to guarantee non-Soviet reliability and performance. Of course, it remained open to question whether the Soviet military could integrate East European conventional forces on the East German pattern. A number of factors which traditionally favored Soviet military control in East Germany since 1945 have not existed in the other strategically vital countries of the Warsaw Pact's Northern Tier – Poland and Czechoslovakia.

First, the status of the East German state still reflects the legacy of Soviet military occupation.[116] Although the NVA's ground force modernization program in the seventies achieved ratios of 285 tanks and 250 armored vehicles per 10,000 men (in contrast to the Polish ground forces with 176 tanks and 250 armored vehicles),[117] the GDR's armed forces remained among the smallest in the Warsaw Pact. Second, the SED in the post-1968 Pact pushed even harder for military integration on the assumption that close cooperation in security affairs with the Soviet state would prevent the Soviets from reopening the German question, or embarking on foreign policies which could impinge on the stability of the GDR's social order.[118] This condition combined with East German socio-economic stability probably led Moscow to see itself as somewhat reliant on the GDR military state which it perceived after 1968 to be an indispensable military clamp ensuring the cohesion of the Soviet Bloc.[119] Third, the

SED's willingness and capacity to support the costs of military modernization was unique in the Pact and this positioned East Germany on the leading edge of military technology and, consequently, in a role calculated to command intrabloc and international respect. The SED's military assistance programs in the Third World also contributed to this process of intrabloc prestige and communist party image-building. Finally, whereas the Czechs, Slovaks and Poles still entertained notions of divesting themselves of Soviet influence and control, in the sixties and seventies the East German population still perceived no alternative to the existing political status quo in Central Europe.[120]

In light of these conditions and of East Germany's military ascendancy, the special Soviet–East German military relationship was articulated in the context of the 1975 Treaty of Friendship, Cooperation and Mutual Aid. Under the new treaty, East Germany's military obligations were extended in a way that permitted the Soviet High Command to deploy East German forces to any military theater.[121]

For all of its military achievements, however, the SED leadership still had profound reasons for concern as the artificial coincidence of Soviet strategic priorities and the GDR's domestic developments placed the GDR state under extreme strains. The proliferation of contacts through television, radio and personal communication eroded the sense of estrangement that Ulbricht's policies of isolation from West Germany had promoted in the sixties. Moreover, the Helsinki process which recognized the GDR's territorial integrity created the foundations for the emergence of a substantial peace and anti-nuclear movement in the East German populace. Although the NVA had not succumbed to the threat of Western political and cultural penetration, the SED's efforts to foster the creation of an East German national consciousness through the use of socialist proletarian internationalism evidently made little progress. Most importantly, the economic productivity which had always been the foundation for social stability in the GDR and a moderate source of legitimacy for the SED showed signs of declining in 1979. How would the SED meet its military obligations to the CPSU if its soldiers questioned the validity of ideological arguments – the *raison d'être* of collaboration with the Soviets? What could be done to minimize the effects of East–West German contacts and sustain real industrial growth?

As it turned out, political and economic developments in neighboring Poland and the Soviet Union's relentless search for security coincided to assist the SED in its bid to remain the "second power in the Warsaw Pact."

4 The Soviet–East German military alliance and Poland

The events leading up to and including the declaration of martial law in Poland on 13 December 1981 had a direct bearing on bilateral Soviet–East German military relations and the conduct of Soviet regional security policy. The consistent failure of the Polish communist leadership to forge a national base for political and economic stability changed East Germany's position in the Pact dramatically. After a forty-year hiatus, the Soviet Union and another German military state became allies in the effort to manage or, if necessary, suppress Polish resistance to Soviet political hegemony in Eastern Europe.

By 1981 the growth and integration of Soviet and East German military power in the GDR had made East Germany the bulwark of the Soviet regional security system. Poland's military position had slipped precipitously as economic stagnation detracted from Polish political prestige and military modernization (see GNP and Defense Expenditure Tables in the Appendix). Politically, there was also evidence during 1981 that unlike Poland's work force, East German workers perceived the GDR state to be the guarantor of their standard of living and security. As the region's most faithful replica of the Soviet state and the Pact's most efficient centrally planned economy, the GDR also proved to be Soviet-style socialism's most ardent defender.

With the reappearance of the "Polish Problem" in 1980, these factors began to reanimate a more traditional array of mutually complementary national political and security interests in Soviet–East German relations. Historically, Germans and Russians have been Poland's chief political and military adversaries. In the most important instances of Russo-German military collaboration, Poland was the catalyzing influence for the external conditions which promoted cooperation. It was not without justification that many Polish citizens viewed the sudden intensification of the campaign to rehabilitate Prussian militarism in the GDR as an attempt to revitalize a set of military and political symbols with an unmistakably anti-Polish stamp.[1] To the Polish population this suggested that a new reactionary, pro-Russian, anti-Polish military state had emerged along the periphery of the Soviet imperium.[2] To observers in the West, Polish instability demonstrated that without the GDR the Warsaw Pact was probably an irrelevant actor on the international scene.[3] Still, few analysts grasped the real significance of the GDR's surge in military and political influence; as long as the GDR remains economically and politically stable Soviet political control of Central-East Europe cannot be successfully challenged anywhere in the region.

The legacy of conflict

Every Russian government since the time of Catherine the Great has insisted on Russia's preponderance in Poland's domestic and foreign affairs. Russian and German military power cooperated in the truncation and ultimate dissolution of the Polish state four times between 1772 and 1939. In each instance, the Russians were obliged to compensate the Prussians with Polish territory in return for their support of Russia's claim to the lion's share of Poland.[4] While the resulting partitions of Poland in 1772, 1793 and 1794 helped to forge an alliance with Prussia that endured for nearly a century, Russia's unusually harsh suppression of Polish independence in the years that followed the partitions created an equally strong legacy of anti-Russian sentiment in Poland.[5]

Soviet dominance of Poland was regarded in Soviet elite circles as vital to the CPSU's future control of Eastern Europe during World War II.[6] When the Red Army finally reached Warsaw in January 1945, the Soviet failure to support the Warsaw rising and the memory of Soviet duplicity during the German invasion of 1939 prevented the Soviet liberation of Poland from ever symbolizing a genuine reconciliation of the two peoples. Fully one-third of pre-World War II Poland still remains under Soviet control as a consequence of the Soviet Union's pact with Hitler, Germany's defeat in World War II and Western acquiescence in the territorial changes associated with the Yalta accords. Today, as in the past, any threat to Soviet security along a 1,000 kilometer line of communications that stretches from the Ukraine and Byelorussia across Poland to Berlin could weaken or jeopardize Soviet strategic interests in Germany, Czechoslovakia and Hungary. Thus, contemporary Soviet military strategy toward Europe continues to be based on ideological concerns and security interests that reflect a great emphasis on control of Poland.

Prussian–German sensitivity to traditional Russian security interests in Poland combined with an ideological distrust of Polish nationalist and democratic aspirations underpinned a compulsive opposition in Berlin to any degree of uncontrolled political change in Poland. For the most part, this made any German answer to demands for Polish independence other than repression impossible. Field Marshal von Boyen, who had commanded Prussian and Russian armies in the wars against Napoleon probably best expressed German elite sentiment when he advised his countrymen that "by contributing to an independent Poland, Prussia would be digging her own grave."[7]

In this respect, it is also relevant to reflect on the historical German view of Poles as people. In Germany, Poland's image has been rather negative. In the emotionally charged atmosphere of nineteenth-century European nationalism, the German public was presented with the view that the Poles were lazy, incompetent and incapable of governing themselves.[8] During Poland's armed conflicts with Russia for independence in 1848 and 1863, Bismarck warned that the Poles really aimed to: "incite Slav and Teuton against each other in the hope of creating a new Polish kingdom at their expense, no matter which side be victorious ... the Pole is an intriguer, hypocritical, untruthful and unreliable, quite incapable of maintaining a state organization."[9]

What happened in Poland under Nazi occupation to poison Polish–German relations is too well known to require detailed review. Nazi brutality left a lasting impression on the Polish psyche and had the effect on many Poles of merging the Polish national identity with anti-German nationalism. With the defeat of Germany, direct Soviet political control was extended to both German and Polish territory. In return for Poland's territorial losses to the Soviet Union, Poland was compensated with most of the German territory East of the Oder and Neisse rivers. In effect, this arrangement made Poland permanently reliant on the Soviet Union for its security and territorial integrity. Gradually, the rump of Brandenburg-Prussia was incorporated into the Warsaw Pact system as the GDR. However, the GDR's postwar communist leadership was not spared the attacks of anti-German Polish nationalism.

During the Warsaw Conference in May 1955, at which the GDR's communist leadership hoped to gain permission for East German rearmament, disputed borders and the whole question of a rearmed

German state became an issue. The Polish and Czechoslovak delegations demanded a series of treaties that guaranteed the postwar borders between them and the GDR before agreeing to the formal creation of an East German military establishment. Eventually, after the SED's recognition of the new territorial limits, and Soviet reassurances to the Polish party leadership in January 1956 that the new East German military establishment would remain subordinate to Soviet command and control, the SED's People's Police were redesignated the National People's Army and an East German ministry of defense was established.[10]

Not surprisingly, the SED under Ulbricht's leadership tended to view postwar manifestations of Polish nationalism with a mixture of fear and contempt. Władysław Gomułka's brand of national Polish communism evoked a visceral response from the SED in the fifties and the East German reaction to Polish social and political unrest in succeeding years continued to be very militant.[11]

The thaw which followed Khrushchev's speech to the Twentieth Party Congress in 1956 created opportunities for Poland's new indigenous communist leadership to assert its national interests and new problems for the SED and the CPSU. Gomułka committed the Polish United Worker's Party (PUWP) to liberal, social and economic policies while justifying these policies to Moscow as temporary expedients.[12] These promising steps in the direction of greater cultural and intellectual freedom included: (1) the discontinuance of police terror; (2) a relative freedom of creative activity; (3) a modus vivendi between church and state; and (4) the guarantee of private ownership in agriculture.[13] Under Gomułka's "national" communist leadership, the PUWP led the East European fight against consolidation of a common ideological line within the Bloc, while Ulbricht's SED adhered strictly to the Soviet line.

Partly inspired by Gomułka's example, a small number of East German communists under the leadership of Wolfgang Harich attempted the legal removal of Ulbricht from power on the grounds that the SED should be reformed on true Marxist–Leninist principles.[14] While the net effect of this experience probably stiffened Ulbricht's resistance to "de-Stalinization," the events of 1956 did not endear Poland's communist leadership to him either. East Berlin already had its hands full with liberalizing influences from the West without having to contend with equally destabilizing influences from the East! Ulbricht realized that the new GDR state was also potentially the Soviet Bloc's open wound. Unlike Gomułka, who initially enjoyed some measure of popularity as a victim of "Stalinism," Ulbricht had no illusions about the disenchantment with communism in the GDR and instead of liberalizing resorted to domestic and foreign policies that were designed to closely align the SED with the CPSU. This tended to poison relations between the GDR and Poland. The antipathy which had characterized Poland's relations with Prussia–Germany reasserted itself through the Gomułka regime in Warsaw. Anti-German sentiment in Poland was so pronounced in the sixties that it detracted from Polish–East German military relations as well.

Tensions in Polish–East German military relations

Stalin's efforts to "stuff the Polish goose" initially gained a valuable ally in the Polish people and the Polish military establishment. Gomułka's leadership emphasized certain historical continuities with the past: fierce nationalism, the traditional military symbols so dear to the hearts of the Poles and, most importantly, the historic hatred of the Germans.[15] The direct involvement of the Polish military elite in the process of de-Stalinization and liberalization after 1956, and especially their willingness to defend Gomułka's national communist regime, enhanced their role as the defender of the new anti-German postwar political order.[16] The postwar period during which the Soviet General Staff granted the Poles substantial military autonomy and independent responsibility for a Warsaw Pact front was bound up with Polish control of former German territory: "[The Polish People's Army] soldier defended the recovered independence and he participated in establishing a new social order; he cleared the land of mines and divided it among the peasants in the agricultural reform: *and he helped the settlers arriving in Warmia and Mazury and in the rebuilding of Warsaw.*"[17]

The willingness of the Polish military to defend the new Soviet-imposed territorial status quo did not, however, include ready acceptance of the GDR and cooperation with the East German military elite. A former East German air force officer who spent several months during 1966 at the Soviet air academy recalled the curious set of "international" relations which evolved in the school's multinational student body. Despite some initial difficulty with the Russian officers whose experiences in the war made them understandably reluctant to rapidly develop close relations with the East Germans, eventually the East Germans and Russians got along rather well.[18] Apparently, the same could not be said for the Polish officers.

In the fifties and sixties, hostility in the Polish military establishment toward the German communist state greatly exceeded anti-Soviet sentiment. On one occasion, the East German major recounted the verbal abuse that the Poles directed at the East Germans during a New Years' Eve party:

Exhausted from the party, we [East Germans] collapsed onto our beds. Suddenly a Polish Lieutenant Colonel screams "You German pigs! We will club you to death yet! You are nothing but Moscow's miserable satellites!" Again and again, we had political confrontations with the Polish officers in the course. They don't like us and often demonstrate their hostility. At the same time, we have endeavored to be especially friendly towards them. Guilty feelings concerning treatment of the Poles by the Germans are not unknown to younger East German officers. We are ashamed of the crimes committed during the war. It is, however, of no use at all. The Poles dislike us anyway.[19]

Anti-German sentiment, however, did not prevent the Polish communist leadership from seeking a normalization of relations with the West Germans. Gomułka's crowning foreign policy achievement was symbolized by the Bonn–Warsaw Treaty of December 1970 which sought to normalize relations between the two states and to resolve the Polish–German border dispute. Again, the SED's opposition to this policy must have added to their resentment toward Gomułka. The series of inter-German and Soviet–German treaties in 1971 and 1972 recast the Federal Republic in a much more favorable light and seriously eroded the credibility of the imperialist German threat from the German Federal Republic which the East Germans deemed so essential to the success of their domestic social and economic programs. However, within a few short weeks the outbreak of food riots and anti-government violence in Szczecin (Stettin) and Gdansk (Danzig) removed Gomułka from office. His failure to deliver on many of his promises of reform and liberalization and a downturn of the Polish economy made his continuation in office impossible.

In contrast to Gomułka's departure, Ulbricht's removal from power was accomplished entirely at the insistence of the Kremlin. When Ulbricht's unrelenting opposition to detente with the West Germans contradicted Soviet foreign policy aims, the Soviet Ambassador to the GDR, Piotr Abrasimov, quietly intervened to install Erich Honecker in office. Public East German influence over the leadership change in the GDR was non-existent when compared to events in Poland. Thus, Gierek and Honecker received similar mandates from Moscow for different reasons. Though the reasons for their appointments were different, the thrust of their announced domestic policies was fundamentally the same: to raise living standards in order to

meet the higher expectations of a new and more demanding generation of workers in Poland and East Germany.

Poland's economic and military decline

After consolidating power, Gierek moved quickly to restructure the
government and party apparatus. The political significance of these
reforms was two-fold: first, the reforms promoted a massive renova-
tion of the Polish party administration; second, they altered the
distribution of power by strengthening central leadership control.[20]
These reforms provided the framework for a massive economic
recovery with expanded imports and foreign financial credits as the
primary stimulants for domestic development.[21]

At first, Gierek's prescription for economic success produced
impressive results. By the end of 1975, Poland's gross national
product had increased by 59 percent over the 1970 level. The annual
growth rate rose to 8 percent and the accompanying material wealth
and expanding job market fostered a sense of material security and
improved social mobility.[22] Worker membership in the PUWP grew
to an unprecedented 45.6 percent of the party's total membership
during 1975. Gierek's uneasy truce between the PUWP and Polish
society seemed to be working.

However, unanticipated economic developments in the West and
an inability to effectively manage economic growth and expansion
robbed the Polish economy of its sustained growth. In 1976, foreign
indebtedness reached nearly 9 billion dollars. Productivity declined
through the remainder of the decade and pressure to reform the
central-pricing mechanism underpinning the economy assumed new
dimensions. The unresolved conflicts with the trade unions over
responsibilities and demands for autonomy became more acute after
the promulgation of the 1975 labor code which attempted to emascu-
late Polish trade unionism.[23] Until Gierek's departure from the Polish
political scene in September 1980, the PUWP pursued a desperate
strategy of alternating between concessions in the private sector and
repressive measures against the advocates of reform.

While modernization of the Polish economy was to be the central
feature of Gierek's domestic policy, his foreign policy was marked by
continuity rather than change. Gierek relentlessly pursued the realization of the Helsinki Final Act during 1972–75 which largely
legitimated Soviet gains in Eastern Europe as a result of the war. Still,
Gierek proved unable to build a party consensus in foreign affairs
after 1975. Opposition to Soviet dominance in Poland's internal

affairs was so strong within the PUWP that it resulted in changes to the wording of the Polish constitution which described Poland's relationship with the Soviet Union. In contrast to the East German constitution which proclaimed that the GDR is "forever and irrevocably allied with the USSR," the 1976 Polish constitution simply affirmed that Polish foreign policy would be based on "strengthening friendship and cooperation with the Soviet Union."[24]

Gierek's failure to curb anti-Soviet sentiment in the PUWP, to modernize the Polish economy with West German assistance, and to satisfy growing consumption demands also had an effect in the Polish armed forces. While the Gierek regime succeeded in manipulating the nationalist military trappings of Polish statehood and in insulating the Polish Army from Polish society's anti-communist sentiment, the decline in economic growth and productivity which had commenced in 1978 also influenced Polish force development. Polish tank and artillery forces tended to be at least one or two generations behind similar Soviet and East German formations.[25] As part of the Warsaw Pact's offensive exercises, the Polish Army continued to constitute a relatively autonomous front as they had during the intervention into Czechoslovakia in 1968. However, the preponderance of towed artillery and aging T-54/55s suggested that only a small number of the Polish divisions could sustain the attack tempo of GSFG–NVA operations. Although the Polish ground forces were still more numerous than the East German Army, in 1980 its army of 210,000 men remained the same size as in 1975.[26] Moreover, the Poles exercised less frequently with the Soviets than did the East Germans and Poland's conscripts were often openly sympathetic to the aims of Gierek's nemesis, Solidarity.

The Honecker era: economic growth and German nationalism

As a result of the inter-German treaties which were designed to normalize relations between the two German states Honecker was able to extract substantial economic credits and technical benefits from the FRG in return for domestic political concessions in the GDR. As Honecker was probably concerned with the specter of unrest in Poland, these concessions may not have seemed excessive and clearly supported his goal of raising living standards throughout the country.[27]

In contrast to Gierek, West German investment was carefully managed and overall productivity rose. Consequently, greater internal control and this skillful use of West German financial backing alleviated much of the pressure on the SED to reform economically. Economic growth continued to reach 4.2 percent per annum between 1976 and 1980.[28] The SED's consumer socialism survived the economic setbacks of the seventies and appeared to refute the thesis that planned economies ultimately restrain growth. Militarily, the GDR's economic growth enabled it to sustain continuous force modernization and expansion. Items of equipment such as T-72 tanks, 152mm artillery and BMPs (infantry fighting vehicles) were delivered within a year of their appearance in the GSFG and between 1970 and 1980 the NVA added another 45,000 men to its forces.[29] Policies favoring high pay, enrollments and equipment in the East German forces, advantageous post-military state positions, and the like tended to result in higher social prestige for the East German officer, in marked contrast to his Polish counterpart, and thus a substantial commitment to the GDR state.[30]

In the sphere of Soviet–East German economic relations, "integrative bilateralism," the basic principle in regard to the development of overall GDR–USSR relations contained in the 1975 Soviet–East German Treaty of Friendship, Cooperation and Mutual Aid, had produced a series of significant bilateral understandings.[31] The most important of these established a joint GDR–USSR government "Commission for Economic and Scientific–Technological Cooperation," reminiscent of the "Society for the Promotion of Industrial Enterprises" or "GEFU" which von Seeckt had created in 1922 to strengthen Russia economically in return for Soviet military support.[32] The formal documents included:

Program of 5 October 1979 Concerning Production Specialization and Cooperation Between the GDR and the USSR up to 1990 ("Program 1990").

Protocol of 5 February 1980 Concerning Coordination Results of the National Economic Plans of the GDR and the USSR.

Long-term Agreement of 19 March 1981 on Reciprocal Services and Trade Between the GDR and the USSR.[33]

An analysis of GDR–Soviet trade indicated that the Soviet Union was drawing more and more strongly on the GDR's economic power to help solve pressing economic problems at home. For the most part, the commodity structure of GDR–Soviet trade consisted of an exchange of Soviet raw materials for large East German shipments of machinery and equipment (see structure of USSR–GDR trade, Table 2 in the Appendix). In its official comments on the Alliance Pact of 7 October 1975, the SED indicated that the political, military, economic and ideological processes taking place in the Warsaw Pact and in CMEA were to be extended and intensified through bilateral relations between the Soviet Union and the GDR – relations oriented primarily toward Soviet interests.[34]

In sum, East Germany, because of its contribution to the Soviet military, economic and political effort in the region had become much more important to Soviet regional strategy than People's Poland. Whereas Soviet and German national interests seemed once again inextricably intertwined, Polish and Soviet national interests seemed to be diverging.

German nationalism and the NVA

The SED had struggled for years with the problems of nationality and statehood. Honecker had begun his term as First Secretary with a program to deemphasize the "Germanness" of the German Democratic Republic.[35] However, the conditions of *rapprochement* with West Germany which Soviet strategic priorities had forced on the SED after 1971 had made the party acutely aware of the problem of Western penetration of GDR society. With more than 80 percent of the East German population watching West German television and with more than one-third of the GDR's citizens having close relatives on the other side of the border with common traditions, culture and history, the SED leadership had to take some interest in the German historical past.[36]

When Frederick the Great's equestrian statue was ceremoniously returned from Potsdam to its traditional place of honor in Berlin during 1979, the act marked the resurrection of a set of military traditions which new generations of East German soldiers could identify with and appreciate. More importantly, Prussia's historical relationship with Russia made possible the acquisition of some historical and political legitimacy in the NVA without destabilizing Soviet–East German military relations. In retrospect, the resonance which the SED's creative historical interpretations evoked in the East German forces was impressive.

Although lip service to Soviet military prowess and superiority continued to be paid in the open press after 1979, the resurgence of Prussian–German nationalism in uniform did lead East German officers to reflect more and more on the military achievements of their ancestors. Outwardly, the NVA, like the Soviet Army, had always resembled its ancestor the Reichswehr. The Prussian goosestep, military tattoo, rank structure and uniforms had been introduced into

Russia's military establishment by German officers in the service of Peter the Great.[37] Consequently, the retention of the same military trappings which World War II had restored to the Soviet Army was not denied the East German forces. However, the cut and color of uniforms could not substitute for the essential military attributes of national pride and self-respect that socialist proletarian internationalism had failed to induce. Soviet-style socialism had, moreover, divided the East German people into party members and non-members. Prussian military nationalism, on the other hand, had a much better chance of uniting them.[38]

The NVA leadership seized upon this opportunity quickly. In no time, articles in East German military journals on the military reform and political activities of the Prussian reformers Gneisenau, Scharnhorst and Clausewitz began to appear.[39] The NVA's unit museum rooms, not unlike those found in the West German Army, began displaying the accoutrements, uniform accessories and weapons of the Prussian Army alongside the required Soviet Army relics.[40]

In contrast to Polish or Hungarian military history, the German military record could easily be edited to emphasize the advantages of cooperation with Russia. Other communist military establishments in Eastern Europe had always been hard pressed to find tangible historical evidence that supported military collaboration with Russia. But since respected figures in German history such as Frederick the Great, Scharnhorst, Stein and Bismarck had been strong exponents of Russo–German military and diplomatic cooperation they could be rehabilitated within the framework of Soviet–German friendship.

Simultaneously, undesirable features of Russo-German military history such as the Hitler–Stalin Pact and the German military triumphs over Russia in both world wars could be sacrificed in favor of Russo–German exploits against primarily West European opponents and Poland.[41] At any rate, this new approach probably made more sense to the East German soldier and officer than obscure references to the relatively insignificant role that Germany's interwar communist party played or to the revolutionary upheavals of 1848 and the middle ages.[42] General Scharnhorst, who was the subject of an East German television documentary drama in 1980, became one of the first targets for rehabilitation in the program of regime-directed nationalism. The sudden reversal in the NVA's policy of deemphasizing the "Germanness" of the NVA was explained by Lieutenant General Wiesner, professor and head of the NVA's top military academy.

Scharnhorst and Clausewitz, among others, belong to the progressive heritage and therefore are also at home with us. And we are justifiably proud of the fact that our military academy bears the Scharnhorst medal, the highest military honor of our republic. Moreover, let us be led by Lenin's suggestion that one can correctly understand and assess each phenomenon only in its historical context. Thus, to the Prussian army also belongs the activity of the men around Scharnhorst, who at the beginning of the previous century, as Prussian reformers, attempted to execute the bourgeois revolution from above.[43]

Lenin's contribution to historical revisionism notwithstanding, when the need and the opportunity arose, Honecker and his government did not hesitate to resort to nationalist symbols in order to improve morale and discipline in the NVA. This was hardly an East German innovation. From the beginning of the Soviet regime, many features of historical tradition and Russian culture have strongly influenced the Soviet interpretation of Marxism.[44] Stalin used nationalist slogans, Tsarist military practices, uniforms and decorations to reinvigorate the fighting spirit of the Red Army in World War II.[45] Today, some of the Soviet Union's top military leaders – Marshals Kulikov, Ogarkov and Sokolov – are thought to be Russian nationalist sympathizers.[46]

In light of the Soviet experience, the East German decision to try and field a politicized armed force embodying an incipient Prussian–German national consciousness is not surprising. As the repository of national values, the NVA could serve in the same capacity as the Soviet Army does: as an important source of support for the GDR state. On the other hand, the fact that official Soviet and Polish histories often attribute Hitler's "misguided" crusade against Bolshevism to the excesses of German nationalism does give the Western observer pause to wonder about the future impact of this nationalist revival.[47]

East Germany and the Polish crisis

The first violent manifestations of public discontent with the Gierek regime were evident in June of 1976. The announced price increases of foodstuffs precipitated social unrest in Poland's coastal cities. In addition, discontent was accompanied by outbursts of anti-Soviet sentiment. Public demonstrations in memory of the 1939 Soviet massacre of the Polish officer corps in the Katyn forest were reported in several Polish cities.[48] Gierek's apparent retreat from unpopular economic and social policies appeared to convey the impression to both the Polish populace and her neighbors that Poland's communists had chosen to reach an unwritten accommodation with the growing opposition.[49]

The SED reacted by issuing statements concerning "hostile activities that were directed against socialism" and by intensifying military security precautions by the NVA and the paramilitary Workers' Militia. Observers in East Berlin suggested that the induction of reservists up to thirty-five years of age as well as the alert exercises that were carried out in factories and industrial centers were connected with the alarming situation in Poland.[50] As the violence seemed to subside, the East German military posture was relaxed. Within a few years, however, the situation, in Polish and East German eyes, became more critical.

After 1980, there was no social sector, no organization, and no profession in Poland that was not extensively influenced by Solidarity.[51] This influence even extended to Poland's military establishment. Political unrest was reported in a number of military districts as Poland's conscript manpower eagerly read the leaflets that Solidarity members were circulating in the barracks.[52] Colonel Kuklinski, a former Polish General Staff officer who fled in December 1981 before the imposition of martial law, recalled during an interview in the spring of 1987 that Solidarity's influence within the Polish armed forces had provoked grave concern among the Soviet military elite. According to Colonel Kuklinski, the Soviet military leadership was well aware that by 1980 nearly one-third of the Polish soldiers in active service had either been Solidarity sympathizers or had taken part in some form of social protest organized by the union. When the spring cohort of conscripts joined the Polish armed forces in 1981 this number probably swelled to more than half of Poland's military manpower.[53] However, as Colonel Kuklinski points out in the passage below, Soviet concern about the reliability of the Polish forces was not limited to the conscripts: what may have filled them with even greater fear is that Solidarity's ideas were shared by an overwhelming majority of the officer corps. Even some party organizations among the military had given their direct or indirect support to Solidarity.[54] The readmission of Polish nationalism to the ranks of the postwar Polish Army also began to reinforce the anti-Soviet tone of Solidarity's democratic programs. Of the new units in the first and second Polish Armies, most were named after men who had become national heroes because they had fought the Russians. Names were selected from a pool of individuals who had opposed Russian dominance of Poland in a series of campaigns between 1794 and 1863.[55]

In this atmosphere of growing anti-Soviet nationalism, transparent efforts to raise the specter of the West German bogey before the Polish people had little effect. PUWP attempts in 1979 to commemorate the Nazi invasion of Poland by ignoring the Soviet Union's participation in Poland's dismemberment failed to reduce the incidence of anti-Soviet outbursts. Spokesmen for Polish human rights activists and patriotic organizations contended publicly that "any normalization of relations between the Soviet Union and Poland would come only on the basis of recognition of crimes committed by the Red Army on Polish territory."[56] Trade-unionism was becoming open rebellion against a political system that was identified with Poland's main historical adversary – Russia.

Stanislaw Kania, a communist of peasant origins from south-east Poland, emerged as Gierek's successor in a moment of extreme emergency for the party. Gierek's failure to resist institutionalization of political participation outside the limits defined by the party left little room for Kania to maneuver. Despite Soviet pressure to do otherwise, Kania proposed a cautious strategy of cooperation with all groups, both inside and outside the party.[57] Kania apparently recognized the need for social change, but vigorously rejected the use of force to effect his policy of "socialist renewal." He stated, "It is no longer possible to use the old methods, and the need for renewal arises from a critical analysis of past experiences."[58]

Unsurprisingly, external Soviet and East German pressure on the PUWP's new leadership to suppress internal political dissent did not abate. Always alert to the spread of politically dangerous viewpoints and behavior, the SED responded to the outbreak of social unrest and labor strikes with the same ferocity that had characterized their reaction to events in Czechoslovakia. During the Warsaw Pact conference that was convened in Moscow on 5 December 1980 to discuss the events in Poland, a GDR delegation reportedly argued for Pact military intervention into Poland to restore domestic order. Other delegates to the conference from the GDR included key members of the East German military–security elite; Army General Heinz Hoffmann and State Security Chief Army General Mielke.[59] While it became clear later that the East German recommendation was rejected in favor of an internal Polish military solution, there were grounds in the Fall of 1980 for the East Germans to anticipate Soviet military action against Poland. A number of top Soviet military elite members, including the GSFG commander, seemed to favor some form of military action against Poland.[60]

Established military procedure suggests that the commanders of

Soviet ground forces in Eastern Europe were consulted on the feasibility and the advisability of invading Poland. This had certainly been the case with the visits of Marshal Konev and Yepishev to Czechoslovakia in 1968. Along with several other key military actors such as Army General Pavlovskiy, commander-in-chief, ground forces and army General Yazov, CGSF commander, General Ivanovskiy, the GSFG commander, appears to have argued strongly in favor of intervention and may have influenced the East German political–military elite to support such action as well.[61] Much of this aggressive posturing on the part of the Soviet and East German military elite vis-à-vis Poland may have been a reflection of the fact that Marshal Kulikov, commander-in-chief of Warsaw Pact Forces, was known to have initiated detailed planning for a military invasion of Poland early in the fall of 1980 that involved at least eighteen Soviet, German and Czechoslovak divisions. Colonel Kuklinski has confirmed that Marshal Kulikov championed this idea and had assigned a prominent role to the NPA – a development which profoundly troubled General Jaruzelski and the Polish General Staff.[62] Colonel Kuklinski has also characterized the Soviet determination to employ East German troops over the objections of the Polish military elite as being "ruthless and uncompromising."[63] It appears that Kulikov's invasion plans were rejected only when the Polish delegation to the Moscow summit presented the Soviet leadership with a credible plan for the liquidation of Solidarity with the use of exclusively Polish military and police units.[64]

Although Brezhnev chose to shelve Kulikov's plans in favor of the Polish General Staff's approach, Soviet and East German forces remained in a high state of readiness. In the meantime, it would appear that a few of the more forceful proponents of joint Soviet–East German military action against the Poles – among them the GSFG commander General Ivanovskiy – were reassigned to lesser posts. In fact, Ivanovskiy's removal was announced without any prior mention or notice on 4 December 1980, only the day before the conference in Moscow was set to convene.[65]

Meanwhile, the East German population was being bombarded with news of the deteriorating economic conditions inside Poland. On 3 February 1981, *Neues Deutschland* carried an article with the headline "Solidarity Promotes Chaos and Anarchy."[66] Although the article depicted Solidarity in the usual negative terms, the emphasis was really on the economic consequences of political discontent in Poland. The real aim of the descriptions of empty stores and vanishing consumer goods was to raise the specter of uncertainty in the minds of East German workers about the fragility of their standard of living and to dispel any notions of counterrevolution in the GDR. "A look in the stores is enough for one to recognize the bad effects of counterrevolutionary activity. By early afternoon, stores everywhere in the country have sold all their food. This is particularly true for butter, margarine, cooking oil, dairy products and many other vital foodstuffs."[67]

In a further attempt to discredit Solidarity, *Neues Deutschland* reprinted excerpts from articles that had appeared in the Polish party organ *Zolnierz Wolnnosci*. The articles linked events in Poland with West German subversion of socialism. Through careful editing the East German press appeared to warn West Germans of the "cost to the international atmosphere"[68] of seeking to restore the borders of 1939. Subsequent articles adopted the Polish theme of Western subversion and accused Solidarity of cooperating with "the machinations of the imperialist secret services and their agents."[69]

Despite the Soviet decision not to opt for military intervention in December 1980, events in the spring and summer of 1981 did not encourage the Soviet or East German leaderships to believe that the Polish leadership was any more capable of managing the Solidarity problem then than in 1980. Again, the Soviet–East German response assumed military dimensions.

East German and Soviet GSFG units staged combined maneuvers on 12 February 1981 along the border with Silesia. East German Defense Minister Heinz Hoffmann and his staff joined the new GSFG commander, Army General M. Zaytsev, to observe combat operations involving tank, artillery and missile units. Then, on 10 March, it was announced that "Soyuz 81", a routine combined headquarters exercise with designated units from the combined armed forces, would commence on 17 March 1981.[70] However, "Soyuz 81" was hardly routine. The exercise was one of the largest front-level staff exercises ever conducted with troops. In addition, Polish deputy premier Rakowski indicated another purpose for the exercises when he informed Solidarity leaders who were then threatening strikes in Bydgoszcz that the exercise was to be prolonged because of the tension in the country.[71]

"Soyuz 81" was extended to 7 April 1981 and was billed as taking place on Polish, Czech and GDR soil. In fact, though, the important military activity was taking place in southern and central areas of East Germany. Some East German ground units actually operated on Polish territory and East German naval and air forces supported joint operations in the Baltic with the Soviet fleet off the Polish coast. On

11 April, in a speech to the SED Party Congress, Honecker warned ominously that Poland "was, is and will remain socialist!"[72]

Neues Deutschland carried stories depicting the Solidarity-led strikes as manifestations of "anti-communism bordering on madness."[73] In August 1981, during Kania's visit to Brezhnev in Moscow, "the Soviet leader promised additional economic aid, but also reprimanded the Poles for being soft on the threat of counterrevolution."[74] Marshal Kulikov's visit to Poland in August was also reported in *Neues Deutschland*. According to East German sources, his visit focused on the communications network linking Soviet forces in the Western military districts with those in Poland and the GDR.[75] More probably, he was sent by Moscow to evaluate the capability of the Polish military and political elite to deal with Solidarity. Finally, on 7 September, without specifying why, East Berlin announced that 100,000 Soviet combat troops had taken up positions along Poland's border with Byelorussia.[76]

For members of the East German and Polish armed forces, an explanation was probably unnecessary. Polish officers who had served in the Polish armed forces reported in interviews with A. Ross Johnson that at least one Soviet general made no secret of Soviet intentions during 1981. According to the account, in the course of a Soviet general's visit to a Polish air force installation, the general and members of his staff told their Polish comrades-in-arms the following:

After a few rounds of drinks, the Polish officers asked the Soviets whether they thought that Soviet troops would cross over into Poland. The Soviets replied that they expected Soviet troops to move into Poland and said that sixty fighter planes and a few helicopters were to occupy their airfield. Further, they said, the Polish air force would be grounded, the officers would be confined to barracks, and the Polish air defense would be taken over by Soviets. The General also told the Polish officers that ten thousand Russians died in Hungary in 1956, and even if thirty thousand were to die in Poland, since greater resistance was expected, it would still be worth it to the Soviets, because they would be saving thirty million Poles for socialism. Therefore, it made no sense to put up any resistance, the Polish officers were told.[77]

The bluntness with which Soviet officers addressed the issue of military intervention to their intended victims – the Poles – leaves little doubt that joint NVA-GSFG operations and training during 1981 included similar discussions between Soviet and East German military elites.

At the end of September 1981, the SED adopted a series of measures in support of what appeared to be renewed preparation for a Soviet–

East German invasion and occupation of Poland. East Germany's border was closed and interstate traffic between Poland and the GDR all but ceased completely. Whether the Soviet High Command had ordered these measures to be implemented or not seems to be an irrelevant question. Honecker's 1972 agreement with Gierek to relax border restrictions and permit greater Polish access to GDR markets and society had been effectively abolished when the SED introduced a number of legal restrictions on travel to and from Poland in October 1980. Shortly thereafter, the Soviet government had exercised its diplomatic prerogatives under postwar agreements by prohibiting Western military observers from traveling inside a 400 kilometer strip of East German territory that ran along the length of the Polish border.[78]

Consequently, the military measures in the fall of 1981 to reactivate NVA reservists, alert internal paramilitary forces and mobilize railway and civil defense resources for the movement of NVA military equipment and personnel to the Eastern border may be seen as a final step in a series of steps to prepare the GDR to support the projection of Soviet and East German military power into Poland. In addition to these measures, leave was cancelled and joint NVA-GSFG maneuvers were intensified. Most of this activity was accomplished in a clandestine fashion and many of the reservists were called up as cadre for additional NVA reserve divisions that were not known to exist in 1981.[79]

Simultaneous East German news bulletins avoided any mention of these activities, but sought to explain the militarization of the crisis in newer and more serious terms:

The worsening of the situation in Poland, as shown particularly during the past two weeks, has reached a most dangerous level for the Polish people and the socialist state authorities. This is the direct result of the Solidarity leadership's counterrevolutionary attacks, which embrace the whole country and all social areas. In view of that, the constant yielding by the party and state organs is viewed here with concern and growing incomprehension.[80]

One day later, *Neues Deutschland* insisted that "the political atmosphere in Poland is becoming more explosive. The counterrevolution is making a direct frontal attack on socialist state power."[81] In a speech published on 14 October 1981, General Secretary Honecker warned again that "Poland is and will remain a socialist country," and "Together with our friends in the socialist camp, we will see to that!"[82]

Publicly, the East German populace responded unsympathetically to developments in Poland. Apart from a few isolated cases of support for Solidarity, the outbreak of labor unrest in Poland succeeded only in exacerbating the historical antipathy between Germans and Poles.[83] While there was some undercurrent of sympathy for Solidarity's demands among East German youth, older generations of Germans expressed their deeply felt conviction that the Poles were troublesome, lazy and incompetent.[84] The East German Protestant Church regarded the rise in anti-Polish sentiment in the GDR as serious enough to warrant a public warning against the revival of anti-Polish prejudices.[85] Reminiscent of the Prussian infatuation with hard work and respect for authority, the main body of the East German populace tended to regard greater discipline and industry as the surest path to resolution of the "Polish" crisis.

Polish citizens who traveled between the two states remarked that East German border officials treated them as though they were the citizens of a state at war with the GDR. After their visits to the GDR in 1981, they recounted the derogatory comments and falsehoods about the Poles which seemed to abound in East German society and the press:

In the GDR, ugly jokes were told about us [Poles] that accused us of being lazy and incompetent ... In Neues Deutschland it stated that a crowd numbering in the thousands had set a police official on fire. There was also a statement that Walesa had demanded control of prisons and incarceration processes, while Walesa had personally advocated the inclusion of Union members in the government.[86]

There can be no doubt that the East German regime benefited from the anti-Polish sentiment among the GDR population and the widespread support for some measure of intervention into Poland's affairs in order to resolve the crisis. Moreover, as a precept for resolving the perennial Soviet security problem in Poland, a Soviet scheme to employ German troops in concert with Soviet troops against the Poles would have had some popular appeal. At the same time, the threat of outside military intervention may have even contributed to the success of Jaruzelski's internal resolution of the crisis. Poland's media clearly sought to exploit this fear in a population that was only too conscious of its juxtaposition between two powerful and unsympathetic neighbors.

The imposition of martial law on Poland in December 1981 stilled the alarmist voices in the GDR and Soviet presses. Nevertheless, intensified GSFG–NVA military activity continued into the spring of 1982 indicating that confidence in the capability of Poland's military establishment and internal security organs to destroy the forces of Polish democracy was not great.

Summary

The most important result of the breakdown of political order in Poland was that Soviet policy toward the GDR and Poland became strongly influenced by the asymmetry in the political, economic and military stakes that the Soviet Union had in the two countries. Militarily, East Germany emerged from the Polish crisis as Moscow's undisputed junior military partner in the Warsaw Pact, "filling the vacuum left by Poland's economic weakness and the demoralization of its armed forces."[87] Moscow further discovered that without East Germany and with Poland, the Warsaw Pact as a military alliance would be irrelevant.[88] East Germany had simply become much more important to the USSR in both foreign policy and security terms than Poland. While the GDR's economy was expanding, Poland's economy was beginning to contract. In short, Poland's weaknesses presented more dangers than opportunities to Moscow.

Although the prospect of labor unrest in the GDR and the probability of it ever sparking a similar outburst was less immediate, a victory for Solidarity and the institutionalization of the role of independent unions as a counterweight to the ruling communist party could have become a very serious threat to East Berlin and the Soviet–East German military alliance.[89] In view of the Polish national and ideological menace, the SED turned out to be the CPSU's most trusted and loyal ally in the Soviet Union's determined effort to oppose any form of political liberalization in Eastern Europe.

Understandably, many Poles perceived the official and public East German responses to Solidarity and the events leading to the imposition of martial law in Poland as marking the resurgence of a new reactionary, anti-Polish German military state in Central-East Europe.[90] In this connection, the NVA's military mobilization in 1981–82 and the SED's efforts to appropriate specific elements of Prussian and German history doubtlessly contributed to this perception. It is no accident that the Poles refer openly to the GDR as *das sowjetische Deutschland*.[91] Unfortunately, the economic crisis in Poland was blamed by the SED for a number of economic problems that then threatened to jeopardize East Germany's high standard of living. And in the GDR, where economic prosperity and stability are extremely dependent on the steady flow of energy imports, Polish shortfalls in hard-coal deliveries during 1981–82 tended to "provoke resentment and the fear among East German workers that they would ultimately have to bear the burden of the Poles' extremism."[92]

Meanwhile, questions in the West about how long the SED's unambiguously pro-Soviet line in foreign and security affairs could compensate for East Germany's cultural, financial and economic contacts with West Germany were answered. The mutual distaste for Poland demonstrated that the convictions in Berlin and Moscow concerning issues of internal security were fundamentally the same. As it had in the past, Poland turned out to be a force for cohesion in Soviet–East German relations. Had the crisis in Poland necessitated Soviet–East German military intervention, it might even have produced a degree of reconciliation between the East German people and their state around the banner of nationalism. Even though Russia's cultural and economic backwardness could not match the attraction of West European culture and civilization for the majority of East Germans, East German society's cultural affinity for the West did nothing to forestall the possibility of East German support in a Soviet confrontation with the Poles in Central Europe. The resurrection of Prussian–German military nationalism did not jeopardize Soviet control of military affairs in the East German state.

As already mentioned, the fact that the coincidence of interest was the result of an earlier Soviet decision to install a ruling elite in Berlin that shared the CPSU's world view does nothing to diminish the military significance of this development for Central Europe. While the tendency of Poland's leadership to identify its interests with the interests of the country has generally led to a conflict of interests with the Soviet Union, the similar tendency in East Germany's leadership after 1979 produced a condominium rather than a conflict of interest with Moscow.

Thus, the Soviet and East German party leaderships turned out to think and behave above all as policemen, trained to think first of internal stability and the continued survival of the existing regional status quo. The demands in Moscow and East Berlin that the PUWP retain its position as the leading force in Polish society and suppress anti-socialist forces did not contradict the historical imperative of Soviet–German relations: the suppression of Polish independence from Moscow. At the same time, just as the geopolitical perspective of the Soviet Union's leadership has generally conformed to an array of security interests that have persisted since the time of Peter the Great, East German behavior during the summer and fall of 1981 reflected an historical German viewpoint, as well as an ideological one.

Together with the regime-directed reemergence of Prussian and anti-Polish nationalism there was a detectable transformation of the official ideological underpinnings of the Soviet–East German military alliance. East Berlin's inclination to adopt popular nationalism for its own internal purposes coincided with the driving imperative of Soviet–East German relations in Central Europe – the Brezhnev Doctrine or the elevation of socialist proletarian internationalism to the level of state-to-state relations. In this context, Poland represented a major challenge to the East German state.

The PUWP's practice of indefinitely deferring unpopular political changes "in the interests of tranquility and productivity"[93] posed a real danger to the SED. Since few Poles believed that Poland's alliance with the Soviet Union enabled Warsaw to implement its vital state and national interests,[94] the SED interpreted the PUWP's reluctance to subdue Solidarity in the period 1980–81 as potentially stimulating to forces elsewhere in the region that operate against Soviet dominance. If unchecked in Poland, social and political forces could jeopardize the artificial political division of Germany and undermine the legitimacy of the Soviet–East German alliance – the raison d'être of the GDR state. Given the GDR's vulnerability to Western influences and its historical origins, anything in a neighboring Pact state that suggests a lack of resolve or will on the part of the ruling party to preserve socialist state power and the relationship with the Soviet Union poses a threat to the SED.

Consequently, neither the SED nor the CPSU were under the illusion that a collapse of communist rule in Poland was impossible. The Soviet and East German state leaderships' respective pronouncements suggested an impressive understanding of the effects and consequences that Poland's collapse would have on the societies in her neighboring states. Even though Solidarity sought to exclude vital Soviet security interests from any public discussion so as not to arouse Moscow's suspicions, the link between anti-Soviet and anti-communist sentiment in Poland was too obvious for Moscow to ignore.

To most Russians both in and out of the CPSU, the Poles are incurably anti-Russian. No solution short of one designed to restore Moscow's absolute control of events in Poland would have been acceptable. A Polish government that held fast to Poland's commitments as a reliable member of the Warsaw Pact and the Council for Mutual Economic Assistance but that was also more responsive to its people would almost certainly have sought closer economic and cultural ties to Western Europe and the United States. Under conditions of reduced Soviet control and penetration, Poland would probably also have developed into an ever greater obstacle to aggressive Soviet military strategy against Western Europe. Thus, there was no evidence insofar as Poland was concerned that the Soviet leadership believed that their security interests would gain from "a less rigid and less heavy-handed approach in Poland or Eastern Europe."[95] Clearly, Poland is not Finland and could never aspire to the autonomy and the freedom that the Finns enjoy.

However, Soviet resistance to a "Finnish" solution for the Polish problem did not necessarily entail another partition of Poland between Russians and Germans. There were probably a number of reasons that militated against a new partition of Poland. First, despite frequently displayed servility and demonstrated loyalty, the functionaries of the SED are seen by the Soviets primarily as Germans, tainted by the suspicion of latent unreliability.[96] Second, the former German territory now under Polish control together with what is the GDR could form the nucleus of a potentially powerful state with its own raw material base in Silesia and fertile land in Pomerania.[97] Third, Western reactions to this reversal of the Helsinki Accords would have made such a decision very costly in regard to Soviet interests.

Although instability in Poland may have given the Soviets pause to reconsider their policies toward Poland, very few Soviet leaders may have thought that an expansion of East German power and influence at the expense of Poland was in the Soviet Union's national interest. Nevertheless, increased Soviet reliance on the East Germans as a result of future events in Poland and Central-East Europe should not be discounted. The evidence suggests that joint Soviet–East German military operations against Poland were under serious consideration in Moscow during 1980 and 1981. It should not be forgotten, however, that East German divisions would probably have moved into Poland on Soviet orders as component parts of the GSFG's armies with or without the SED's sanction.

5 Conclusion

The central theme of this book is that the Soviet–East German military relationship has evolved in a way that contradicted both postwar Soviet and Western expectations.[1] To many thoughtful observers, these expectations seemed to be confirmed when, in the wake of Stalin's death, German workers and soldiers in the Soviet zone of occupation openly rejected the GDR state. This conclusion obscured, however, the real consequences of German resistance to the imposition of Soviet-style communism; the SED's extreme dependence on Soviet military, political and economic support combined with a developing Soviet interest in East Germany's strategic military value led the post-Stalin East German and Soviet leaderships to adopt measures that were designed to improve and strengthen Soviet control of East Germany's political and military development. Politically, Soviet control meant that the GDR had to become a faithful replica of the Soviet state. Economically, this meant an end to reparation payments and Soviet confiscation of East German capital stock. In military terms, Soviet control meant that East German forces were compelled to develop within the larger framework of the Soviet military establishment rather than as an independent national army.

With these points in mind, the preceding chapters have attempted to demonstrate that for reasons of history, convergent elite interests and Soviet control of the internal and external political factors that position the two states in the world arena, it should not be surprising that the GDR has emerged in the region as the Soviet Union's most stable and reliable military ally. This chapter will proceed from that basis to examine the possible evolution of the Soviet–East German military alliance in the 1990s, and will focus on the GDR's military relationship with the Soviet state in order to develop a broader analytical framework for the future study of Soviet-controlled force development in the Warsaw Pact's Northern Tier. It is the central premise of this book that the GDR's current ruling elite regards the military power of the state, and the further development of that power within the framework of the Soviet-East German military alliance, as a prerequisite for the attainment of future foreign and domestic policy objectives. This judgment will have important implications for the conduct of *Soviet* security policy in the 1990s and beyond.

Economic prowess has never been the basis of the Soviet Union's international position and has not been the foundation for Soviet-style socialism in Eastern Europe either. Gorbachev's current domestic agenda for economic and political renewal has already in the late 1980s run into difficulty[2] and the forecast for a similar program of renewal in Eastern Europe is equally uncertain.[3] This state of affairs has suggested to at least one analyst that in the future Moscow will rely increasingly on military power as the Soviet state's primary claim to international prestige and as the chief means of maintaining control of Eastern Europe.[4] If the past is a good guide for the future of Eastern Europe, only the SED seems capable of coping with the political and economic challenges that lie ahead. In the face of conditions of resource stringency and East European instability, an enlarged military and political role for the GDR in Soviet security policy seems unavoidable.

The unanticipated gains of Soviet-controlled development

In East Germany, where authority was never afraid to act and seldom met resistance, the adoption of Soviet political institutions and mechanisms of control not only guaranteed Soviet political control, they also revived the Prussian–German tradition of a powerful authoritarian state. When the factors of German national character and political culture were added to the SED's acute sense of dependency on Soviet military backing it was probably inevitable that from the beginning, the objective of the GDR state, like its model the Soviet state, would be "the continual development of its own power."[5]

However, Soviet occupation policies and postwar military strategy were not initially compatible with the resurrection of German military power in the East. Soviet hostility toward the Germans animated an occupation policy that stripped East Germany of most of its remaining industrial capacity and rendered it militarily ineffective.[6] This resulted from a Soviet interest both in preventing the resurgence of a German military threat to the Soviet Union, and in reconstruction of the Soviet economy. Militarily, this meant that until Sokolovskiy's work on Soviet military thought began to have an impact on Soviet/Warsaw Pact force development, the GDR was not viewed in either the East or West as a particularly important military asset. Forged under the pressure of advancing technology and new strategic concerns, Sokolovskiy's contribution to Soviet military thought tended to reposition the GDR at the center of Soviet military strategy where it has remained ever since. With the appearance of internal threats to Soviet control of Central-East Europe in Hungary, Czechoslovakia and Poland, the GDR gradually emerged as the Soviet Union's chief military partner in the Warsaw Pact. This development suggested that the Soviet and East German state leaderships had begun to see each other as useful vehicles in the pursuit of their interests in the strategic nexus of Central Europe. In sum, the historical underpinnings of earlier patterns of state-to-state relations were restored.

One can argue that the current conditions of Soviet–East German cooperation vividly recall past Tsarist and Soviet efforts to accelerate Russia's modernization with German military and technical assistance. East Germany has again become the Soviet Union's leading trade partner.[7] The vitality and structure of this trade relationship with its emphasis on technology was evident in the remarks of the Soviet minister of the electronics industry, Vladimir Kolesnikov:

The main thing now is the broad development of direct relations between scientific institutions, enterprises, and combines and the formation of joint collectives . . . Cooperation will develop at a fast pace in those sectors which determine scientific–technological progress: microelectronics, the production of industrial robots, numerically controlled machine tools, flexible production systems, processing centers, computer and information technology and new production materials.[8]

The reason for economic cooperation with the East Germans today, as in the past, is not to culturally merge Russians and Germans, but to strengthen a backward Russia in its competition with the West. The fact that the international behavior of the USSR is more and more shaped by an objective force which Soviet theorists term the "scientific–technological revolution"[9] suggests that Soviet–East German scientific–industrial interdependence will continue to expand. The SED has made reliance on the application of modern technology in all of their industries the centerpiece of East German industrial and foreign trade policy[10] and it is equally clear that inter-German trade has become an important element in both Soviet and East German scientific–industrial modernization.[11]

These comments notwithstanding, the enduring legacy of Soviet military control still means that the Soviet–East German military relationship is bounded and constrained by expectations that are different from the content and forms of earlier Russo-Prussian and Russo-German relations. However, the successful transformation of pre-war German society in the Soviet zone of occupation has ensured that disagreements in any area of common interest would never produce irreconcilable conflicts in the given fundamental convictions of the two party leaderships where security issues were involved.[12] It is no accident that the SED insists on regularized cooperation, joint socialization and training of Soviet and East German officer cadres. This is designed to foster a military–political orientation in the East German military elite that is commensurate with the common security needs of the CPSU and the SED. Hence, the emphasis in political training in the Soviet and East German forces on defense of the World War II gains of socialism and the readiness to strike out militarily against any opponent, internal or external, that threatens the territorial and political status quo in Central Europe.[13]

Naturally, this also means that the GDR's political and military leadership must balance itself between the demands for legitimate statehood and national identity among its soldiers and the externally imposed requirement to serve as the political–military bulwark of the Soviet regional security system. Thus far, the GDR's relative economic prosperity, the SED's military programs for regime-directed nationalism and cooperation with the Soviet Armed Forces have been generally successful in managing these conflicting demands.

This observation would support Melvin Croan's contention that the SED's energetic commitment to building close relations with the CPSU leadership has succeeded in transforming Soviet–East German relations from cooperation based entirely on dependence in a "largely one-sided partnership with the Soviet Union into a growing reciprocity of interests."[14] Indeed, Soviet confidence in the East German military contribution to the Soviet Union's strategy in Central Europe and, to a lesser extent, the Third World, probably helps explain the SED's growing margin of political autonomy in inter-German affairs. The departure of Soviet Ambassador Abrasimov from East Berlin after the restoration of domestic order in Poland further testified to the position of trust and loyalty that Honecker's leadership of the SED enjoys in Moscow's eyes. Abrasimov had symbolized direct Soviet intervention in the SED's internal affairs since the end of World War II.

Nevertheless, it is also true that control of events continues to rest ultimately in Moscow rather than in Berlin. The GDR, then, does not enjoy the position of military and economic strength *vis-à-vis* the Soviet Union which an independent Prussia did or a united Germany would. However, the degree to which Soviet–East German military cooperation currently depends on a set of political, economic and strategic relations that have changed little in the past 200 years cannot fail to impress even those to whom the changes wrought since 1945 are more significant than the continuities with the past.

The GDR: military model for the Northern Tier?

The preceding chapters attempted by implication to provide at least a partial answer to this question by stressing the events and conditions that triggered the development of Soviet–East German military cooperation and by suggesting that there was really no direct parallel in the other Warsaw Pact states. However, a discussion of the prospects for the transplantation of specific features of Soviet-controlled force development in the GDR to Czechoslovakia and Poland must also consider other factors. While all the Warsaw Pact states have been forced to adopt Soviet political and military institutions, the evolution of these systems has varied considerably from country to country.[15] Viewed from this standpoint, the pattern of Soviet-controlled force development in East Germany has been similar in form, but decidedly different in content. From the start, the Soviets and their East German comrades adopted measures that resulted in:

the negation of East German political influence over the command, control and organization of East Germany's armed forces;

the development of the NVA as a component part of a larger Soviet front organization;

the containment of the potentially detrimental impact of societal factors on the reliability of East German forces through mechanisms of socialization and joint training;

the sustaining of the economic growth that underpins a stable social system.

Since incorporating the lessons of military history is common practice in Soviet military policy,[16] it seems reasonable to expect the Soviet High Command to attempt to replicate the GSFG–NVA pattern of Soviet-controlled force development. There is evidence to suggest that since the Soviet intervention into Czechoslovakia in 1968 the Soviet military has been engaged in a process of consolidating its influence over the CPA in the same way that it did in the NVA. For the purpose of regaining control of a recalcitrant satellite, the Soviet experience with developing the NVA appears to have provided a useful blueprint for action.

In neighboring Czechoslovakia, Soviet military intervention in 1968 tended to create conditions which were similar to those that had existed in postwar East Germany. The Czechoslovak Communist Party became heavily dependent on Soviet military and political support as it sought to dismantle the popular policies associated with the "Prague Spring." The army's failure on three separate occasions to defend the country from external threats – 1938, 1948 and 1968 – deprived the Czechoslovak armed forces of a strong, independent twentieth-century military tradition. With the installation of the CGSF in Czechoslovakia, the Soviets created the conditions for the resocialization and remodeling of the CPA in the image of the GDR's "coalition army." Most importantly, by linking the key components of the Czechoslovak defense system directly to the CGSF, the CGSF could serve as the fundamental basis of internal politics in Czechoslovakia as it had in the GDR. As a result, the CGSF has become the critical agency for the purpose of foreclosing the option of an independent operational military capability in the CPA.[17]

Within the framework of joint military activity, Czechoslovak forces were conditioned after 1968 to regular cooperation with, and subordination to, Soviet forces. Also, higher Soviet visibility in the key supervisory positions of the Czechoslovak Ministry of Defense indicated that the Soviets planned to control military policy in that country as they had in the GDR.[18] Organizational trends and a reduction in strength in the seventies further suggested that the Czechoslovak forces (CPA) were in a transition to new conditions of structured dependence on the Soviet military establishment in order to augment the Central Group of Soviet Forces on the GSFG–NVA model.[19] Nonetheless, most paramilitary and civil defense activity remains subordinate to local party control. Since it is probable that the Soviets would prefer to consolidate these activities under the CPA, this raises some questions about the military utility of these militia units and the quality of the Czechoslovak military's administrative bodies.[20]

Since the implementation of martial law in Poland, Soviet military policy has attempted to follow a course similar to that taken in the GDR and Czechoslovakia, albeit with far greater difficulty. This is understandable since the important factors which traditionally favored Soviet military control and influence in East Germany have been more difficult to create in Poland.

First, the status of the GDR state and army still reflects the legacy of Soviet military occupation. The total destruction of the German national state and army offered the Soviets the opportunity to erect entirely new structures in their place. While communist Polish forces were organized on Soviet soil during World War II pre-war Polish heroes and traditions found their way back into the Polish military establishment and Home Army veterans have enjoyed some measure of rehabilitation. This was, in part, the consequence of the Polish Communist Party's decision in the fifties to admit the forces of Polish nationalism to the ranks of the armed forces and party. (World War II had discredited German nationalism and so the observance of national traditions in the East German Army was, until recently, limited to the cut and color of uniforms). Second, the Soviets encouraged the Poles to develop an independent Polish front structure within the framework of the Soviet commanded Pact forces. Consequently, the formations and equipment to support this structure were established in the Polish forces during the sixties. This has led to persisting notions of Polish military autonomy within the Pact. Third, the Polish regime can not easily endure the economic costs to Polish society of military modernization.[21] Poland's virtual economic collapse raises questions about the PUWP's ability to keep pace with current Soviet requirements for military modernization without jeopardizing the party's future in Poland. Lastly, whereas the East German population still perceives no alternative to the existing political status quo in Central Europe, the Polish populace continues to entertain ideas about divesting itself of Soviet influence and control.[22]

Not surprisingly, the combination of persistent Polish opposition to Soviet domination and a growing disparity in equipment inventories between the Soviet and Polish military establishments have acted to relegate Polish forces to an increasingly secondary role in Soviet military strategy. This has complicated the traditional employment of Polish forces in a front formation within the Western theater of military operations. Recent Pact exercises indicate that the Soviet High Command is developing alternatives to the Polish front and that only a limited number of category I Polish forces are permanently assigned to a first strategic echelon role in the Western theater of military operations (TVD).[23]

The extent to which the Poles in and out of the Polish military establishment have resisted Soviet control and influence before and since 1945 is too well known to recount here.[24] As mentioned in chapter 4, the suppression of Solidarity and the threat of Soviet intervention have greatly contributed to a revival of interest in Poland's anti-Soviet and anti-Russian past.[25] Polish military victories over the Soviets and Soviet atrocities committed against the Poles at Katyn and other locations are remembered privately and publicly in Poland. Communist efforts to revise the historical record in these areas have failed completely.

While this has not prevented the Soviets from subverting and controlling Polish command structures or from deploying Polish forces facing West rather than East, these developments have severely inhibited collaboration with the Soviets on the East German pattern. In fact, the Soviet and Polish military presses still allude to persisting Polish resistance to military cooperation with the Soviet military establishment.[26]

Organizationally, Polish forces are also too numerous to simply reconfigure as augmentation forces for the tiny NGSF. Although it is clear that certain elite forces have been assigned special missions as part of the Pact's combined armed forces in the Western TVD, as already mentioned there is evidence to suggest that the bulk of Poland's conscript forces are being given a secondary operational role. This is understandable. Modern equipment in certain key categories is sadly lacking. One Western analyst estimates that according to Soviet organizational norms the traditional Polish front structure is short 68 battalions of artillery. Moreover, much of the Polish tank fleet is at least one generation behind Soviet and East German forces and the independent tank regiments and battalions that are normally found in Soviet motorized rifle divisions do not exist in the Polish People's Army![27]

Despite the short-term success in achieving the goal of destroying the organized forces of democracy in Poland, the failure of Poland's military–political elite to reinvigorate the moribund Polish Communist Party or to spur Polish force development must be a source of extreme disappointment to the Soviet High Command in Moscow. For the moment, Soviet efforts have produced a regional strategy with overambitious goals.

This does not mean that greater Soviet reliance on the GDR will detract from the Soviet Union's relentless efforts to achieve absolute control of military affairs in Poland and elsewhere in the region. On the contrary, the unavoidable requirement for the Soviet military establishment to adapt its operations to some degree of resource scarcity[28] and Marshal Ogarkov's emphasis on sustained, high-tech theater offensive operations dictate a continued East European contribution to Soviet regional military strategy.[29] However, it is clear that only the East German model for military integration, modernization and war mobilization embraces all of the key elements in the process of Soviet-controlled force development. The external factors which position the other East European parties and the CPSU in the world arena may not be as conducive as the Soviet–East German bilateral relationship to effective military cooperation. In contrast to the GDR, the remaining Pact countries are confronted with deteriorating economic situations and more acute consumption demands at home than either the Soviets or the East Germans face. An immense military buildup on the scale of the late sixties and early seventies simply violates their own narrow political interests and threatens to sabotage domestic economic consumption.[30] While the militarization of East German society has proven to be a useful means of minimizing the effects of West German cultural and political influence, similar attempts at societal militarization have failed miserably in Hungary, Poland and, to a lesser extent, in Czechoslovakia.

Therefore, the Soviets will probably opt increasingly for a regional policy of selective modernization limited to mission-essential, non-Soviet ground formations. In addition, the Soviets may seek to increase the role of Soviet forces in the western Soviet military districts in Central European strategy and to expand the Groups of Soviet Forces' capacity to absorb additional Soviet military manpower in the event of a crisis mobilization. When supplemented with frequent joint maneuvers and the constant schooling of non-Soviet officer cadres in the Soviet Union,[31] this policy would coincide with the Soviet interest in gaining permanent operational control of the Pact's best non-Soviet formations and also compensate for the diminished operational capabilities of the Polish armed forces.[32]

In Eastern Europe, the political requirement to preserve social and economic stability has coincided with a developing Soviet military interest in transforming the Warsaw Pact's doctrine for coalition warfare into a rationale for tightly organized and Soviet-controlled multinational armed forces.[33] One consequence of this interest has been the emergence of the theater of military operations orientation and increased reliance on "forces-in-being" in Soviet military thought.

Command and control has always received as much attention in the Soviet armed forces as the development of any weapon system.[34] Soon after the Nazi invasion of the Soviet Union began in the summer of 1941, Stalin created the State Defense Committee whose job it was to organize mobilization and exercise command of the armed forces through the Supreme High Command of the Soviet armed forces of "Stavka." However, the Stavka proved increasingly incapable of coping with the enormous span of control that ensued as new fronts and armies were created to stop the advancing Germans.[35] In order to reduce the burden on the Stavka without diminishing Moscow's control of operations, the Soviet High Command began the practice of sending senior officers from Moscow directly to the critical fronts where they could coordinate operational details and exert decisive influence over events on the battlefield. It would appear that this practice resulted in more formalized, intermediate command structures by the end of the war.

According to Soviet and Western sources, Marshal Vasilievskiy, the commander of Soviet forces in Manchuria at the end of the war, was instrumental in the process of designing an intermediate operational command structure that guided the clandestine mobilization and attack of large mobile combat formations.[36] His victory focused attention on a number of important points. Of these, Marshal Ogarkov, the current Western TVD commander, has stressed the requirement for ground and air forces to achieve a high state of readiness in a forward deployed posture and the importance of an intermediate strategic leadership that associates a level of command with a geographical area of responsibility.

Marshal Ogarkov has been the main proponent of the view which envisions the subordination of integrated, multi-national Pact fronts to a new theater command within specific geographical limits. These limits define the scale of the operations and, in the case of directions and zones of advance, indicate the locations of objectives. The Soviet and East European forces in the GDR, Poland, Czechoslovakia and the western Soviet military districts constitute the assets of the Western theater of strategic military action or TVD. Furthermore, Marshal Ogarkov has assumed responsibility for the development of Pact command and control structures to facilitate Soviet operational control of all Pact forces in "time of peace."[37]

In the drive to forge a more cohesive and responsive Pact force structure, Marshal Ogarkov has chosen to emphasize the technological modernization and integration of Soviet and non-Soviet forces in Central Europe. Ogarkov's demand that these forces attain the highest possible state of combat readiness in "time of peace" and be prepared to move within twenty-four to forty-eight hours notice against the West also suggests that the Soviets' former reliance on total mobilization has given way to new notions of pre-war mobilization in which a conflict in the European theater would be decided primarily by the Warsaw Pact's tank-heavy "forces-in-being" with the aid of new generations of high technology conventional weapons.[38]

Colonel General Gareev, Deputy Chief of the Soviet General Staff, has given considerable thought to the notion of pre-war mobilization and the tactical and strategic measures which would presumably compensate for the absence of overwhelming numerical superiority. In his book, *M. V. Frunze: Military Theorist*, he suggests that:

a majority of the measures to cover, mobilize, concentrate and deploy the armed forces in the theater of military operations can be carried on ahead of time and merely completed in the threatening period ... early strategic deployment of the armed forces prior to the start of a war, regardless of the benefits of this in purely military terms is not always feasible out of military–political considerations. A mobilization, let alone the entire range of measures related to strategic deployment, has always been considered tantamount to a state of war and it is very difficult to achieve a return from it back to a peacetime status ... Considering all of this, the present system of strategic deployment cannot be oriented solely on one of the most advantageous variations for us, but should be more flexible and provide the organized deployment of the troops under any conditions when the imperialist aggressors initiate a war.[39]

While seeking to minimize uncertainty about the enemy's capability to respond through the achievement of surprise in a short-warning attack is not necessarily new, this line of thought does place less importance on traditional Soviet concepts of mobilization for total war. According to Gareev, mobilization potential is no longer as important as it once was to victory in a conventional arms-only campaign limited to the European theater of strategic military action. Moreover, General Gareev's discussion of future war and Marshal Ogarkov's demand for higher states of readiness and tighter integration of Soviet and non-Soviet ground forces in the Pact's forward deployed formations suggest that the Soviet attack scenario for which NATO is best prepared may be the least likely contingency. Historically, NATO's military response to a Soviet-led Pact offensive against the West has been predicated on the detection of a Warsaw Pact mobilization within four days of it beginning.[40]

General Gareev and Marshal Ogarkov appear to have concluded that a deliberate Soviet attack with fully mobilized forces is the kind of war with which NATO is best prepared to cope. This interpretation is supported by the Soviet General Staff's acute sensitivity to the potential consequences of incautious war mobilization and the Soviet opinion that standing forces rather than mobilized reserves will play the decisive role in a crisis situation. These remarks also reveal Soviet confidence in the view that the West will not launch an unprovoked assault on their homeland. While there is room for discussion concerning how far the existing Soviet force posture has already moved in the direction of this new doctrinal goal, the aim is unmistakable. Soviet military thought is based on the assumption that if the alternative were ignominious retreat from the "gains of socialism" in a crisis, the Soviet state would like to be able to opt for a military solution in Central Europe and to strike before NATO were even partially mobilized and, therefore, more survivable.[41]

Viewed in the context of Ogarkov's and Gareev's remarks, the congruity of thought and action in the contemporary Soviet approach to conventional force development is really quite striking. The emphasis on non-nuclear conflict has been evident for some time in the scenarios which Warsaw Pact maneuvers employ in joint field training of Soviet and non-Soviet ground forces.[42] Also, the Soviet desire to adopt the measures that General Gareev deems critical to success in a future conflict have led to fundamental changes in the Soviet–East European military relationship within the framework of the Warsaw Pact military alliance.

Changes in the new Soviet view of future war have underpinned a military policy which seeks to permanently modify command relationships between the Soviet and non-Soviet forces in the Western TVD in order to exclude the local ruling parties from operational control of their respective military establishments. According to Ryszard Kuklinski, a former Polish General Staff officer who fled to the West in 1981, this policy has resulted in what the military leadership of the Warsaw Pact calls the "wartime statute." In the following excerpt from a longer interview given by Colonel Kuklinski in the spring of 1987, the émigré details the consequences for the operational command, control and development of the Polish armed forces:

The Soviet commands will give their orders and instructions directly to the Polish armies subordinate to them, bypassing national command. In practice, this means that the USSR has the unrestricted right to dispose of the Polish People's Army without any prior consultation with the PPR's [Polish People's Republic] leadership ... The role of the national leadership of the PPR will be limited solely to the functions of ensuring all-round supplies to the Polish troops fighting under Soviet command, to training material and making up for human and material losses.[43]

In 1977, SED First Secretary, Erich Honecker alluded to the structure of Soviet command, control and mobilization which, in later years, the Soviet High Command sought to replicate regionally. Careful examination suggests that the Pact's recent efforts to tighten Soviet control over the region's capacity to mobilize its military resources have their antecedents in the development of Soviet–East German military cooperation.[44]

Of course, Soviet attempts to transplant the most prominent features of Soviet–East German military cooperation to the Pact's other Northern Tier states have met with limited success. Still, even partial Soviet success suggests that the Soviet High Command will attempt to construct a system of Soviet control on the same principles in Poland's armed forces. Future Soviet measures to reform the Polish military establishment on the East German pattern may include

- the gradual elimination of those military units which were formed in the sixties to support a Polish front. This would tend to induce greater Polish dependence on the Soviet military establishment for indirect fire, intelligence and logistical support in order to ease the progressive integration of Polish formations into the larger Soviet-dominated front structures of the Western TVD;
- higher Soviet visibility and control in the key supervisory positions of the Polish Ministry of Defense and command apparatus. While this will create new points of friction in Soviet–Polish military relations, the Soviets have shown some sensitivity to Polish nationalist sentiment;[45]
- closer cooperation in the framework of Pact exercises and intra-army comrades-in-arms relations with Soviet units from the GSFG and western Soviet military districts. This will probably include exercise activity in which Polish forces are integrated with second-echelon Soviet armies;[46]
- stepped-up selection of Polish officers for extended training and education in the Soviet Union's military educational system;
- increased pressure for the Soviet High Command to extract the Polish armed forces from their current public administrative duties.

Based on the Soviet military's efforts to consolidate Soviet control and influence within the East German and, more recently, the Czechoslovak forces, the Soviets may feel capable of coping successfully with Polish resistance to closer integration into the Soviet-controlled force structure. As already mentioned, the political conditions in the GDR do not apply universally in Eastern Europe. Nevertheless, there is evidence that the Soviets are attempting to create the conditions in Poland which have been beneficial to Soviet influence and control in the East German polity.

Poland's social and economic difficulties have made the restoration of communist political institutions in Poland impossible without the threat of Soviet military intervention. This condition has induced extreme dependence in the PUWP on the CPSU for survival. The Polish regime's dependence on Soviet support in the late 1980s has forced a similar degree of diplomatic and military cohesion on the bilateral Soviet–Polish party-military relationship which led the East German and Czechoslovak communists to abdicate responsibility for national security affairs to the Soviet military establishment.[47] This developing state of affairs increases the probability that the Soviets will achieve some success in their attempts to apply the lessons which history has taught them. However, they undoubtedly realize that they will encounter much more resistance to the extension of the East German pattern for Soviet-controlled force development to Poland than they did in Czechoslovakia.

Future prospects: constraints and opportunities

It is clear that two of the most important proximate causes of the emergence of the GDR as the Soviet Union's chief military ally in the Warsaw Pact have been East European resistance to the imposition of Soviet-style communism and the centrality of military power in the Soviet strategy to gain international power and influence.[48] This raises the question of whether future Polish and East European political and economic instability, as well as new Soviet doctrine and strategy will be a catalyzing influence for the further development of Soviet–East German military cooperation? The answer to this question would seem to depend primarily on two factors: (1) the probability that opposition to Soviet control and influence in Poland and elsewhere in the region will survive the measures taken against it; and (2) the GDR state's capacity to sustain the East German contribution to the regional Soviet military effort and to cope with potential internal challenges to the GDR's political order.

Although the Soviets have recognized the need to strengthen and improve their political, economic and military relationship with Eastern Europe, they have had extreme difficulty in doing so. The combination of persistent anti-Russian sentiment and a mediocre leadership that will not risk substantial political and economic innovation in the region has made the Polish, Czechoslovak and past Hungarian regimes increasingly reliant on the use of force and the ultimate threat of Soviet military intervention to maintain control.[49] With the exception of the current Polish regime, the others have cautioned against any hasty, wholesale adoption of Mikhail Gorbachev's proposals for systemic reform. The Czechoslovak party has tended to emphasize the differences between Prague's notion of economic restructuring and Gorbachev's.[50] Similar sentiments were also expressed by the Hungarian Central Committee Secretary Matyas Szuros when he suggested that "only time will reveal the essential significance of everything [going on in the USSR], but we can tell right now that any imitation by Hungary would be a mistake."[51] Predictably, the SED leadership has insisted that the economic steps which Gorbachev now wants to take have already been taken in the GDR and that the Soviet exercise in *glasnost* is inapplicable to the GDR society and state.[52] It may be that with most of the GDR's population religiously watching West German television, any more *glasnost* could prove extremely dangerous.

Conscious of its grave domestic problems, the Polish response to Gorbachev's program has been very different. Jaruzelski has not only enthusiastically applauded the "new political thinking" in Moscow, he is entertaining proposals for economic reform that, according to one account, are so "revolutionary that Gorbachev's 'reconstruction' looks like mere cosmetics by comparison."[53] Part of the reason for this behavior may be the regime's acute dependence on Soviet support for survival and Jaruzelski's need to seek some new accommodation with the Polish people. However, neither reform nor repression are likely to automatically spare the PUWP from further social unrest.

Since the declaration of martial law in Poland, the Polish population has continued to find ingenious, non-violent ways to assert their defiance of Jaruzelski's government. Despite efforts to arrest its development, a society has evolved that is very resistant to party control. More than six years after the imposition of martial law, "Poland's leaders face a united, independent society – a situation unprecedented in Eastern Europe."[54] In short, the best that Jaruzelski can hope for is a temporary, uneasy truce with the Polish people.[55]

Meanwhile, the economic statistics for 1985, the last year for which full data were available, contain little indication that Poland's economic situation is improving. While Poland's population increased by 6.5 percent between 1978 and 1985, national income at the end of 1985 was 12 percent below what it had been in 1978.[56] More importantly, the economic situation in Poland is not expected to improve in the near future and this has important implications for the entire Bloc which has generally failed to keep pace with the Western world's rising prosperity. For example, in 1960 when per capita income of the Warsaw Pact and NATO countries was $3,865 and $6,977 respectively, Warsaw Pact per capita income represented 55.4 percent of NATO's per capita income. In 1985 per capita income in the Pact still only represented 59 percent of NATO's per capita income.[57]

While these economic conditions post no great challenge to NATO, they do create problems for Moscow. As Dr Jeffrey Simon of the National Defense University in Washington has pointed out:

One only has to recall Nikita Khrushchev's rhetoric at the 22nd Congress of the Communist Party of the Soviet Union in October 1961 when the CPSU First Secretary claimed that the USSR would achieve the advanced stage of communism in twenty years, 1981, or his threats at the United Nations boasting to the West that "we will bury you." Khrushchev's statements reflected an optimism about the Soviet political and economic system and the Warsaw Pact vis-à-vis the United States and NATO that, only twenty-five years later, has all but dissipated.[58]

In essence, Gorbachev's attempt to reinvigorate the Soviet state is an explicit recognition of the Soviet failure to match the vitality and productivity of the West.

Of course, the long-run prospects for Gorbachev's success are uncertain at best. What is certain, however, is that the "Polish problem" and the East European problem in general are perpetual.[59] A recent Rand study emphasized this point by noting that in the 1990s, the political convulsions that have become a regular occurrence in Poland and Eastern Europe are likely to continue.[60]

Thus, the Soviets will probably have to incur large economic and military costs to preserve their future political control of Poland and the rest of the region. Moreover, military power will remain the ultimate guarantor of Soviet-style socialism in Eastern Europe. Under these circumstances, will the Soviet–East German military alliance continue to play a key role in the effort to delay the decline of Soviet hegemony over Central-East Europe? The answer to this question would appear to be a qualified "yes." Qualified because there is some doubt about the GDR's capacity to sustain the East German contribution to the regional Soviet military effort at current levels.

Since the founding of the GDR in 1949, the country has experienced a steady decline in the size of the population. Prior to 1950, more than 18,000,000 Germans lived in the former Soviet zone of occupation. By 1984 this number had fallen to 16,600,000 inhabitants.[61] While much of this decline may be attributed to continued legal and illegal migration to the West, most of the decrease may be traced to a birthrate that has been declining for some time. In 1985, the number of live births fell to 227,436 compared with 298,867 in 1964.[62] In an effort to revive the German population's fecundity, the regime has provided numerous aids and incentives to encourage both families and single women to have children. As of the late 1980s it is difficult to forecast the results of these efforts, but the future impact on the GDR's capacity to man its armed forces at current levels and to sustain its reserve of military manpower will be severe in the 1990s.

Table 9 in the appendix illustrates the unavoidable manpower dilemma which will confront the GDR in the decade ahead. As mentioned earlier, the GDR's armed forces are among the Pact's smallest. Peacetime figures are, however, misleading if the state's military mobilization potential is included in the estimate. NVA reserves total 400,000, with 330,000 men in the ground forces. The soldiers of the reserve thus constitute 65 percent of the East German Army's total force of 619,000 troops.[63] When the additional armed organs of the state are added to this number, the total number of men under arms during full mobilization swells to a massive 1.272 million. In the German Federal Republic, a similar state of mobilization produces 1.045 million.[64]

Clearly, the current structure of the GDR's armed forces institutionalizes East German dependence on reserve mobilization. The basis for the reserves is a cadre system with a nucleus of trained professionals engaged in training draftees for eighteen months. The conscripts currently represent roughly 55 percent to 60 percent of the total number of serving soldiers, sailors and airmen.[65] East German reports suggest that most arrive for duty in a high state of physical readiness.[66] Much of the remaining professional cadre is expected to serve during mobilization as cadre for the NVA's four additional reserve divisions and supporting units. Still, with virtually the entire male population already serving in the GDR's armed forces at one time or another, a decline in the male population reaching the age of eighteen each year represents a serious threat to the GDR's military effort.

Since more than 80 percent of the nation's military-eligible youth is called upon each year to serve in the NVA, manipulating age cohorts to compensate for the reduction in the number of eligible men produces marginal results at best. In view of this point, spokesmen for the NVA main staff have indicated that new laws will mandate an increase in the number of extended term and career soldiers. Free German Youth (FDJ) functionaries and authorities from the NVA military commands have already intensified their efforts to convince GDR youth to voluntarily extend their military service or to pursue military careers. One incentive for GDR youth to voluntarily serve longer than the prescribed eighteen months is the high probability of being called to serve for additional periods because of demographic circumstances if they do not! Most young people in the GDR understandably regard service later in life as professionally disadvantageous.[67]

An equally plausible solution that should not be dismissed would be to selectively draft and employ women in activities that do not require men. Already there have been indications in the Soviet and GDR military press that this solution may be under serious consideration. Army General D. T. Yazov, Soviet Minister of Defense, recently addressed the employment of women as officers in the Soviet armed forces. If the past is any guide, the NVA will move quickly to embrace his remarks:

Women may serve as officers, for example, at computer centers, in radiotechnical flight support units, in legal or medical establishments, in the Signal Troops, in the editing and publishing system, and other positions. Women officers have performed well in office work, in military psychology and sociology, and in many other fields.[68]

Nevertheless, what cannot be changed is the growing number of men in the reserves who will be thirty-five and over. Despite the SED's emphasis on youth in the NVA's mobile combat formations, the limited numbers of young men available to serve in combat roles cannot help but moderately degrade the NVA's offensive striking power. War is not an old man's game! In sum, the GDR state confronts a demographic challenge to its military potential in the 1990s which it will have difficulty meeting no matter what measures it adopts.

However, one must also emphasize that in contrast to Poland or Czechoslovakia, the GDR's military–political elite does not have to fear outright political opposition to its rule, but rather a continuing assault on the credibility of the state – "ideological softening-up" as it is referred to in the NVA.[69] In Prussia, opposition to the existing political order never came from the peasants, but from a small minority of professors and officials.[70] Internally, the SED has had to contend with an unruly peace movement composed of students and a handful of professional people who have generally resisted the government's attempts at cooptation.[71] But this has been hardly more than a minor irritant to either the GDR state or the NVA.

This is not to say that the East German military leadership is unaware of the possibility that West German or Polish influence could have a destabilizing effect on their conscript forces,[72] but they understand that the more important gap between economic promise and performance has not precipitated internal revolt and the peace movement will not either.[73] Today, everyone in the GDR is aware that the new socialist society has not, in fact, come about and assurances that communism will yet be built generally evoke disinterest among East German citizens.[74]

Western analysts should not lose sight of the fact that the key factor in Prussia's avoidance of revolution and internal disorder was that the educated classes identified with the state because the state had become their *raison d'être*.[75] This coincidence of interest seems to describe the NVA's relationship with the GDR state.

The East German military establishment is not likely in the short-run to become a source of nationalist opposition to Soviet domination. The demonstrated desire of the Soviet and East German military–political elite to retain stringent control over the East German armed forces and the re-emerging Prussian tradition of military participation in government[76] probably precludes such a development.

This is not to say that the GDR has not produced its own political opposition. The GDR's reform-oriented intelligentsia who reside in the West have argued that the GDR state is out of touch with the German people in the East who desire to find expression through more popular forms of political participation.[77] For them, freedom and national independence would mean abandoning the GDR's military–bureaucratic subordination to Soviet national security interests and the centrally planned economy. It is not impossible that future generations of East German military elites will recognize that a more just social order and greater freedom from Soviet political hegemony will not be attained as long as the Soviet–East German military alliance is firm. Generational change should not be ruled out as a potential source of initiative in the direction of self-determination. East Germany's current military–political ruling elite is, after all, a gerontocracy. In 1988, the Minister of Defense, Army General Heinz Kessler, was sixty-seven years of age; Willi Stoph, Chairman of the Council of Ministers was seventy-three; and Kurt Hager, Secretary of Culture and Science and for International Liaison was seventy-five.[78] In view of this fact and the selection of a younger man, Gorbachev, to head the CPSU, numbers of Western analysts have speculated that there might be a movement toward new blood in the rest of the Soviet bloc.[79] Thus, the impact of new blood in the NVA's senior leadership positions should not be under-estimated.[80]

However, this presupposes that a new generation of military elites would be more willing to risk an existence without Soviet support than their predecessors. Since military interests in the GDR are inextricably intertwined with the interests of the communist political system, this development seems improbable. The fact that the SED regime has worked tirelessly to tie military class interests to the Soviet-sponsored system's survival suggests that East German military elites will be reluctant to sacrifice their fringe benefits, upward social mobility and prestige for the uncertainty of a different social system.[81] Nowhere has this point been demonstrated more emphatically than in Poland during the imposition of martial law in December and January 1981–82. Very few Western scholars and analysts accurately assessed the loyalty, discipline and reliability of the Polish internal security and elite military units. Nearly everyone underestimated the commitment of the Polish military elite to the tenets of orthodox communism.[82]

A highly centralized, militant political system like the GDR assigns a premium to strict control, hierarchical organization and authoritarian chains of command. The underlying ideological conflict with an intransigent Western enemy and the military alliance with the Soviets help rationalize the mobilization of diverse social, economic and political entities under the SED's control. This conforms to a military elite preference for a degree of social order and stability that serves a purely military purpose. This convergence of military conservatism and bureaucratic elitism seems to reinforce the imperative to preserve rather than change the GDR's social order. While this does not exclude the possibility that a withdrawal of Soviet forces from the GDR might merge East Germany as readily with West Germany as Prussia was joined with the rest of Germany in 1871, it does question the validity of any statement that discounts the reliability of East Germany's military establishment under Soviet command and control in a conflict.[83]

This recognition is especially important for those students of international affairs who are understandably alert to potential crises that could lead to a confrontation between the two superpowers in Central Europe. One such study called *Inadvertent War in Europe: Crisis Simulation* conducted in the spring of 1984 at Stanford University revolved around a hypothetical US–Soviet crisis in which an NVA division revolts and deposes its commander.[84] As already mentioned, institutionalized cooperation and regular joint planning with the Soviet military establishment make this possibility remote. Moreover, East German force modernization within the framework of the GSFG seems to be slowing down more and more.[85]

Lastly, beyond the East German military role in the stabilization of the GDR state, a break in Soviet–East German military cooperation would be contingent on an equally unlikely Soviet retreat from the World War II "gains of socialism." On this point there is widespread agreement in Moscow and Eastern Europe.

Soviet control of East Germany and the rest of Eastern Europe still represents an important affirmation for what the communist elites in Eastern Europe believe is an historical process that ordains the imperative of history in a predetermined direction. Western analysts should be careful not to interpret discussions in the Soviet and East German press to mean fundamental movement on the part of the SED toward real independence in the areas touching on the GDR's security relationship with the Soviet Union.[86] These pronouncements are as misleading in the context of security as those alluding to a restoration of warm military ties between the Polish and East German armed forces![87] It is not the aim of the SED to surmount the status quo in Europe unless it would be in the direction of an East German sphere of influence in Eastern Europe in the form of a "condominium" shared with the Soviets. The true aim is to transform the existing situation into a permanent territorial arrangement in order to solidify the GDR as "an irrevocable element of a European order of equilibrium"[88] and to further delay the decline of Soviet regional hegemony. In fact, former border guards who now reside in the West have reported that the prototype for a new high-technology barrier system for the inter-German border already exists and is scheduled for installation in the 1990s![89] Comments that Germans in the East and West are trying to achieve reunification "on the sly"[90] ignore the conditions of hostility that the GDR state's internal order and external relations with the Soviet Union create between the two German states. SED First Secretary Erich Honecker took great pains during his September 1987 visit in Bonn to disabuse Germans in the East and the West from believing that the GDR's ruling elite has any intention of liquidating itself through the reunification of the German nation.

At the official reception in Bonn, I pointed out that unification of the two German states is equally as impossible to effect as the uniting of fire and water. This comes about just from the fact of the differing social systems. Socialism and Capitalism cannot be united. This may occur in fireside dreams, but in reality, such dreams have no substance![91]

However, hard dialectical reasoning in Moscow and East Berlin keeps the door open, at least in theory, for a rearrangement of the

European status quo. In fact, Europe may be entering the period which history may well judge as the beginning of the end of the post-World War II world order. As events in Poland in the 1980s have demonstrated, much of Eastern Europe is already in the advanced stage of a process of organic rejection of a system and an ideology that were artificially transplanted to the region after World War II.[92]

This comment notwithstanding, Lenin always emphasized that men can determine within fairly wide limits the cost and duration of an inevitable social change.[93] For the Soviets who will be concerned with minimizing any loss of influence or control in the states of Eastern Europe, this means that the GDR's political stability and military support will be important to the success of the Soviet Union's efforts to maintain political control of the region. The conservative nature of the SED regime and the insecurity which a contiguity of borders with West Germany implies for the GDR state guarantee that the SED elite will work endlessly to prolong and promote Soviet political control of the states that border the GDR. For the CPSU and the SED, this means that no balance of military power is immutable and no agreement on arms limitations will end Soviet–East German military cooperation in the defense of communism.

Appendix Selected data tables

Table 1a. *Events in Russo-German military relations, 1709–1829*

1709	Peter the Great defeats the Swedes at Poltava and forms a defensive alliance with Brandenburg–Prussia.
1714	In a secret treaty with Frederick I, Prussia guarantees support for Russia's acquisition of Lithuania.
1715	Prussian troops cooperate with Russian troops against the Swedes at Stralsund.
1719/20	Prussia and Russia are parties to the Treaty of Stockholm in which Sweden concedes territory to both.
1762	Tsar Peter III withdraws Russian support from Austria in the Seven Years War and transfers Russian military support to Frederick the Great.
1764	Prussia agrees to an eight-year defensive alliance with Russia which includes provisions for the right of both powers to intervene in Poland should the Polish regime change.
1772	Russia, Prussia and Poland agree to the first partition of Poland.
1789	Russia underwrites and supports Prussia's preparations to oppose the armed forces of the French Revolution.
1793	Russia and Prussia partition Poland for a second time.
1794	Russian and Prussian troops cooperate against Polish revolutionary forces.
1795	Prussia and Russia declare Poland ungovernable and complete the liquidation of Poland.
1807	In the Peace of Tilsit, Russia prevents France from liquidating Prussia. Thanks to Russian insistence, a diminished Prussia remains on the map of Europe.
1812	Tauroggen: Prussia's General Yorck agrees to cooperate with Russian armies under the command of General Diebitsch (who is advised by Clausewitz). Prusso-Russian military collaboration to defeat Napoleon begins in earnest.
1813–15	Russia acquires Polish territory and Prussia acquires Saxony and Westphalia as a result of the Russian Tsar's influence over the Congress of Vienna.
1829	Prussia intercedes on behalf of Russia to facilitate the Peace of Adrianople.

Table 1b. *Events in Russo-German military relations, 1830–1939*

1830	Prussia supports Russian repression of the Polish insurrection in Warsaw.
1854	Prussia remains neutral during Russia's war with Turkey, France and Britain in the Crimea.
1863	Prussia and Russia agree to cooperate against a new Polish insurrection
1870	Russia reassures Prussia that an Austrian attempt to attack Prussia's rear during war with the French will be met by 300,000 Russian troops.
1871	Bismarck supports Russia's demand for a Black Sea fleet at the Pontus conference in London.
1887	Bismarck arranges a secret treaty with Russia which guarantees the neutrality of both powers in the event that either party engages in a war with a third power.
1890	The new German Kaiser removes Bismarck and allows the secret treaty with Russia to lapse.
1917	With the help of the German General Staff, Lenin returns to Russia.
1920	Karl Radek begins negotiations with the German Army leadership on the subject of cooperation. Agreements are also reached on the exchange and repatriation of Soviet and German prisoners of war.
1922	The Weimar German government recognizes the Soviet delegation in Berlin as the legitimate representative of Russia and signs agreements to regulate Russo-German trade.
1922	The treaty of Rapallo between the Soviet Union and Germany establishes formal diplomatic relations, and economic cooperation and absolves both parties of responsibility for war reparations. Clandestine Russo-German military cooperation begins within a military–industrial framework.
1926	Russia and Germany sign accords on friendship and neutrality.
1933	Hitler dismantles the German military presence in Russia and technical–military cooperation ultimately ceases.
1939	Hitler and Stalin agree to cooperate in the liquidation of Poland. Russia eventually acquires Lithuania, Latvia, Estonia, all Polish territory east of the Vistula to include part of Galicia, and occupies Bessarabia.

Table 2. *The USSR as a market for GDR products 1980–84*[a]
USSR share of the respective GDR community exports (%)

Commodity item	1980	1981	1982	1983	1984
Machines for processing					
plastic and elastic materials	61.4	63.3	71.5	77.6	76.6
Machine tools	42.3	63.7	62.2	65.9	70.0
Fishing vessels	100.0	100.0	100.0	100.0	100.0
Office equipment	51.6	64.1	59.9	46.1	40.1
Textile machines	33.1	39.9	38.8	43.2	46.8
Agricultural machines					
and tractors	54.1	60.9	54.4	58.4	59.0
Ocean-going and coastal					
ships	14.8	17.5	28.3	26.3	16.7
Lifting and handling devices	54.7	55.2	48.1	55.1	53.7
Plant-protective agents	42.1	46.4	41.5	41.3	43.7
Photochemical products	36.0	33.3	32.5	32.0	32.6
Products of the precision					
mechanics and glass industries	17.7	15.3	19.6	20.2	21.2
Furniture (incl. upholstered					
furniture)	41.7	45.9	52.3	51.2	47.1
Textile floor covering	63.0	52.0	66.7	54.2	45.3
Men's wear	57.5	66.9	65.7	67.2	61.3
Ladies' wear	65.8	67.2	61.9	65.0	63.1
Toys	39.9	43.3	40.9	39.3	42.7

Note: [a] Data based on value. Measured against the total export volume of the respective commodity, the percentage rates quoted in East German statistics for GDR products exported.
Sources: Statistical Yearbooks of the German Democratic Republic, 1984 and 1985. *JPRS–EER–86–012–L*, 11 Aug. 1986. Percentages determined by calculation.

Table 3. *Selected data on GDR military capabilities, 1962–88*
German Democratic Republic (GDR)

Population and forces	1962	1967	1971	1975	1979	1982	1988
Population	17,280,000	17,200,000	17,150,000	16,990,000	16,700,000	16,750,000	16,250,000
Total regular forces:	85,000	127,000	126,000	143,000	159,000	167,000	179,000
Ground forces	65,000	85,000	90,000	98,000	107,000	113,000	123,000
Motorized divisions	2	2	4	4	4	4	4
Tank divisions	2	2	2	2	2	2	2
Tanks	1,800	1,800	2,200	2,000	2,500	2,500	2,800
T-34	Mainly	Mainly	Some	Sev 100 res			
T-54/55	Mainly	Mainly	Mostly	Yes	+600 storage	+1,600 stor.	1,800
T-62			Some	Yes	All	Yes	Yes
T-72							Yes
Airborne divisions					1 Battalion	1 Bn	1 Bn
Amphibious assault division							
Air force/Air defense	9,000	25,000	20,000	28,000	36,000	38,000	40,000
Fixed-wing combat	300	300	290	330	335	359	337
MiG-17s			32	36	35	35	
MiG-21s			256	294	300	300	100
MiG-23s							200
Su-22/MiG-23MF						12	24
Vertical-lift a/c			20	85	110	125	150
Mi 1			Yes	Yes			
Mi 4			Yes	Yes	40	40	Yes
Mi 8			Yes	Yes	70	70	Yes
Mi 24				Yes		15	70
Navy	11,000	17,000	16,000	17,000	16,000	16,000	16,000
Internal security/border	60,000	70,000	70,000	70,000	71,500	70,200	77,500
Paramilitary forces (Worker's Combat Groups)	n.a.	n.a.	n.a.	350,000	400,000	400,000	500,000
TOTAL MILITARY FORCES	145,000	197,000	196,000	213,000	230,500	237,200	239,000
TOTAL MILITARY PLUS PARAMILITARY FORCES				563,000	630,500	637,200	739,000

Sources: IISS, *The Military Balance*, for data for 1962, 1967, 1975, 1979, 1982, 1986, 1987. More recent figures were provided to the author by US Delegation to MBFR, Vienna.

Table 4. *GDR foreign trade with major partners, 1970–82*

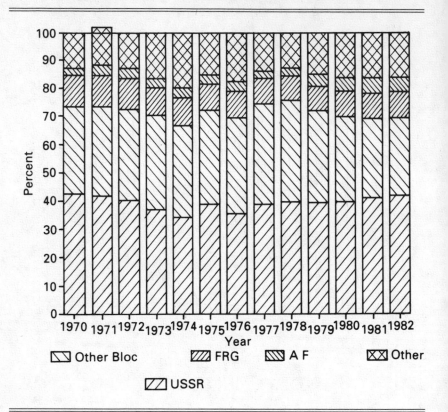

Source: Statistics published by the GDR and reproduced in ULF MARWEGE'S *Neuorientierungim Westhandel der DDR?* (Bonn: Europa Union Verlag, 1984), p. 111.

Table 5. *Defense expenditures, 1974–84 (percent of GNP)*

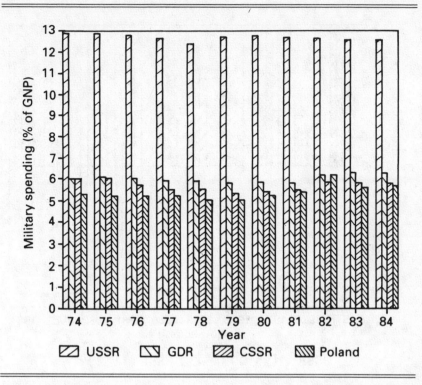

Source: World Military Expenditures and Arms Transfers , 1986 (Washington, DC: US Arms Control and Disarmament Agency, 1986), pp. 75, 90, 93.

Table 6. *Annual growth rates of real GNP, 1975–84 (percent)*

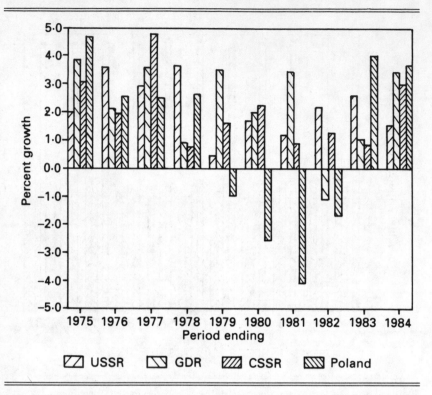

Source: *World Military Expenditures and Arms Transfers*, 1986 (Washington, DC: US Arms Control and Disarmament Agency, 1986), pp. 75, 90, 91, 93.

Table 7. *Geographical proximity of GSFG and NVA combat divisions*

2nd Guards Army	Fuerstenberg/Havel
16th Guards Armored Division	Neustrelitz
21st Motorized Rifle Division	Perleberg
94th Guards Motorized Rifle Division	Schwerin
207th Motorized Rifle Division	Stendal
8th NVA Motorized Rifle Division	Schwerin
9th NVA Armored Division	Eggesin
("Heinz Hoffmann")	
3rd Assault Army	Magdeburg
7th Guards Armored Division	Dessau-Rosslau
10th Guards Armored Division	Altengrabow
12th Guards Armored Division	Neuruppin
47th Guards Armored Division	Hillersleben/Altmark
20th Guards Army	Eberswalde
25th Armored Division	Vogelsang
32nd Guards Armored Division	Jueterbog
90th Guards Armored Division	Bernau bei Berlin
35th Motorized Rifle Division	Doeberitz bei Potsdam
1st NVA Motorized Rifle Division	Potsdam
8th Guards Army	Weimar-Nohra
79th Guards Armored Division	Jena
27th Guards Motorized Rifle Division	Halle/Saale
39th Guards Motorized Rifle Division	Ohrdruf
57th Guards Motorized Rifle Division	Naumburg
11th NVA Motorized Rifle Division	Halle
4th NVA Motorized Rifle Division	Erfurt
1st Guards Armored Army	Dresden
9th Armored Division	Riesa
11th Guards Armored Division	Dresden-Klotzsche
20th Guards Motorized Rifle Division	Grimma
7th NVA Armored Division	Dresden

Sources: Ltc. Guenter Lippert "Die GSTD – vier Jahrzehnte Sowjettruppen in Deutsch-land," *Soldat und Tachnik*, No. 11, November 1986, pp. 620–39, and William Mako's *US Ground Forces and the Defense of Central Europe* (Washington, DC: The Brookings Institute, 1983), pp. 127–29.

Table 8. *Major Pact exercises involving East German participation (exercises involving more than 15,000 troops)*

Major exercise	Dates	Location
*No name given	1–7 Mar. 1969	GDR
Vesna	30 Mar. – 4 Apr. 1969	POLAND
No name given	23 July – 2 Aug. 1969	POLAND
Oder-Neisse	21–28 Sept. 1969	POLAND/GDR
Staff exercise	10–16 Oct. 1969	GDR
Zenith 70	13–17 July 1970	PACT-wide
Comradeship-in-arms	13–18 Oct. 1970	GDR
Visla–Elbe	12–21 July 1971	POLAND/GDR
Autumn Storm	13–18 Sept. 1971	GDR
No name given	25 Feb. – 4 Mar. 1972	GDR/POLAND
*No name given	19–24 June 1972	GDR
Shield 72	4–16 Sept. 1972	CSSR/GDR
Baltica 72	Summer 1972 (naval)	BALTIC
No name given	26 June – 5 July 1973	GDR/POLAND
No name given	4–13 Sept. 1974 (naval)	BALTIC
Shield 76	9–16 Sept. 1976	GDR/POLAND
Val 77	July 1977 (naval)	BALTIC
No name given	Apr. 78 (naval/ASW)	BALTIC
*Tarcza	3–8 July 1978	GDR
*No name given	14 Feb. 1980	GDR
*No name given	21 Mar. 1980	GDR
*No name given	2 Apr. 1980	GDR
Spring 80	26 May – 4 June 1980	POLAND
*No name given	10–16 July 1980	GDR
Comradeship-in-arms	4–12 Sept. 1980	GDR
No name given	12 Feb. 1981	GDR, USSR
Soyuz 81	17–22 Mar. 1981	GDR, POLAND
No name given	30 June 1981	GDR, USSR
No name given	6–18 July 1981	GDR, POLAND

NVA/GSFG troops mobilized periodically during Sept./Nov./Dec. 1981 in connection with Polish crisis

Friendship 82	13–20 Mar. 1982	POLAND
Defense 82	18–21 Oct. 1982	GDR, CSSR
Druzhba 83	10–11 Mar. 1983	POLAND
No name given	18–23 Mar. 1983	GDR
Soyuz 83	30 May – 10 June 1983	GDR, POLAND
No name given	7–14 July 1983	GDR
No name given	21–29 Aug. 1983	N. SEA
Druzhba 84	29 Feb. – 2 Mar. 1984	POLAND
YUG-84	27–31 Mar. 1984	GDR
Shield-84	6–14 Sept. 1984	CSSR
No name given	8 Feb. 1985	GDR
No name given	6–14 July 1985	GDR
Yug 85	21–30 Aug. 1985	GDR
Druzhba 85	6–9 Sept. 1985	POLAND

Several joint Soviet–East German exercises held, but none involving more than 25,000 Soviet and East German ground forces in 1986.

*No name given	23–30 Mar. 1987	GDR
*No name given	21–28 June 1987	GDR
*No name given	10–12 June 1987	GDR
*No name given	26–31 July 1987	GDR, POLAND

* Exercises in which only Soviet and East German forces participated.

Table 9. *GDR manpower (militarily eligible men)*

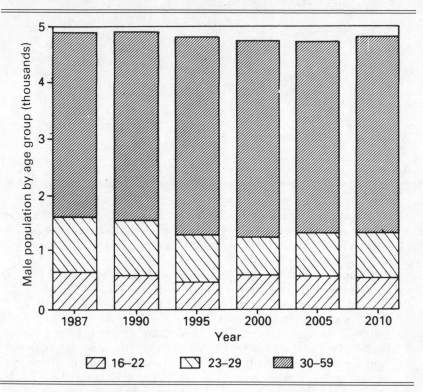

Source: Raw data from US Bureau of the CENSUS for the World Population Project (MAY 1987).

Notes

Introduction

1 Ivan Volgyes, "Troubled Friendship or Mutual Dependence? Eastern Europe and the USSR in the Gorbachev Era," *Orbis*, Summer 1986, p. 343.

2 Charles Gati, "Gorbachev and Eastern Europe," *Foreign Affairs*, vol. 65, no. 5, Summer 1987, p. 969.

3 See Thomas Ammer's "Menschenrectnisverletzungen in der DDR," *Deutschland Archiv*, vol. 18, no. 9, pp. 949–59.

4 "Warsaw Pact Forces in Europe: A New Survey," *Jane's Defense Weekly*, vol. 7, no. 14, 11 Apr. 1987, p. 669.

5 Reinhold August Dorwart, *The Administrative Reforms of Frederick William I of Prussia* (Westport, Conn.: Greenwood Press, 1953), p. 195.

6 John Starrels, Anita Mallinckrodt, *Politics in the German Democratic Republic* (New York: Praeger, 1975), p. 5. Also see Boris Meissner's "Die sowjetische Deutschlandpolitik," in *Sowjetunion: Aussenpolitik I, 1917–1955* (Cologne/Vienna: Böhlen Verlag, 1972), pp. 467–79.

7 Thomas O. Cason, "The Warsaw Pact Today: The East European Military Forces," in *The Warsaw Pact: Political Purposes and Military Means*, R. Clawson and L. Kaplan, eds. (Wilmington, Del.: Scholarly Resources Press, 1982), p. 151; Dale Herspring and Ivan Volgyes, "Political Reliability in the East Europe Warsaw Pact Armies," *Armed Forces and Society*, vol. 6, no. 2, Winter 1980, pp. 270–96; and Thomas Forster, *The East German Army* (London: George Allen and Unwin, 1981). For a more pessimistic assessment of the NVA's striking power see Ivan Sylvain, "The German Democratic Republic," in Christopher Jones and Teresa Rakowska-Harmstone *The Warsaw Pact: Question of Cohesion* (Ottawa: Canadian Department of National Defense, 1984), pp. 272–347.

8 For example, see Robert W. Dean, "The GDR Military," in A. Ross Johnson, Alex Alexiev and Robert Dean, *East European Military Establishments* (New York: Crane, Russak, 1982), pp. 100–2.

9 See Colonel Ryszard Kuklinski's comments in Michael Kaufman, "Bloc Was Prepared to Crush Solidarity, A Defector Says," *New York Times*, 16 Apr. 1987, p. A–9.

10 See Ronald Asmus' comments concerning the East German role in twenty-year Soviet SDI research program in the *RFE/RL Report* dated 31 Oct. 1985, comments in the CDU/CSU's *Pressedienst*, 25 Oct. 1985 and report of the international news agency Reuters on 20 Feb. 1986.

11 See "INF Negotiations and Soviet Nuclear Missiles in the GDR and Czechoslovakia," *RFE/RL Background Report/148*, 21 Oct. 1986, "GDR Submits Proposal on Anti-Satellite Weapons Ban," *FBIS-EEU-87-151*, 6 Aug. 1987, p. BB1.

12 See "Observers Arrive," reported by East Berlin ADN International Service in Germany, 27 July 1987, translated in *FBIS-EEU-87-145*, 29 July 1987, p. AA1.

13 Smith and Meier, "Ogarkov's Revolution: Soviet Military Doctrine for the 1990s," *International Defense Review*, no. 7, 1987, pp. 872–73.

14 Thane Gustafson and Dawn Mann, "Gorbachev at the Helm: Building Power and Authority," *Problems of Communism*, May–June 1986, p. 18.

15 Vladimir Kusin, "Glasnost in Eastern Europe," *RAD Background Report/ 15*, 5 Feb. 1987, p. 1.

16 See Kansan Uutiset's "Reform Debate Not Considered Necessary, GDR Confident in Its Economic Policy," *JPRS-EER-87-106*, 10 July 1987, p. 67. Also, see Margot Honecker's remarks rejecting an open society in *FBIS-EER-DR*, 24 June 1987, p. G–1.

17 See Barbara Donovan, "The GDR's Attitude Toward the Soviet 'Reforms,'" *RAD Background Report/23*, 20 Feb. 1987, pp. 1–5 and Yevgeniy Kapustin's article "Perfecting the System of Management, Planning and Economic Accountability in the GDR," *Voprosy Ekonomiki*, no. 3, Mar. 1987, *JPRS-EER-87-012–2*, 15 June 1987, pp. 43–55.

1 The legacy of success

1 Helmuth Wolfgang Kahn, *Die Deutschen und die Russen: Geschichte ihrer Beziehungen* (Cologne: Pahl Rugenstein, 1984), p. 44.

2 James Billington, *The Icon and the Axe* (New York: Random House, 1970), pp. 111–12.

3 Ibid., p. 182.

4 Elise Kimerling, "Soldier's Children, 1719–1856: A Study of Social Engineering in Imperial Russia," in *Forschungen zur Osteuropäischen Geschichte* (Wiesbaden: Otto Harrassowitz, 1982), vol. 30, p. 92.

5 Dorwart, *Administrative Reforms*, p. 194.

6 Ibid., p. 196.

7 Otto Büsch, *Militärsystem und Sozialleben im alten Preussen, 1713– 1807* (Frankfurt: Ullstein, 1962), pp. 17–18.

8 Dorwart, *Administrative Reforms*, p. 195.

9 Isabel de Madariaga, *Russia in the Age of Catherine the Great* (New Haven, Conn.: Yale University Press, 1981), pp. 584–85.

10 Bruce W. Menning, "Russia and the West: The Problem of Eighteenth Century Military Models," in *Russia and the West in the Eighteenth*

Century, A. G. Cross, ed. (Newtonville, Mass.: Oriental Research Partners, 1983), p. 290.

11 Walter N. Pintner, "Russia's Military Style, Russian Society, and Russian Power in Eighteenth Century," in *Russia and the West in the Eighteenth Century*, ed. A. G. Cross, p. 264.

12 De Madariaga, *Russia*, pp. 445–46.

13 Ibid., p. 448.

14 Volcker Hentschel, *Preussens streitbare Geschichte 1594–1945* (Düsseldorf: Droste, 1980), pp. 115–29.

15 Wolfgang Venohr, *Preussische Portraits* (Hamburg: Christian Wegner, 1969), pp. 15–19 and Hentschel, *Preussens streibare Geschichte*, pp. 101–56.

16 Fritz Epstein, "Friedrich Meinecke on Eastern Europe," in Robert Byrnes, ed. *Fritz Epstein: Germany and the East* (Bloomington, Ind.: Indiana University Press, 1973), p. 29.

17 Lesley Blanch, *The Sabres of Paradise* (New York: Carroll & Graf, 1960), p. 24.

18 See Leo Sievers, *Tausend Jahre gemeinsame Geschichte: Deutsche und Russen* (Augsburg–Munich: Wilhelm Goldman, 1983), p. 357.

19 See John Shelton Curtiss, "The Army of Nicholas I: Its Role and Character," *American Historical Review*, vol. 63, no. 4, 1958, pp. 880–86.

20 Edward C. Thaden, *Russia Since 1801: The Making of a New Society* (New York: John Wiley and Sons, 1971), p. 360.

21 Edward Crankshaw, *Bismarck* (New York: Viking Press, 1981), pp. 394–414.

22 Fritz Epstein, "East Europe as a Power Vacuum," pp. 57–58.

23 Werner Mosse, *Alexander II and the Modernization of Russia* (New York: Collier Books, 1962), pp. 127–31.

24 Hans Roger, *Russia in the Age of Modernization and Revolution: 1881–1917* (London: Longman, 1983), p. 171.

25 Gordon Craig, *The Politics of the Prussian Army* (Oxford: Clarendon Press, 1955), pp. 268–70.

26 Roger, *Russia in the Age of Modernization*, p. 172.

27 Albert Hirschman, *National Power and the Structure of Foreign Trade* (Berkeley, Cal.: University of California Press, 1980), p. 31.

28 Roger, *Russia in the Age of Modernization*, p. 107.

29 Harold Ingle, *Nesselrode and the Russian Rapprochement with Britain, 1836–1844* (Berkeley, Cal.: University of California Press, 1976), p. 5.

30 Ibid., p. 31.

31 Roger, *Russia in the Age of Modernization*, p. 133.

32 D. C. B. Lieven, *Russia and the Origins of the First World War* (New York: St. Martin's Press, 1983), p. 16.

33 Klemens von Klemperer, *Germany's New Conservatism: Its History and Dilemma in the Twentieth Century* (Princeton, N.J.: Princeton University Press, 1968), p. 139.

34 See Arno Mayer's work on the subject, *The Politics and Diplomacy of*

Peacemaking, Containment and Counterrevolution at Versailles, 1918–1919 (New York: Vintage Books, 1967).

35 Telford Taylor, *Sword and Swastika* (Chicago, Ill.: Quadrangle Books, 1969), p. 46.
36 Robert C. Tucker, "The Emergence of Stalin's Foreign Policy," *Slavic Review*, Dec. 1977, p. 565.
37 E. H. Carr, *The Bolshevik Revolution*, vol. 3 (London: Penguin, 1953), p. 182.
38 Ibid., pp. 118–19.
39 M. K. Dziewanowski, "Joseph Pilsudski," *East European Quarterly*, vol. 2, no. 4, Jan. 1969, p. 379.
40 Quoted by Norman Davies, *White Eagle, Red Star* (London: Macdonald, 1972), p. 114.
41 Barton Whaley, *Covert German Rearmament, 1919–1939: Deception and Misperception* (Frederick, Md.: University Publications of America, 1984), p. 78.
42 Hans W. Gatzke, "Russo-German Military Collaboration During the Weimar Republic," *The American Historical Review*, vol. 63, Apr. 1958, pp. 565–70.
43 John Erickson, *The Soviet High Command: A Military–Political History, 1918–1941* (Boulder, Col.: Westview Press, 1984), pp. 303–6.
44 Whaley, *Covert German Rearmament*, p. 78.
45 Academic Publications, *The Development of The Soviet Armed Forces, 1917–1977* (Maxwell AFB, Ala.: Air University Press, 1977), p. 21.
46 Whaley, *Covert German Rearmament*, p. 79.
47 Taylor, *Sword and Swastika*, p. 49.
48 Erickson, *The Soviet High Command*, pp. 280–81.
49 Ibid., p. 281.
50 Karl Spalcke, "Begnungen zwischen Reichswehr und Roter Armee: 1924–1933, Ein Rückblick," *Aussenpolitik*, no. 9, 1958, pp. 506–9.
51 Helm Speidel, "Reichswehr and Rote Armee," *Vierteljahreshefte für Zeitgeschichte*, Jan. 1953, pp. 9–43.
52 Academic Publications, *Development*, pp. 21–22.
53 Quincy Wright, *A Study of War* (Chicago, Ill.: University of Chicago Press, third edition, 1971), pp. 1280–81.
54 See Wojtech Mastny, "The Militarization of the Cold War," *International Security*, vol. 9, no. 3, Winter 1984–85, pp. 109–29.
55 Tucker, "The Emergence of Stalin's Foreign policy," p. 574.
56 Ibid., pp. 573–78.
57 Ibid., p. 573.
58 Ibid., p. 571.
59 Michael H. Kater, *The Nazi Party: A Social Profile of Members and Leaders, 1919–1945* (Cambridge, Mass.: Harvard University Press, 1983).
60 Quoted by Tucker, "The Emergence of Stalin's Foreign Policy," p. 23.
61 Ibid., p. 573.
62 General Ernst Koestring, *General Ernst Koestring, Der militärische Mittler*

zwischen dem deutschen Reich und der Sowjetunion, 1921–1941,
Hermann Teske, ed. (E. S. Mittler und Sohn, 1963), p. 126.

63 Ibid., p. 85. Recently there has been some discussion concerning the
   preemptive nature of the German attack on Russia in light of Stalin's
   supposed readiness to launch a surprise attack against Hitler. See Bernd
   Stegemann's "Geschichte und Politik: Zur Diskussion über den
   deutschen Angriff auf die Sowjetunion 1941," *Beiträge zur Konfliktfors-
   chung*, no. 1, 1987, pp. 73–93.
64 Telford Taylor, *Sword and Swastika*, p. 322.
65 Koestring, *General Ernst Koestring*, p. 145 and Taylor, *Sword and Swastika*, p. 343.
66 Seweryn Bialer, *Stalin and His Generals* (Boulder, Col.: Westview Press,
   1984), p. 59.
67 See John Erickson's chapter "We are being fired on. What shall we do?,"
   in Erickson, *The Soviet High Command*, pp. 565–75 and General
   Koestring's comments on pages 1–16 and especially p. 70 (*General Ernst
   Koestring*).
68 Norman Davies, *Heart of Europe: A Short History of Poland* (Oxford:
   Clarendon Press, 1984), pp. 66–67.
69 Albert O. Hirschman, *National Power*, p. 149.
70 Wojtech Mastny, *Russia's Road to the Cold War* (New York: Columbia
   University Press, 1979), p. 77.
71 J. Engleman, *Manstein: Ein Stratege und Truppenführer* (Friedberg:
   Podzun-Pallas-Verlag GmbH, 1970), pp. 121, 125 and 153.
72 Julius Epstein, *Operation Keelhaul The Story of Forced Repatriation
   from 1946 to the Present* (Old Greenwich, Conn. Devin-Adair, 1974),
   p. 61.
73 George H. Stein, *The Waffen SS, Hitler's Elite Guard at War* (Ithaca, N.Y.:
   Cornell University Press, 1966), pp. 168–96.
74 Herzogin Viktoria Louise, *Im Strom der Zeit* (Göttingen–Hannover:
   Göttinger Verlagsanstalt, 1974), pp. 31–32.

2 The East German rise to military prominence, 1956–1969

1 See Colonel N. Martsikh's remarks in a review of *The Organizational
  Development of the Armies of the European Socialist Commonwealth
  Nations*, *JPRS–UMA–85–56*, Sept. 1985, pp. 11–15.
2 Thomas Wolfe, *Soviet Military Power and Europe, 1945–1970* (Baltimore, Md.: Johns Hopkins Press, 1970), p. 148.
3 John Yurechko, "Command and Control for Coalitional Warfare: The
  Soviet Approach," *Signal*, December 1985, pp. 14–15.
4 The current East German Minister of Defense, Colonel General Heinz
  Kessler, was among the very few German soldiers who, at the beginning of
  the war, deserted to the Soviets and spent the war working with this
  organization.
5 Forster, *The East German Army*, p. 20 and Kater, *The Nazi Party*, p. 160.

6 Stefan Brant, *The East German Rising* (New York: Praeger, 1957), pp. 149–50.

7 Heinz Koehler, *Economic Integration in the Soviet Bloc; With an East German Case Study* (New York: Praeger, 1965), p. 8.

8 J. P. Nettl, *The Eastern Zone and Soviet Policy in Germany, 1945–1950* (London: Oxford University Press, 1951), p. 200.

9 Koehler, *Economic Integration*, p. 12.

10 Nettl, *The Eastern Zone*, p. 204.

11 Koehler, *Economic Integration*, p. 38.

12 Nettl, *The Eastern Zone*, p. 206.

13 Forster, *The East German Army*, p. 19.

14 See David Childs, *The GDR: Moscow's German Ally*, p. 273 and Robert Dean, "The GDR Military," pp. 65–67.

15 Samuel Huntington, *Political Order in Changing Societies* (New Haven, Conn.: Yale University Press, 1968), p. 144.

16 Robert Dean, "The GDR Military," in *The Warsaw Pact Northern Tier*, p. 70. None of the treaties on friendship, reciprocal assistance and cooperation between the USSR and GDR in 1964, 1975 or 1985 modifies this arrangement in any way.

17 Arthur Hanhardt Jr, *The German Democratic Republic* (Baltimore, Md.: Johns Hopkins Press, 1968), p. 65.

18 John Keegan, *World Armies* (New York: Facts on File, Inc., 1979), p. 236.

19 Major General Hans Pilster, *Soldat und Technik*, vol. 21, no. 10, Oct. 1978, p. 517.

20 Gerhard Wettig, *Community and Conflict in the Socialist Camp: The Soviet Union, East Germany and the German Problem 1965–1972* (New York: St. Martin's Press, 1975), p. 4.

21 J. F. Brown, "Relations Between the Soviet Union and Its East European Allies: A Survey," *Rand Report R–1742–PR* (Santa Monica, Cal.: Rand Corporation, 1975).

22 Zvi Gitelman, *Change in Communist Systems* (Stanford, Cal.: Stanford University Press, 1970), p. 263.

23 Martin McCauley, *The German Democratic Republic Since 1945* (New York: St. Martin's Press, 1983), pp. 68–69; The GDR's extensive uranium deposits are still exploited by the last remaining joint Soviet–German Corporation (SDAG) Wismut. All East German uranium is still shipped to the USSR, both the volume and the terms are state secrets. See Jochan Bethenhagen, "FRG Study on Soviet, GDR, CMEA Energy Policy, Prospects," in *JPRS–EER–87–011*, 26 Jan. 1987, p. 16.

24 Zbigniew K. Brzezinski, *The Soviet Bloc* (Cambridge, Mass.: Harvard University Press, 1981), pp. 173–74.

25 Christopher D. Jones, *Soviet Influence in Eastern Europe* (New York: Praeger, 1981), pp. 8–9.

26 A. Ross Johnson, "The Warsaw Pact: Soviet Military Policy in Eastern Europe," *Rand Paper P–6583* (Santa Monica, Cal.: The Rand Corporation, 1981).

27 Andrzej Korbonski, "The Polish Army," in *Communist Armies in Politics*, edited by J. Adelman (Boulder, Col.: Westview Press, 1982), p. 116.

28 For an excellent discussion of these events see Jones, *Soviet Influence*.

29 Richard Mills, "The Soviet Leadership Problem," *World Politics*, July 1981, vol. 32, p. 597.

30 Woodrow Kuhns, "Political Nationalism in Contemporary Eastern Europe," in Jeffrey Simon and Trond Gilberg, eds., *Security Implications of Nationalism in Eastern Europe* (Boulder, Cal.: Westview Press, 1985), p. 91.

31 Hartmut Zimmerman, "The GDR in the 1970s," *Problems of Communism*, Mar.–Apr. 1978, p. 8.

32 McCauley, *German Democratic Republic*, pp. 103–48.

33 Klaus von Beyme, *Economics and Politics in Socialist Systems* (New York: Praeger, 1982), p. 212.

34 Ken Booth, "The Military as an Instrument of Soviet Foreign Policy," in John Baylis and Gerald Segal, editors, *Soviet Strategy* (London: Croom Helm, 1981), p. 83.

35 Booth, "The Military Instrument," p. 75.

36 Vojtech Mastny, "Militarization of the Cold War," pp. 109–29.

37 William E. Odom, "The Soviet Approach to Nuclear Weapons," *Annals*, AAPSS, no. 469, Sept. 1983, p. 116.

38 Yurechko, "Command and Control," p. 8.

39 See William E. Odom's comments in "Soviet Force Posture: Dilemmas and Directions," *Problems of Communism*, July–Aug. 1985, p. 5.

40 Mark Urban, "Red Flag Over Germany," *Armed Forces*, March 1985, p. 71.

41 Major General S. A. Tyushkevich, *The Soviet Armed Forces: A History of Their Organizational Development*, translated by CIS Multilingual Section, Secretary of State, Canada (Washington: US Govt. Printing Office, 1978), p. 411.

42 Urban, "Red Flag Over Germany," p. 71.

43 McCauley, *German Democratic Republic*, pp. 108–11.

44 "Einige Entwicklungsprobleme der Landstreitkräfte der NVA in den sechzigen Jahren," *Militärgeschichte*, no. 4, 1978, pp. 418–26.

45 Gerhard Lux, "Die Entwicklung der motorisierten Schützentruppen der NVA in der ersten Hälfte der sechzigen Jahre," *Militärgeschichte*, no. 2, 1978, p. 163.

46 Oleg Penkovsky, *The Penkovsky Papers* (Garden City: Doubleday, 1965), pp. 221–23.

47 Urban, "Red Flag Over Germany," p. 71.

48 Army General Heinz Kessler, Minister of Defense, "Three Decades of the NVA Reflect the Unity of the People, Party and Army," *JPRS–EER–86–042*, 21 Mar. 1986, p. 60; also, see Peter Ludz, *The Changing Party Elite in East Germany* (Cambridge, Mass.: MIT Press), 1972, pp. 35–43.

49 Richard Martin, "Warsaw Pact Modernization: A Second Look," in Simon and Gilberg, eds., *Security Implications of Nationalism in Eastern Europe*, p. 210.

50 See Günter Lippert, "Warschauer Pakt: Die Nationale Volksarmee der DDR" (Warsaw Pact: The National People's Army of the GDR), *Wehrtechnik*, no. 10, Oct. 1980, pp. 49–50 and 56–57, in *JPRS 76945*, 5 Dec. 1980. Also see Günter Lippert's "The GSFG – Four Decades of Soviet Troops in Germany," *Soldat und Technik*, no. 11, Nov. 1986, pp. 620–39.

51 See *The Soviet Army: Troops, Organization and Equipment FM 100–2–3* (Washington, HQTRS, Dept. of the Army, 1984), pp. 4112–17.

52 Christopher Jones, "Agencies of the Alliance: Multilateral in Form, Bilateral in Content," in Simon and Gilberg, eds., *The Security Implications of Nationalism in Eastern Europe*, p. 180.

53 Ulrich Ruehmland, *Die NVA in Stichworten* (Bonn–Röttgen, Bonner Druck– und Verlagsgesellschaft, 1978), pp. 203–4. Also see William Lewis, *The Warsaw Pact: Arms, Doctrine and Strategy* (New York: McGraw-Hill, 1982), p. 179.

54 Karl Greese, Guenter Schulz, Alfred Voerster, "Zur Aufstellung moderner Verbände der Landstreitkräfte der NVA im Jahre 1956," *Militärgeschichte*, no. 4, 1967, pp. 389–99, and David Childs, *East Germany* (New York: Praeger 1969), p. 246.

55 E. Waldman, "The Other Side of the Hill II: The Military Policy of an Archetypal Soviet Satellite, the German Democratic Republic," *Canadian Defence Quarterly*, vol. 5, no. 4, Spring 1976, p. 47.

56 William Corson and Robert Crowley, *The New KGB* (New York: William Morrow, 1986), pp. 263–64.

57 Kurt Leissler, "How Moscow is Spying in the GDR: A High KGB Officer Fled and Is Now Revealing Secret Service Practices of the East," *Die Welt*, 27 Dec. 1975, p. 3, *JPRS 66774*, 11 Feb. 1976, p. 9. Also see Aleksei Myagkov, *Inside the KGB* (London: New Goswell Printing, 1976).

58 See Herspring and Volgyes, "The Military as an Agent of Political Socialization in Eastern Europe", *Armed Forces and Society*, vol. 3, no. 2, Feb. 1977, pp. 261–65, for a description of this period in Pact military development.

59 Forster, *The East German Army*, p. 73.

60 Colonel General Horst Stechbarth, "Thirty Years of Reliable Protection in the Service of Peace," *Horizont*, no. 2, Feb. 1986, *JPRS–EER–86–072*, 9 May 1986, p. 85.

61 General Gribkov on "Warsaw Pact Responsibilies," from *Voyenno-Istoricheskiy Zhurnal* in *JPRS–UMA–85–051*, 5 Sept. 1985.

62 See Fjodorowitsch's and Smirow, "Die Verteidigung des sozialistischen Vaterlands als Grundprinzip der sowjetischen Verfassung," *Militärgeschichte*, no. 4, 1978, pp. 427–30.

63 Herman Müller, Karl-Heinz Schulz, Paul Wollina, *Warschauer Vertrag: Schild des Sozialismus* (East Berlin: DDR Militaerverlag, 1975), p. 135.

64 McCauley, *German Democratic Republic*, p. 117.

65 Heinz Marks, *Die Kampfgruppen der Arbeiterklasse* (Cologne: Markus, 1970), p. 10.

66 Laszlo Revesz, *Militärische Ausbildung in Osteuropa* (Bern: W. Steiger, 1975), p. 227.
67 Jeffrey Simon, *Warsaw Pact Forces: Problems of Command and Control* (Boulder, Col.: Westview Press, 1985), p. 21.
68 Karl Wilhelm Fricke, "Okkupanten oder Waffenbrueder? Die Gruppe der sowjetischen Streitkräfte in Deutschland," *Deutschland Archiv*, vol. 15, no. 3, Mar. 1982, pp. 269–76.
69 McCauley, *German Democratic Republic*, p. 231, and *JPRS–EER– 86–012–L*, 11 Aug. 1986, p. 6.
70 Fricke, "Okkupanten oder Waffenbrueder?," p. 6.
71 Simon, *Warsaw Pact Forces*, p. 33.
72 Ibid., p. 38.
73 Von Beyme, *Economics and Politics*, pp. 146, 165 and 188.
74 Jiri Valenta, "Soviet Decisionmaking on Czechoslovakia, 1968," in *Soviet Decisionmaking for National Security*, Jiri Valenta and William Potter, eds. (London: George Allen and Unwin, 1984).
75 Johnson, Alexiev, Dean, *East European Military Establishments*, pp. 28–31.
76 According to Viktor Suvorov, *Inside the Soviet Army* (New York: Macmillan, 1982), pp. 12–16, this type of Soviet officer held commissions in both armies at the same time.
77 Simon, *Warsaw Pact Forces*, p. 45.
78 A. Ross Johnson, "The Warsaw Pact: Soviet Military Policy in Eastern Europe," *Rand Paper P–6583* (Santa Monica, Cal.: The Rand Corporation, 1981), p. 12.
79 Andrzej Korbonski, "Eastern Europe," in *After Brezhnev*, Robert K. Byrnes, ed. (Bloomington, n.d.: Indiana University Press, 1983), pp. 310–11.
80 Egon Winkelmann, "A New Kind of Alliance," *Einheit*, vol. 35, no. 5, May 1980, *JPRS 76395 EE No. 1812*, 10 Sept. 1980, p. 46.
81 Simon, *Warsaw Pact Forces*, pp. 64–65.
82 Klaus-Ulrich Keubke, Toni Nelles and Heinz Oeckel, "Zur Entwicklung der Waffenbruederschaftsbeziehungen zwischen der Nationalen Volksarmee der DDR und der Sowjetarmee in den siebziger Jahren", *Militärgeschichte*, no. 1, 1978, p. 24.
83 See Karl Greese, Peter Schramm, Alfred Voerster, "Die Waffenbruederschaftsbeziehungen der NVA zur Polnischen Armee in den siebziger Jahren", *Militärgeschichte*, no. 3, 1980, pp. 279–89.
84 Dean, "The GDR Military," p. 71.
85 David Eisenhower, *Eisenhower at War 1943–1945* (New York: Random House, 1986), p. 652.
86 East Germany really consists of those former German territories in Polish and Soviet hands.
87 Ronald Asmus, "The GDR in 1983: New Issues to the Fore," *Soviet-East European Survey*, Wojtech Mastny, ed. (Durham, N.C.: Duke University Press, 1985), p. 241.

88 Dale Herspring, *East German Civil-Military Relations: The Impact of Technology 1949–1972* (New York: Praeger, 1973), see Chapter 8.
89 Thomas Ammer, Gunter Holzweissig, *Die DDR* (Bonn: Bundesministerium der Verteidigung, 1979), pp. 12–14.
90 Peter Christian Ludz, *Parteielite im Wandel* (Cologne: Westdeutscher Verlag, 1970), pp. 6–7.
91 See Robert Tucker's *The Lenin Anthology* (New York: W. W. Norton and Co., 1975), p. 433.
92 Wolfgang Mommsen, "Wandlungen der nationalen Identität," *Die Identität der Deutschen*, Werner Weidenfeld, ed. (Darmstadt: Carl Hanser, 1983), p. 201.
93 Colonel General Yevdokiy Mal'tsev, "With Thoughts of the Party and Country," *Sovetskiy Voin*, no. 1, Jan. 1971, pp. 2–4, *JPRS 52428*, 19 Feb. 1971, p. 16.
94 J. Gruemmert, "Die Waffenbrüderschaftsbeziehungen eines Panzerverbandes der NVA zu seinem Partnerverband der GSSD 1970–1976," in *Militärgeschichte*, no. 2, 1980, pp. 169–76.
95 John R. Thomas, "Soviet Foreign Policy and Conflict within Political and Military Leadership," Paper for U.S. Dept. of Defense, RAC–P–61, Sept. 1970, p. 8, unpublished.
96 See Marshall Ogarkov's comments in *Krasnaya Zvezda*, 9 May 1984, pp. 2–3.

3 Soviet–German military collaboration in the post-1968 Pact

1 Wettig, *Community and Conflict*, pp. 74–75.
2 Ibid., p. 76.
3 Zimmerman, "The GDR in the 1970s," p. 13.
4 Quoted by Lt. Col. G. Graebner, "Internationalist Character of GDR Military Policy Explained," *Zeitschrift für Militärmedizin*, no. 4, 1972, pp. 181–83, *JPRS 57386*, pp. 13–18.
5 Thomas Wolfe, *Soviet Power and Europe*, (Baltimore, Md.: Johns Hopkins Press, 1970), p. 451.
6 Joseph Douglass, Jr., *Soviet Military Strategy in Europe* (New York: Pergamon Press, 1980, pp. 176–79).
7 Alfred Monks, *Soviet Military Doctrine: 1960 to the Present* (New York: Irvington Publishers, 1984), p. 79.
8 Ibid., p. 79.
9 Then General V. Kulikov, "High Military Preparedness – A Critical Condition for the Reliable Defense of the Homeland," *Kommunist Vooruzhenyh Sil*, no. 6, Mar. 1973, p. 15 in Alfred Monks' *Soviet Military Doctrine*, p. 80.
10 James M. McConnell, *The Soviet Shift in Emphasis From Nuclear to Conventional – the Mid-term Perspective* (Alexandria, Va.: Center for Naval Analyses, 1983), pp. 18–19.

11 Ibid., p. 20.
12 Dale Herspring, "Detente and the Military," *The German Democratic Republic: A Developed Socialist Society*, Lyman Letgers, ed. (Boulder, Col.: Westview Press, 1978), pp. 199–200.
13 Ronald Asmus, "Honecker: The Man and his Era," *RFE Background Report/174*, 30 Aug. 1982, p. 3.
14 Ibid., p. 3–4.
15 Ibid.
16 Ulf Marwege, *Neuorientierung im Westhandel der DDR? Die Wirtschaftsbeziehungen mit der Bundersrepublik Deutschland, Frankreich, Japan und Österreich* (Bonn: Europa Union, 1984), pp. 51–53.
17 Asmus, "Honecker," p. 3.
18 Karl Wilhelm Fricke, "Der Verteidigungshaushalt der DDR," *Deutschland Archiv*, vol. 10, no. 2, Feb. 1977, pp. 169–68.
19 "Military Spending Rates in East Europe," *Aviation Week and Space Technology*, 19 Sept. 1977, p. 21.
20 Simon, *Warsaw Pact Forces*, p. 102.
21 This information is taken from Heinz Hoffmann's remarks in "Our Achievements Are Reliably Protected," *Einheit*, vol. 29, no. 9/10, 1974, pp. 1085–95, and Simon, *Warsaw Pact Forces*, pp. 222–23.
22 Pierre Darcourt, "Large-scale Maneuvers in East Germany," *Le Figaro*, 7 July 1978, p. 1; *JPRS 71672*, 14 Aug. 1978, p. 2.
23 Simon, *Warsaw Pact Forces*, p. 79.
24 Dr Col. G. Jokel, Dr Col. T. Nelles, K. U. Keubke, "Zur Entwicklung der Waffenbrüderschaftsbeziehungen zwischen der NVA und der Sowjetarmee in den ziebziger Jahren," pp. 65–71 and Ltg. Horst Stechbarth's comments in "Higher Quality of Combat Training," *Volksarmee*, 9 Feb. 1976, p. 3; *JPRS 67076*, 2 Apr. 1976, pp. 17–18.
25 Darcourt, "Large-scale Maneuvers," p. 2.
26 Quoted in *Der Spiegel*, Oct. 1984.
27 "Civil Defense of the GDR Under NVA Command," *Informationen*, (Bonn), no. 8, Apr. 1977, p. 7.
28 Günter Holzweissig, "DDR–Zivilverteidigung reorganisiert," *Deutschland Archiv*, vol. 11, no. 2, Feb. 1978, pp. 172–77.
29 See General William Odom's essay "The Militarization of Soviet Society," *Problems of Communism*, Sept.–Oct. 1976, p. 47.
30 See "Details Provided on Reservists' Training," translated from *Der Kämpfer, JPRS 66556 EE No. 1184*, 12 Jan. 1976, pp. 27–29.
31 "Plans for Civil Defense Mobilization," *Der Spiegel*, 13 June 1977, p. 18DW; *JPRS 69293*, 22 June 1977; and Simon, *Warsaw Pact Forces*.
32 Gunter Holzweissig, "DDR–Zivilverteidigung Reorganisiert" (GDR Civil Defense Reorganized), *Deutschland Archiv*, vol. 11, no. 2, Feb. 1978, pp. 172–77.
33 Dietrich Wagner, "Organisation, Auftrag und militärischer Stellenwert der Kampfgruppen der Arbeiterklasse in der DDR," *Europäische Wehrkunde*, July 1981, p. 320.

34 Dr Gerd Meyer, "On the Sociology of the GDR Power Elite," *JPRS–EPS–85–083*, 14 Aug. 1985, p. 84.

35 Ibid., p. 84.

36 Ivan Sylvain, "The German Democratic Republic," *Warsaw Pact: Question of Cohesion, Phase II* (Ottawa: Department of National Defense, 1984), p. 280.

37 Claus-Einar Langen, "GDR Border Troops Superior to those of FRG," *Frankfurter Allgemeine*, 4 Sept. 1975, p. 3.

38 The line of demarcation extends from Hof into the Mecklenburg Bay opposite West Germany.

39 Claus-Einar-Langen, "Activity of Warsaw Pact's Western Flank Reported," *Frankfurter Allgemeine*, 23 Apr. 1977, p. 3; *JPRS 29266*, 16 June 1977, pp. 1–2.

40 Ibid., p. 2.

41 *Krasnaya Zvezda*, 14 Apr. 1981, p. 1; *JPRS 78250*, 8 June 1981, p. 15.

42 Army General Mikhail Zaytsev, *Neues Deutschland*, 23 Feb. 1982, p. 3; *FBIS–USSR–DR*, 25 Feb. 1982, p. V–3.

43 "I Lost My Illusions," *Der Spiegel*, no. 9, 21 Feb. 1977, pp. 38–52; *JPRS 68866*, 1 Apr. 1977, pp. 50–53.

44 G. Jokel, T. Nelles, K. U. Keubke, "The Development of Combat Collaboration Between the GDR NPA and the Soviet Army During the 70s," *Voyenno-Istoricheskiy Zhurnal*, no. 7, July 1978; *JPRS 72066*, 18 Oct. 1978, pp. 45–46.

45 Melvin Croan, "The Development of GDR Political Relations with the USSR," in the edited volume *GDR Foreign Policy* (London: M. E. Sharpe, 1982), p. 72.

46 Army General Heinz Hoffmann, *Neues Deutschland*, 29 Sept. 1972, p. 4; *JPRS 57274*, 17 Oct. 1972, p. 17. See the regulations printed in *Militärgeschichte*, 1980, no. 2, p. 207.

47 Ibid.

48 Admiral V. Werner, "The Indissolvable Fraternity in Arms with the Soviet Armed Forces is the Basic Principle of SEPG Military Policy," *Kommunist Vooruzhenyh Sil*, no. 5, 1974, p. 80; *JPRS 61753*, 15 Apr. 1974, p. 6.

49 Lieutenant General Joachim Goldbach, chief of the military Bezirk of Neubrandenburg, "Soldiers of the People Defend Peace and Socialism," *Bauern Echo*, 14/15 Feb. 1976, p. 7; *JPRS 67076*, 2 Apr. 76, p. 2.

50 Ltg. Streletz, "Interview," *National Zeitung*, 7 Apr. 1977, p. 3; *JPRS 69141*, 24 May 1977, p. 42–43.

51 Ltg. Horst Bruenner, "Active Party Work – A Prerequisite of High Combat Readiness," *Neuer Weg*, vol. 32, no. 5, 1977, pp. 199–202; *JPRS 68920*, 12 Apr. 1977, p. 16.

52 J. Gruemmert, "Die Waffenbrüderschaftsbeziehungen eines Panzerverbandes der NVA zu seinem Partnerverband der GSSD 1970–1976," *Militärgeschichte*, no. 2, 1980, pp. 169–76.

53 Ibid., p. 172.

54 Confirmed in the author's conversations with former NVA personnel. Ivan Sylvain also makes this observation, "The German Democratic Republic," pp. 323–24.
55 Sylvain, "The German Democratic Republic," p. 317.
56 Dean, "The GDR Military," p. 86.
57 A. Ross Johnson and Alex Alexiev, "East European Military Reliability: An Emigré-Based Assessment," *Rand Report R-3480* (Santa Monica, Cal.: The Rand Corporation, 1986), p. 57.
58 Forster, *The East German Army*, p. 81.
59 See the interview with Stechbarth in *JPRS 70616*, 9 Feb. 1978, p. 16.
60 See his speech in *FBIS-EEU-DR*, 12 Feb. 1986, pp. E-2–E-3.
61 Rakowska-Harmstone and Jones, *Warsaw Pact's Northern Tier*, p. 190.
62 See Erich Honecker's remarks at a reception held for GDR-USSR military academy graduates on 6 Sept. 1985, *FBIS-EEU-DR*, 9 Sept. 1985, p. E-1.
63 Johnson and Alexiev, "East European Reliability," p. 58.
64 Ibid.
65 Col. A. Khorev, "The New Traditions are Growing Stronger," *Krasnaya Zvezda*, 27 May 1975, p. 3; *JPRS 65099*, 27 June 1975, p. 32.
66 *Krasnaya Zvezda*, 14 Apr. 1981, p. 1; *JPRS 78250*, 8 June 1981, p. 16.
67 Major General Ernst Hampf, *Neues Deutschland*, 29 Sept. 1972, p. 4; *JPRS 57274*, 17 Oct. 1972, p. 17.
68 Lieutenant General Joachim Goldbach, chief of the military, Bezirk of Neubrandenburg, "Soldiers of the People," p. 7; *JPRS 67076*, 2 Apr. 1976, p. 2.
69 Ltg. P. Shkidchenko, Deputy Commander GSFG, "Build Up Efforts," *Krasnaya Zvezda*, 26 Aug. 1977, p. 2; *JPRS 69932*, 7 Oct. 1977, p. 45.
70 See Ltc. V. Devin, GSFG, "No Changes Occurred," *Krasnaya Zvezda*, 18 Jan. 1978, p. 2; *JPRS 70975*, 19 Apr. 1978, p. 23.
71 Ltc. Bogdanovskiy, GSFG, "The Horse Never Left the Gate," *Krasnaya Zvezda*, 31 Mar. 1981, p. 2; *JPRS 78975*, 12 Sept. 1981, p. 22.
72 Col. Gen. Horst Stechbarth, "Achieving Higher Performance Through Efficient Leadership," *Volksarmee*, no. 34, 1985; *JPRS-EPS-85-124*, 24 Dec. 1985, p. 24.
73 Childs, *The GDR*, pp. 281–82.
74 From talks with former East German soldiers now living in the West.
75 See Suvorov's comments in *Inside the Soviet Army*, pp. 220–23.
76 Ltg. Hans Wiesner, Commandant, Friedrich Engels Military Academy, *JPRS 072822 EE* No. 1635, 15 Jan. 1979, p. 11.
77 Martin van Creveld, *Fighting Power: German and U.S. Army Performance, 1939–1945* (Westport, Conn.: Greenwood Press, 1982), p. 129.
78 Ernst Leghahn; "White on the Inside, Red on the Outside – Combat Strength, Combat Morale and Ideology in the GDR National People's Army," *Die Welt*, 15 Oct. 1977, p. 3, *JPRS 70234 EE 1498*, 28 Nov. 1977, p. 38.
79 Unattributed article, "Mangel der Disziplin" *Soldat und Technik* (Frankfurt am Main), May 1972, p. 256.

80 Lt. Col. Dietmar Mann, "Border Troop Defector on Reliability, War Plans," *Die Welt*, 20 Jan. 1987, p. 4, *JPRS-EER-87-055*, 7 Apr. 1987, pp. 95–97.

81 Martin (German soldier), "I Lost My Illusions," *Der Spiegel*, no. 9, 21 Feb. 1977, pp. 38–52; *JPRS 68866*, 1 Apr. 1977, p. 50.

82 Ltg. Horst Brünner, "Soldiers' Comradeship: Combat Strength," *Volksarmee*, no. 31, July 1979, p. 3; *JPRS 74310*, 4 Oct. 1979, p. 16.

83 *Der Spiegel*, no. 9, 21 Feb. 1977, pp. 38–52; *JPRS 68866*, 1 Apr. 1977, p. 47.

84 Ltg. Joachim Goldbach, "Working and Living Conditions – Factors of Combat Readiness," *Volksarmee*, no. 21, 1980, pp. 4–5; *JPRS 76635*, 16 Oct. 1980, p. 24.

85 D. Dieter, "Answers to Questions Arising After 7 Weeks' Service in the NVA," *Volksarmee*, 23 June 1975, p. 3; *JPRS 65840*, 3 Oct. 1975, p. 23.

86 "New Disciplinary Regulations for National People's Army Soldiers," *Informationen* (Bonn), no. 23, Nov. 82, pp. 13–14.

87 From the author's discussions with US Army officers who had been stationed in Potsdam. Major Howard Berner and Lt. Col. Michael Peters.

88 See Col. Gen. Horst Stechbarth's remarks in "Ground Forces Chief Cites Training Deficiencies," *JPRS-EPS-85-124*, 24 Dec. 1985, pp. 23–26.

89 Colonel General Heinz Kessler, "Shield of Socialism," *Einheit*, vol. 30, no. 4/5, Apr.–May 1975, p. 454; *JPRS 64867*, 29 May 1975, p. 41.

90 See Col. Heinz Schlitter's "Strong Political Effort in NVA Needed to Dispel Illusions," *Volksarmee*, no. 2, Mar. 1972; *JPRS 55749*, 18 Apr. 1972, p. 50.

91 *IWE Tagesdienst*, 24 Nov. 1972; *JPRS 57870*, 29 Dec. 1972, p. 16.

92 Ltg. Horst Bruenner, "Active Party Work – A Prerequisite of High Combat Readiness," *Neuer Weg*, vol. 32, no. 5, 1977, pp. 199–202; *JPRS 68920*, 12 Apr. 1977, p. 18.

93 Guenter Rahn, "Das Feindbild der NVA in der sozialistischen Wehrerzeihung," *Deutschland Archiv*, vol. 10, no. 5, May 1977, pp. 494–505.

94 Forster, *The East German Army*, p. 68.

95 Ulrich Ruehmhand, "Hasserziehung," in *NVA der DDR in Stichworten*, p. 89.

96 "SED Influence on FDJ," *JPRS 70234*, 28 Nov. 1977, p. 63.

97 General Heinz Hoffmann, "Our Achievements Are Reliably Protected," *Einheit*, vol. 29, no. 9, Oct. 1974, pp. 1085–95.

98 "GDR-Soviet Military Cooperation Reviewed," *National Zeitung*, 28 Oct. 1972, pp. 1–2; *JPRS 57600*, 27 Nov. 1972, p. 8.

99 Christian Walther, "Warum östliche Armeen ein westliches Feindbild brauchen," *Europäische Wehrkunde*, Sept. 1984, pp. 523.

100 See interview with Lt. Col. Dietmar Mann published in *Die Welt* on 20 Jan. 1987 and translated in *JPRS EER-87-055*, 7 Apr. 1987, p. 96, and Robert Dean's "The GDR Army," p. 102.

101 "GDR–Soviet Military Cooperation Reviewed," *National Zeitung*, 28 Oct. 1972, pp. 1–2, *JPRS 57600*, 27 Nov. 1972, p. 8.

102 Ibid., p. 8.
103 Sylvain, "The German Democratic Republic," p. 318.
104 Ibid., p. 318.
105 Quoted in an article in the section "Bilder und Zeiten," *Frankfurter Allgemeine*, 15 Feb. 1975, p. 3.
106 Quoted by Johnson and Alexiev, "East European Reliability," p. 61.
107 From interviews with US Army officers stationed at the US Military Liaison Mission in Potsdam, East Germany.
108 Ibid.
109 Zimmerman, "The GDR in the 1970s," p. 37.
110 Munich ARD television interview with Otto Ponert, former NVA Major, *FBIS-DR-EEU*, 15 Aug. 1985, p. E-1.
111 Col. Gen. Fleissner, "Sixty Years Soviet Army: Comradeship-in-Arms With the Soviet Army – Basis for Continually Increasing Fighting Power and Combat Readiness of the National People's Army," *Militärtechnik*, no. 1, Jan. 1978, pp. 1–3, *JPRS 70672*, 22 Feb. 1978, p. 49.
112 F. Stephen Larrabee, *The Challenge to Soviet Interests in Eastern Europe R3190–AF* (Santa Monica, Cal.: Rand Corporation, 1984), p. 9.
113 Col. Gen. Fleissner, "On the 25th Anniversary of the Founding of the National People's Army," *Militärtechnik*, no. 6, 1980, pp. 281–83, *JPRS 77484*, 2 Mar. 1981, p. 5 and p. 7.
114 Eberhard Schneider, *JPRS 69616*, 17 Aug. 1977.
115 Erich Honecker, *JPRS 80734*, 5 May 1982, p. 5.
116 See discussion of GSFG political role and title change in Lt. Col. Günter Lippert, "Nach 40 Jahren in Deutschland," *Soldat und Technik*, no. 6, June, 1985, p. 369.
117 Thomas Cason, "East European Military Forces," in Clawson and Kaplan, eds., *The Warsaw Pact*, p. 150.
118 Stephan Tiedtke, "Detente and the Warsaw Pact," in *Germany Debates Defense: NATO at the crossroads*, Michel Vale and Rudolf Steinke, eds. (Armonk, N.Y.: M. E. Sharpe, 1983), p. 57.
119 Gerhard Wettig, *JPRS-EER-86-003-L*, 6 Feb. 1986, p. 53.
120 Based on the author's conversations with East Germans who emigrated in May 1984.
121 McCauley, *German Democratic Republic*, p. 189.

4 The Soviet–East German military alliance and Poland

1 George Schoepflin, "Poland and Eastern Europe," in *Poland: Genesis of a Revolution*, Abraham Brumberg, ed. (New York: Vintage Books, 1983), p. 133.
2 Nicholas Andrews, *Poland 1980–1981* (Washington, DC: National Defense University Press, 1985), p. 275.
3 Larabee, *The Challenge to Soviet Interests in Eastern Europe, R-3190-AF*, p. 110.

4 From Catherine's own writings. See de Madariaga, *Russia in the Age of Catherine the Great*, p. 449.

5 Norman Davies, *Heart of Europe: A Short History of Poland* (Oxford: Clarendon Press, 1984), p. 308.

6 Dimitrii Simes, "Clash Over Poland," *Foreign Policy*, no. 46, Spring 1982, p. 56.

7 Generalfeldmarschall Hermann von Boyen quoted in Byrnes, ed., *Fritz Epstein: Germany and the East*, p. 28.

8 Theodor Schieder, "Der Nationalstaat in Verteidigung und Angriff," in *Probleme der Reichsgründungszeit 1848–1879*, Helmut Böhme, ed. (Cologne: Kiepenheuer und Witsch, 1972), p. 405.

9 H. von Poschinger, *Conversations with Prince Bismarck*, Sidney Whitman, ed. and trans. (London: Harper Brothers, 1900), p. 157.

10 Hanhardt Jr., *German Democratic Republic*, p. 65.

11 Ibid., pp. 65–68 and "GDR Enhances Military Readiness," *JPRS 68178*, 29 Feb. 1977, p. 15.

12 Josef Korbel, *Poland Between East and West: Soviet and German Diplomacy Toward Poland, 1919–1953* (Princeton, N.J.: Princeton University Press, 1963), p. 231.

13 M. K. Dziewanowski, "Joseph Pilsudski," *East European Quarterly*, vol. 11, no. 4, Jan. 1969, p. 379.

14 Hanhardt Jr, *German Democratic Republic*, p. 69.

15 Andrej Korbonski, "Poland: Changed Relationship Between the Polish United Workers' Party and the Polish People's Army," in Simon and Gilberg, eds., *Security Implications of Nationalism in Eastern Europe*, p. 261.

16 "The Party and the Military in Poland," *RFE Research Report "Poland/ 12"*, 26 Apr. 1971, pp. 3–29.

17 Gen. Zygmunt Zielinski, *Rzeczpospolita*, 18 July 1985, in *JPRS-EER-86-033*, 6 Mar. 1986, p. 61.

18 Jörg Lolland, *Zu Befehl, Genosse Unterleutnant: Authentische Berichte aus dem Alltag der Nationalen Volksarmee* (Stuttgart: Seewald, 1971), pp. 167–69.

19 Ibid., p. 168.

20 Jan de Weydenthal, *The Communists of Poland, An Historical Outline* (Stanford, Cal.: Hoover Institution Press, 1978), p. 155.

21 Ibid., p. 155.

22 Ibid.

23 Ibid., p. 158.

24 Peter Raina, *Political Opposition in Poland: 1954–1977* (London: Poets and Painters Press, 1978), p. 221.

25 Richard C. Martin, "Warsaw Pact Force Modernization: A Second Look," in Simon and Gilberg, eds., *Security Implications of Nationalism in Eastern Europe*, pp. 202–7.

26 Simon, *Warsaw Pact Forces*, p. 124.

27 *RFE Background Report/174*, 30 Aug. 1982, p. 2.

28 Ibid., pp. 2–3.

29 Simon, *Warsaw Pact Forces*, p. 239.

30 Dean, "The GDR Military," p. 100.

31 "GDR–USSR Economic Relations Analyzed," *JPRS–EER–86–012–L*, 11 Aug. 1986, p. 7.

32 Ibid.

33 Also see Honecker's central committee report to the 11th SED Congress in *FBIS–EEU–DR*, 21 Apr. 1986, p. E–2, "Scientific-Technological Cooperation Protocol Reviewed," FBIS–EEU–DR, 4 Nov. 1985, p. E–2, "Sci-Tech Cooperation Protocol Signed with USSR," *FBIS–EEU–DR*, 21 Apr. 1986, p. E–3.

34 "GDR–USSR Economic Relations Analyzed," pp. 24–25.

35 For a more complete treatment, see Ronald Asmus' "The GDR and the German Nation: Sole Heir or Socialist Sibling?," *International Affairs*, Spring 1984, pp. 405–18.

36 *RFE Background Report 225*, Jan. 1982, p. 5.

37 Walter Transfeldt and Karl Frhr. von Brand, *Wort und Brauch im deutschen Heer* (Hamburg: Helmuth Gerhard Schulz, 1967).

38 Army officers who have served in Potsdam have suggested that this effort in the NVA has met with more success than similar efforts in the Bundeswehr!

39 See Reinhard Bruehl "Zur militärtheoretischen Leistung Carl von Clausewitz," *Militärgeschichte*, no. 4, 1980, pp. 389–99; Werner Knoll "Zur Entwicklung von Offiziersschulen und Militärakademien in Deutschland Anfang des 19 Jahrhunderts," *Militärgeschichte*, no. 4, 1978, pp. 457–62 and "Eine Rüstungskonzeption des deutschen Generalstabes aus dem Jahre 1934," *Militärgeschichte*, no. 2, 1978.

40 Theo Sommer, "Trip to the Other Germany: Visit to the People's Army; Would Germans Shoot Germans?," *Die Zeit*, 27 June 1986, p. 13.

41 The most recent example widely circulated in both East and West is Kahn, *Die Deutschen und die Russen*.

42 See Mehlhorn and Quaiser, "Fahnen deutsch-sowjetischer Freundschaft 1924–1929," *Militärgeschichte*, no. 1, 1978, p. 93. Also, Ltc. E. Doehler and Ltc. R. Falkenberg, *Militärische Traditionen der NVA* (East Berlin: Militärverlag der DDR, 1979), pp. 10–15 and "Wahrhaft progressive und volksverbundene Streitkräfte," in *Bundeswehr Aktuell*, pp. 2–3.

43 Ltg. Hans Wiesner, "To be an Officer – What Does this Mean Today? Scharnhorst–Example for the NVA General?," *Sächsische Zeitung*, 2–3 Dec. 1979, in *JPRS 072822*, 15 Jan. 1979, p. 10.

44 Helène' Carrère d'Encausse, *Decline of an Empire* (New York: Harper and Row, 1978), p. 274.

45 Bialer, *Stalin*, Introduction.

46 John Dunlop, "Russian Nationalist Spectrum," *Canadian Review of Studies in Nationalism*, Vol, 11, no. 1, 1984, p. 66.

47 Ernst Leghahn, "White on the Inside, Red on the Outside – Combat Strength, Combat Morale and Ideology in the GDR National People's Army," *Die Welt*, 15–16 Oct. 1977, JPRS 70234, 28 Nov. 1977, p. 39.

48 *Daily Telegraph*, Sept. 30, 1977, as reported in *FBIS–DR–EEU*, 30 Sept. 10, 1977, p. G-1–G-2.

49 Vladimir Wozniuk, Ph.D. dissertation, University of Virginia, 1984, p. 118.

50 From *Die Welt*, 2 Feb. 1977, p. 1, reported in *JPRS 68178*, 29 Feb. 1977, p. 15.

51 Eligiusz Naszkowski, "The Darkest Chapter: The War of the Intelligence Organization Against Solidarity," *JPRS–EPS–85–097*, 23 Sept. 1985, p. 17.

52 Rakowska-Harmstone, "Poland," in Jones and Rakowska-Harmstone, *Warsaw Pact*, p. 127.

53 See Colonel Ryszard Kuklinski's remarks in "The War Against the Nation Seen From the Inside" or "Wojna z narodem widziana od srodka" in the Polish émigré journal published in Paris *Kultura*, no. 4/475, 1987, p. 33. Translation of the interview was provided to the author by the Defense Intelligence Agency.

54 Ibid., p. 33.

55 See Rakowska-Harmstone, "Poland," in Jones and Rakowska-Harmstone, *Warsaw Pact*, pp. 168–69.

56 Quoted from *Le Monde* by Vladimir Wozniuk, in dissertation, p. 147.

57 See *RFE BR/241 Poland*, 10 Oct. 1980, p. 12.

58 *RFE BR/242 Poland*, p. 2.

59 Fred Oldenburg, "Die DDR und die polnische Krise," *Osteuropa*, vol. 12, no. 12, Dec. 1982, p. 1007.

60 Richard D. Anderson, Jr., "Soviet Decision-Making and Poland," *Problems of Communism*, Mar.–Apr. 1982, p. 24.

61 Ibid., pp. 24–26.

62 See Michael Kaufman's "Bloc Was Prepared to Crush Solidarity, A Defector Says," *New York Times*, 16 Apr. 1987, p. A–9.

63 Kuklinski interview, "The War Against the Nation Seen From the Inside," in Simon and Gilberg, eds., *Security Implications of Nationalism in Eastern Europe*, p. 17.

64 Ibid., p. 18.

65 Anderson, Jr., "Soviet Decision-Making and Poland," pp. 24–26.

66 Paul Weinreich, "Solidarnosc provoziert Chaos und Anarchie", *Neues Deutschland*, 3 Feb. 1981, p. 2.

67 Ibid., p. 2.

68 Gerhard Kovitski, "Warschauer Zeitungen verurteilen verstärkte Aktivitäten der Revanchisten in der BRD," *Neues Deutschland*, 3 Feb. 1981.

69 "Report on Katowice PZPR Declaration Cited," *FBIS-EEU-DR*, 3 June 1981, p. E–1.

70 Simon, *Warsaw Pact Forces*, p. 168

71 According to Colonel Kuklinski, the Soviets never withdrew the command, control and communications elements from Poland that had been placed there during "Soyuz 81." See the interview, p. 29.

72 *FBIS-EEU-DR*, 14 Apr. 1981, p. E–9.

73 *FBIS-EEU-DR*, 10 Aug. 1981, p. E–1.

74 Dimitrii Simes, "Clash over Poland," *Foreign Policy*, no. 46, Spring 1982, p. 53.

75 See "Soviet Military Maneuvers Near Poland Reported," *FBIS-EEU-DR*, 8 Sept. 1981, p. E–5. Kuklinski indicates that Marshal Kulikov "carried the main burden of direct contacts and talks with the Party-military leadership of the PPR." See the interview, p. 33.

76 *FBIS-EEU-DR*, 8 Sept. 1981, p. E–5.

77 Johnson, Alexiev, "East European Reliability."

78 Reported in the East Berlin ADN International Service 1139 GMT 21 Sept. 1981 in *FBIS-EEU-DR*, 22 Sept. 1981, p. E–1.

79 See Sylvain, "The German Democratic Republic," p. 293.

80 *FBIS-EEU-EU*, 23 Sept. 1981, p. E–1.

81 Quoted by Andrews in *Poland 1980–1981*, p. 84.

82 Jan de Weydenthal, B. Porter, K. Devlin, *The Polish Drama, 1980–1982* (Lexington, Mass.: Lexington Books, 1983), p. 156.

83 Joachim Nawrocki, "A Turn Away From the Party," in *Die Zeit*, 19 Mar. 1982, *FBIS-EEU-DR*, 22 Mar. 1982, p. E–6.

84 Ibid.

85 De Weydenthal, *et al.*, *The Polish Drama*; p. 157.

86 Wolf Oschlies, "Ich fürchtete Unmutsäusserungen ... Polen und die DDR 1981," *Deutschland Archiv: Kommentare und aktuelle Beiträge*, Oct. 1981, p. 1014. Also see P. J. Winter's comments in "Angst vor dem polnischen Bazillus," in *Deutschland Archiv*, Oct. 1981, pp. 1009–11.

87 Larrabee, *Challenge to Soviet Interests*, p. 93.

88 Ibid., p. 93.

89 Seweryn Bialer, "Poland and the Soviet Imperium", *Foreign Affairs*, vol. 59, no. 3, 1981, p. 523.

90 Andrej Korbonski, "Poland: Changed Relationship Between the Polish United Workers' Party and the Polish People's Army," in Simon and Gilberg, eds., *Security Implications of Nationalism in Eastern Europe*, pp. 271–73.

91 From discussions with Polish émigrés now living in Vienna and Munich.

92 Larrabee, "Challenge to Soviet Interests," p. 110.

93 Walter Connor, *Socialism, Politics, and Equality* (New York: Columbia University Press, 1979), p. 69.

94 See "The Polish Raison d'Etat" (anonymous), reprinted from *Rzeczywistosc*, in FBIS-EEU-DR, 27 Oct. 1986, p. G–2.

95 Dimitrii Simes, "Clash Over Poland," *Foreign Policy* no. 46, Spring 1982, p. 56.

96 Gerhard Wettig, "The Smaller Warsaw Pact States in East-West Relations," *JPRS–EER–86–003–L*, 6 Feb. 1986, p. 53.

97 McCauley, *German Democratic Republic*, p. 1. A joint Soviet–East German partition of Poland has been the subject of Western and Polish speculation. "Westteil Polens an SED-Staat," *Allgemeine Zeitung*, Mainz, 25 Feb. 1982.

5 Conclusion

1 *Ulbricht: A Political Biography*, trans. by Abe Rarbstein (New York: Praeger, 1965), introduction.

2 Mark d'Anastasio, "Gorbachev Fights Conservative Elite," *The Wall Street Journal*, 15 Jan. 1987, p. 26.

3 Keith Crane, "The Soviet Economic Dilemma of Eastern Europe," *R–3368–AF* (Santa Monica, Cal.: Rand Corporation, May 1986), pp. 59–62.

4 See Condoleeza Rice's comments in "The Soviet Military Under Gorbachev," *Current History*, Oct. 1986, p. 342.

5 See Col. V. A. Zubkov's remarks in "CPSU Concern for Strengthening the Economic Basis of Socialist State Military Might," in *Voyenno-Istoricheskiy Zhurnal*, no. 3, Mar. 86, pp. 3–8 in *JPRS–UMA–86–047*, 20 Aug. 1986, p. 1.

6 Koehler, *Economic Integration*, pp. 36–37.

7 Dr Herbert Weiz, "New Dimensions of Socialist Integration", *Einheit*, vol. 41, no. 4–5, Apr.–May 1986, *JPRS–EER–86–087*, 13 June 1986, p. 23.

8 See "Soviet Minister Toasts Honecker," in *FBIS–EEU–DR*, 2 Sept. 1986, p. E–6. Also see "FRG Study on Soviet, GDR, CEMA Energy Policy Prospects," *JPRS–EER–87–011*, 26 Jan. 1987, p. 8.

9 Erik Hoffman and Frederic Fleron, eds., *The Conduct of Soviet Foreign Policy* (Hawthorne, N.Y.: Aldine, 1980), p. 291.

10 "Technology Still Viewed As Panacea For Productivity Gaps," *JPRS–EER–86–160*, 24 Oct. 1986, p. 30.

11 See Ronald D. Asmus' data in "Bonn and East Berlin: The New German Question," *Washington Quarterly*, Winter 1986, p. 52.

12 Bernard von Plate, "Maneuvering Room and Interests in GDR Foreign Policy," *JPRS–EER–86–106*, 21 July 1986, pp. 73–75.

13 German Defense Minister, *Ideologischer Kampf der Warschauer-Pakt-Staaten gegen Wehrbereitschaft, Bundeswehr und NATO* (Bonn: Ministry of Defense, Apr. 1985), pp. 22–31.

14 Melvin Croan, "The Development of GDR Political Relations with the USSR," in Schulz, Jacobsen, Leptin and Scheuner, eds., *GDR Foreign Policy* (London: M. E. Sharpe, 1982), p. 186.

15 George Schoepflin, "Poland and Eastern Europe," in *Poland*, ed., p. 132.

16 See Jerry Hough, "The Historical Legacy in Soviet Weapons Development," in *Soviet Decisionmaking for National Security*, Jiri Valenta and William Potter, eds. (London: George Allen and Unwin, 1984), pp. 87–115.

17 Christopher Jones, "Czechoslovakia" in Jones and Rakowska-Harmstone, *Warsaw Pact*, p. 344.

18 See Condoleeza Rice, *The Soviet Union and the Czechoslovak Army 1948–1983: Uncertain Allegiance* (Princeton, N.J.: Princeton University Press, 1984).

19 Richard C. Martin, "Warsaw Pact Force Modernization: A Second Look," in Gilberg and Simon, eds. *Security Implications in Eastern Europe*,

20 See Vladimir Kusin's comments in "Czechoslovak People's Army 1945–1985: An Analytical Overview;" a paper presented at the Carleton University Conference on the Warsaw Pact in Ottawa during March 1986.

21 Michael Checinski's comments in "Poland's Military Burden," *Problems of Communism*, May–June 1983, p. 34.

22 From the author's conversations with the military representatives of the Warsaw Pact's East European delegations to the MBFR talks and former Solidarity members in Vienna during March 1986.

23 See Jeffrey Simon's assessment of "Soyuz 83" and "Soyuz 84" in his paper "Problems of Military Cohesion of the Warsaw Pact," prepared at the INSS, MCDC, National Defense University, Washington, DC, 1986, pp. 40–41 and "Foreign Threat and Cooperation Among Member States," from *Zarubezhnoye Voyennoye Obozreniye* in *JPRS–UMA–85–040*, 15 July 1985, pp. 23–24.

24 T. Rakowska-Harmstone, "Poland," *Warsaw Pact: Question of Cohesion*, vol. 2 (Ottawa: Canada DND, 1984), pp. 128–30.

25 Jan de Weydenthal, Bruce D. Porter, Kevin Devlin, *The Polish Drama: 1980–1981* (Lexington, Mass.: Lexington Books, 1983), p. 167. *Zolnierz Wolnosci*, 14 Apr. 85, p. 5 in *JPRS–EPS–85–077*, 19 July 1985, pp. 63–65.

26 Joachim Goerlich, "Polnische August: Die Sowjetische Gruppe Nord und Polens Volksarmee," *Europäische Wehrkunde*, Apr. 1981, pp. 162–63.

27 Martin, "Warsaw Pact Force Modernization," pp. 204–7.

28 Rebecca Strode, "The Soviet Armed Forces: Adaptation to Resource Scarcity," *The Washington Quarterly*, Spring 1986, pp. 55–69.

29 Odom, "Soviet Force Posture," p. 5.

30 Larrabee, "Challenge to Soviet Interests," pp. 114–16.

31 Army General Heinz Kessler, "Three Decades of the NVA Reflect the Unity of the People, Party and Army," *JPRS-EER-86-042*, 21 Mar. 1986, p. 63.

32 Army General Gribkov, "Warsaw Pact Responsibilities," from *Voyenno-Istoricheskiy Zhurnal*, in *JPRS-UMA-85-051*, 5 Sept. 1985, pp. 36–37.

33 Yurechko, "Command and Control," pp. 14–15.

34 Joseph Douglass, *Soviet Military Strategy in Europe* (New York: Pergamon Press, 1980), p. 117.

35 I. Bagamyan and I. Vyrodov, "The Role of Representatives of Headquarters, Supreme High Command, STAVKA VGK, During the War Years. Organization and Methods of their Work," *Voyenno-Istoricheskiy Zhurnal*, 22 July 1980, trans. in *JPRS 76953 USSR Report: Military Affairs*, 19 Apr. 1985, p. 27.

36 John Hines and Phillip Petersen, "Changing the Soviet System of Control: Focus on Theater Warfare," *International Defense Review*, vol. 3, 1986, pp. 281–89; and John Despres, "The Timely Lessons of History: The Manchurian Model for Soviet Strategy," *Rand Report R-1825-NA* (Santa Monica, Cal.: Rand Corporation, July 1976).

37 John Hines and Phillip Petersen, "Is NATO Thinking Too Small? A Comparison of Command Structures," *International Defense Review*, no. 5, 1986, pp. 563–71.

38 Hines and Petersen, "Changing the Soviet System of Control," pp. 281–89.
39 Col. Gen. M. A. Gareev, *M. V. Frunze, Military Theorist* (English translation, New York: Pergamon-Brassey 1988), p. 218.
40 Richard K. Betts, *Surprise Attack: Lessons for Defense Planning* (Washington, DC: The Brookings Institute, 1982), pp. 152–89.
41 Dennis Gormley, "A New Dimension to Soviet Theater Strategy," *Orbis*, Fall 1985, p. 557.
42 Simon, *Warsaw Pact Forces*, pp. 217–18.
43 Ryszard Kuklinski, "Wojna z narodem widziana od srodka" (The War Against the Nation Seen From the Inside), *Kultura*, no. 4/475, Paris, 1987, p. 51, translation provided by the Defense Intelligence Agency.
44 Erich Honecker, *Reden und Aufsätze* (East Berlin: 1976), 17 Aug. 1977, in *JPRS 80734*, 5 May 1982, p. 5.
45 Goerlich, "Polnische August," pp. 162–63.
46 See report on Soviet–East German–Polish joint exercise activity in *FBIS-EEU-DR*, 26 Aug. 1986, p. E-2.
47 "U.S. Policy Toward Eastern Europe, 1985," 2 and 7 Oct. 1985, *Committee on Foreign Affairs House of Representatives* (Washington, GPO, 1986), pp. 206–10.
48 Seweryn Bialer, *The Soviet Paradox: External Expansion, Internal Decline* (New York: Alfred Knopf, 1986), p. 343.
49 Zvi Gitelman, "Power and Authority in Eastern Europe," *Change in Communist Systems*, Chalmers Johnson, ed. (Stanford, Cal.: Stanford University Press, 1970), p. 259.
50 See Adenek Sedivy's (Director of Central Institute for National Economic Research in Prague) comments in the Viennese paper *Die Presse*, 14–15 Feb. 1987, p. 10, also reported in *FBIS-EER-DR*, 17 Feb. 1987, p. D-3.
51 Quoted by Vladimir Sobell, "Eastern Europe's Adjustment to Gorbachev's Reform Program," *RAD Background Report/43*, 25 Mar. 1987, p. 2.
52 E. Kautsky, "Gorbachev's Reforms and the GDR," *RAD Background Report/32*, 6 Mar. 1987, p. 2.
53 See article by Stefan Dietrich, "Jetzt oder niemals in Polen" (Now or Never in Poland), *Frankfurter Allgemeine*, 22 Apr. 1987, p. 12 and translated in *JPRS-EER-87-121*, 6 Aug. 1987, pp. 113–14.
54 Susan Osnos, "Poland, Five Years After Martial Law," *New York Times*, 12 Dec. 1986, p. A32.
55 Andrzej W. Malachowski, "Nomenklatura Practices Weaken Public Faith in System," *JPRS-EER-86-089*, 17 June 1986, pp. 57–65.
56 See *Situation Report Poland*, RFE/RL, vol. 12, no. 3, 23 Jan. 1987, p. 15.
57 Data compiled by Dr Jeffrey Simon at the Institute of Strategic Studies, National Defense University, Fort McNair, Washington DC for a conference at NDU on comparative mobilization capabilities in the Warsaw Pact and NATO, 3–4 Nov. 1987, p. 6.
58 Jeffrey Simon in his paper "NATO/Warsaw Pact Institutional Developments," presented to the conference held at the National Defense University, Washington, DC, 3–4 Nov. 1987.

59 Odom, "Soviet Force Posture," p. 5.

60 Crane, "Soviet Economic Dilemma," p. 61.

61 Sophia Miskiewicz, "Demographic Policies and Abortion in Eastern Europe," *RFE/RL Background Report 179/86*, 19 Dec. 1986, p. 4.

62 Ibid., p. 4.

63 Harald Zulanj, "Being a Reservist in the GDR," *Loyal*, Bonn, Aug. 1986, p. 14–15, 1 Nov. 1986, p. 21.

64 "The East German Army – An Integral Part of the Conventional Threat to NATO," *International Defense Review*, vol. 20, no. 4, 1987, p. 403.

65 Ibid., pp. 401–4.

66 Colonel Dr M. Drechsler, "Statistics on Health Defects of Draft Age Youth," *Zeitschrift für Militär-medizin*, vol. 26, no. 3, June 1985, pp. 126–27, trans. in *JPRS-EPS-85-085*, 21 Aug. 1985, pp. 73–76.

67 "Personnel Shortages Seen in Coming Years for NVA," *JPRS-EER-86-164*, 30 Oct. 1986, p. 99.

68 Army General D. T. Yazov, "An Authority Replies: Permit Us to Join the Formation: What Young Women Who Want to Become Officers Say," *Komsomolskaya Pravda*, 1 Apr. 1987, p. 2, *JPRS-UMA-87-040*, 18 Aug. 1987, p. 56.

69 See "SED Problems with Peace Movement, Youth Viewed," in *FBIS-EEU-DR*, 22 Mar. 1982, E-5.

70 William J. Bossenbrook, *The German Mind*, p. 263.

71 "Peace Group Demands Nuclear Power Referendum," *Der Spiegel*, vol. 40, no. 27, 30 June 1986, p. 47 and p. 50.

72 Dr Hans-Juergen Trommer, "On Political and Social Stability in Developed Socialism," *Deutsche Zeitschrift für Philosophie*, vol. 34, no. 3, Mar. 1986, pp. 193–200.

73 See "Relative Buying Power of Mark Compared to D-Mark in 1985," in *JPRS-EER-86-111*, 28 July 1986, pp. 28–29; Ivan Volgyes, "Do Systemic Variables Make A Difference? Causes of Successes and Failures in Communist States," in *Europe and the Superpowers*, Steven Bethlen and Ivan Volgyes, eds. (Boulder: Westview Press, 1985), p. 114.

74 See "GDR Futurologist Predicts Transition to Communism," in *Informationen*, no. 12, 20 June 1986, pp. 6–7.

75 William Doyle, "Prussian Officers," *German Book Review*, Fall 1986, p. 81.

76 See "Honecker Promotes Major General, Colonels," in *FBIS-EEU-DR*, 2 Oct. 1986, p. E-3.

77 See "No Illusions Left at the Age of Twelve," *JPRS-EPS-85-022*, 15 Feb. 1985, pp. 37–39.

78 Joachim Nawrocki, "Honecker at the Zenith of His Power," *JPRS-EER-86-010*, 24 Jan. 1986, p. 71.

79 Jürgen Engert, "The Man Behind Honecker," *JPRS-EPS-85-975*, 15 July 1985, p. 14.

80 Dr Gerd Meyer, "On the Sociology of the GDR Power Elite," *JPRS-EPS-85-083*, 14 Aug. 1985, p. 84.

81 Mark Kramer, "Civil–Military Relations in the Warsaw Pact: The East European Component," *International Affairs*, vol. 61, no. 1, Winter 1984/85, pp. 52–53.

82 Bialer, *The Soviet Paradox*, p. 225.

83 See Theo Sommer's remarks in "Trip to the Other Germany," p. 13.

84 Alexander George, David Bernstein, Gregory Parnell and Philip Rogers, *Inadvertent War in Europe: Crisis Simulation* (Stanford, Cal.: Stanford Center for International Security and Arms Control, 1985).

85 Major General Lorenz, "30 Years of NVA – 30 of Constant Concern by Our Party About Providing it with Modern Combat Equipment and Arms," *JPRS-EER-86-072*, 9 May 1986, p. 87.

86 "GDR, Hungary Promote Detente Policy," *FBIS-SU*, 3 June 1986, p. F-2.

87 See Army General Kessler's remarks in "GDR Defense Minister's Speech in Silesia," *JPRS-EER-86-165*, 31 Oct. 1986, pp. 59–61.

88 Gerhard Wettig, "Flexibility, Intent in Inner German Relations Assessed," *JPRS-EER-106*, 21 July 1986, p. 81.

89 See the article by Dieter Dose concerning the suspension of shooting orders during Honecker's visit to West Germany in *Die Welt*, 12 Aug. 1987, p. 1.

90 William Safire, "The Germanys: Trying Reunification on the Sly," *International Herald Tribune*, 14 Aug. 1984.

91 See the interview with Honecker in *Neues Deutschland*, 29 Sept. 1987, pp. 3–4, translated in *FBIS-EEU-87-189*, 30 Sept. 1987, p. 24.

92 From the text of a speech by Zbigniew Brzezinski in Berlin, Germany on 16 Sept. 1987, p. 7.

93 Alexander George, "The Operational Code: A Neglected Approach to the Study of Political Leaders and Decision-Making," *The Conduct of Soviet Foreign Policy*, Hoffman and Fleuron, eds. (New York: Aldine, 1982), p. 176.

Select bibliography

Academic Publications. *The Development of the Soviet Armed Forces, 1917–1977*. Maxwell AFB, Ala.: Air University Press, 1977.

Adelman, Jonathan, ed. *Communist Armies in Politics*. Boulder, Col.: Westview Press, 1982.

Ammer, Thomas, "Menschenrechtsverletzungen in der DDR," *Deutschland Archiv*, 18, (1985).

Anderle, A. Rosenfeld, G. "Die Erforschung der deutschsowjetischen Beziehungen in der Weimarer Republik," *Zeitschrift fü Geschichtliches Wissen*, Aug. 1960, Sonderheft.

Anderson, Richard D., Jr. "Soviet Decision-Making and Poland." *Problems of Communism*, Mar.–Apr. 1982.

Arnold, Karl. "Waffenbrüderschaft mit der Sowjetunion Gestern und Heute." *Militärgeschichte*, 2 (1968).

Aslund, Anders. *Private Enterprise in Eastern Europe: The Non-Agricultural Private Sector in Poland and the GDR, 1945–1983*. London: Macmillan, in association with St Antony's College, Oxford, 1985.

Asmus, Ronald D. "The GDR and the German Nation: Sole Heir or Socialist Sibling" *International Affairs*, Spring 1984.

Asmus, Ronald D. "Bonn and East Berlin: The New German Question." *Washington Quarterly*, Winter 1986.

Asmus, Ronald D., ed. *East Berlin and Moscow: The Documentation of a Dispute*. Radio Free Europe Occasional Papers, no. 1. Munich, Radio Free Europe, 1985.

Aspaturian, Vernon. "Soviet Global Power and the Correlation of Forces," *Problems of Communism*, 29, 3 (May–June).

Baylis, Thomas A. *The Technical Intelligentsia and the East German Elite*. Berkeley, Cal.: University of California Press, 1974.

Baylis and Segal, eds. *Soviet Strategy*. London: Croome Helm, 1981.

Bentley, Raymond. *Technological Change in the German Democratic Republic*. Boulder, Col.: Westview Press, 1984.

Betts, Richard K. *Surprise Attack: Lessons for Defense Planning*. Washington, DC: The Brookings Institute, 1982.

Beyme, Klaus von. *Economics and Politics in Socialist Systems.* New York: Praeger, 1982.

ed. *Policymaking in the German Democratic Republic.* New York: St Martin's Press, 1984.

Bialer, Seweryn. *Stalin and His Generals.* Boulder, Col.: Westview Press, 1984.

The Soviet Paradox: External Expansion, Internal Decline. New York: Alfred Knopf, 1986.

"Poland and the Soviet Imperium," *Foreign Affairs,* 59, 3 (1981).

Billington, James. *The Icon and the Axe.* New York: Random House, 1970.

Blanch, Lesley. *The Sabres of Paradise.* New York: Carroll and Graf, 1984.

Boehme, Helmut. *Probleme der Reichsgründungszeit 1848–1879.* Cologne: Kiepenheuer und Witsch, 1972.

Bogisch, Gerhard. "Zum militärischen Bündnis zwischen der DDR und der USSR als wichtigster internationaler Grundlage für die erfolgreiche Militärpolitik der SED." *Militärgeschichte,* 1 (1968).

Borkenau, Franz. *Der Russische Bürgerkrieg: 1918–1921. Von Brest-Litovsk zur NEP.* Berlin: Grunewald, 1954.

Bornstein, Morris, Zvi Gitelman, and William Zimmerman, eds. *East–West Relations and the Future of Eastern Europe: Politics and Economics.* Boston: Allen and Unwin, 1981.

Bruehl, Reinhard, "Zur militärtheoretischen Leistung Carl von Clausewitz." *Militärgeschichte,* 4 (1980).

Bruenner, Horst. "Der proletarische Internationalismus-Grundzug der Erziehung der Armeeangehörigen zur socialistischen Waffenbrüderschaft." *Militärgeschichte,* 34 (1974).

Brumberg, Abraham, editor. *Poland: Genesis of a Revolution.* New York: Vintage Books, 1983.

Bryson, Phillip J. "The GDR in the International Economy." *East Central Europe,* 1979, part 2.

Brzezinski, Zbigniew K. *The Soviet Bloc.* Cambridge, Mass.: Harvard University Press, 1981.

Buesch, Otto. *Militärsystem und Sozialleben im alten Preussen, 1713–1807.* Frankfurt: Verlag Ullstein GmbH, 1962.

Bundesminister der Verteidigung. *Ideologischer Kampf der Warschauer-Pakt-Staaten gegen Wehrbereitschaft, Bundeswehr und NATO.* Bonn: Bundesministerium der Verteidigung, Apr. 1985.

Byrnes, Robert F., ed. *Fritz Epstein: Germany and the East, Selected Essays.* Bloomington: Indiana University Press, 1973.

Byrnes, Robert K. *After Brezhnev.* Bloomington, Ind.: Indiana University Press, 1983.

Carr, E. H. *German–Soviet Relations Between the Two World Wars.* Baltimore, 1951.

The Bolshevik Revolution, vol. 3, London: Penguin Books, 1953.

Childs, David. *The GDR: Moscow's German Ally.* London: Allen and Unwin, 1983.

Clawson, Robert W. and Kaplan, Lawrence S. *The Warsaw Pact: Political Purposes and Military Means.* Wilmington, Del.: Scholarly Resources 1982.

Connor, Walter D. *Socialism, Politics, and Equality: Hierarchy and Change in Eastern Europe and the USSR.* New York: Columbia University Press, 1979.

Craig, Gordon. *Politics of the Prussian Army.* Oxford: Clarendon Press, 1955.

Crane, Keith. "The Soviet Economic Dilemma of Eastern Europe," *R-3368-AF*, Santa Monica, Cal.: Rand Corporation, May 1986.

Crankshaw, Edward. *Bismarck.* New York: Viking Press, 1981.

Croan, Melvin. *East Germany: The Soviet Connection.* Washington Papers, No. 36. Beverly Hills, Cal.: Sage, 1976.

Cross, A. G., ed. *Russia and the West in the Eighteenth Century.* Newtonville, Mass.: Oriental Research Partners, 1983.

D'Anastasio, Mark. "Gorbachev Fights Conservative Elite." *The Wall Street Journal*, 15 Jan. 1987.

Davies, Norman. *Heart of Europe: A Short History of Poland.* Oxford: Clarendon Press, 1984.

Dawisha, Karen and Philip Hanson, eds. *Soviet–East European Dilemmas: Coercion, Competition, and Consent.* New York: Holmes and Meier, 1981.

Dept. of the Army. *The Soviet Army: Troops, Organization and Equipment FM 100-2-3.* Washington, DC: US Govt. Printing Office, 1984.

Despres, John. "The Timely Lessons of History: The Manchurian Model for Soviet Strategy." *Rand Report R-1825-NA*, Santa Monica, Cal.: Rand Corporation, July 1976.

De Weydenthal, Jan. *The Communists of Poland.* Stanford, Cal.: Hoover Institution Press, 1978.

De Weydenthal, Jan, Porter, Devlin. *The Polish Drama: 1980–1982.* Lexington, NY: Lexington Books, 1983.

Doehler, E., Falkenberg, R. *Militärische Traditionen der DDR und der NVA.* Berlin: Militärverlag der DDR, 1979.

Dorwart, Reinhold. *The Administrative Reforms of Frederick William I of Prussia.* Westport, Conn.: Greenwood Press, 1953.

Dziewanowski, M. K. "Joseph Pilsudski," *East European Quarterly*, 2, 4 (Jan. 1969).

Eisenhower, David. *Eisenhower at War 1943–1945.* New York: Random House, 1986.

Eltze, Werner. "Manöver 'Waffenbrüderschaft' – Spiegelbild sozialistischer Wehrerziehung." *Militärgeschichte*, 4 (1971).

Ely, Geoff, "Some Thoughts on German Militarism," *Militär und Militarismus in der Weimarer Republik*, Muller and Opitz, eds. Düsseldorf: Droste, 1978.

Engleman, J. *Manstein: Ein Stratege und Truppenführer.* Friedberg: Podzun-Pallas-Verlag GmbH, 1980.

Epstein, J., "Der Seekt Plan," *Der Monat*, no. 1, 1948/49.

Erickson, John. *The Soviet High Command: A Military-Political History 1918–1941.* Boulder, Col.: Westview Press, 1984.

Fainsod, Merle. *How Russia is Ruled.* Cambridge, Mass.: Harvard University Press, 1970.

Falkenberg, Eberhard, and Guenther, Gerhard. "Die Entwicklung der Offizierschule Ernst Thaelman zur Offizierhochschule." *Militärgeschichte,* 6 (1973).

Farrell, R. Barry, ed. *Political Leadership in Eastern Europe and the Soviet Union.* Chicago, Ill.: Aldine, 1970.

Fischer, Karl. "Zur Waffenbrüderschaft zwischen der Nationalen Volksarmee und der Sowjetarmee." *Militärgeschichte,* 2 (1963).

Fjodorowitsch, Nikolai Bugai and Pawel Spiridonowitsch Smirnow. "Die Verteidigung des sozialistischen Vaterlands als Grundprinzip der sowjetischen Verfassung." *Militärgeschichte,* 4 (1978).

Foreign Broadcast Information Service, Washington, DC: Government Printing Office, 1960–87.

Forster, Thomas M. *The East German Army.* London: George Allen & Unwin, 1980.

Foschepoth, Josef. "Grossbritannien, die Sowjetunion und die Westverschiebung Polens." *Militärgeschichtliche Mitteilungen,* 2 (1982).

Freund, Gerald. *Unholy Alliance: Russian–German Relations from the Treaty of Brest-Litovsk to the Treaty of Berlin.* New York: Harcourt, Brace and World, 1957.

Fricke, Karl Wilhelm. "Okkupanten oder Waffenbrüder? Die Gruppe der Sowjetischen Streitkräfte in Deutschland." *Deutschland Archiv,* 15, 3 (Mar. 1982).

Gareev, Makhmut Akhmetovich. *M. V. Frunze – voennyi teoretik, M.V. Frunze, Military Theorist* in English. New York: Pergamon-Brassey, 1988.

Gati, Charles, "Gorbachev and Eastern Europe," *Foreign Affairs,* 65, 5 (Summer, 1987).

Gatzke, Hans. "Russo–German Collaboration During the Weimar Republic." *The American Historical Review,* 63 (Apr. 1958).

"GDR Foreign Policy (Part 2)." *International Journal of Politics,* 12 (Spring/Summer 1981) (entire issue).

Glass, George, "East Germany in Black Africa: A New Special Role?" *The World Today,* Aug. 1980.

Goerlich, Joachim. "Polnischen August: Die Sowjetische Gruppe Nord und Polens Volksarmee." *Europäische Wehrkunde,* Apr. 1981.

Gormley, Dennis. "A New Dimension to Soviet Theater Strategy." *ORBIS,* Fall 1985.

Graves, A. Karl. *The Secrets of the German War Office.* New York: McBride, Nast and Co., 1914.

Greese, Karl. "Die Bedeutung der ersten gemeinsamen Übung von Truppen der NVA und der Sowjetarmee 1957 für die Entwicklung des Kollektiven Schutzes der DDR und für die Deutsch-Sowjetische Waffenbrüderschaft." *Militärgeschichte,* 1 (1968).

Greese, Karl, Hohn, Hans, Voerster, Alfred. "Zur Entwicklung der Landstreit-kräfte der Nationalen Volksarmee 1960–61." *Militärgeschichte* (1900).

Greese, Karl, Schulz, Günter, Voerster, Alfred. "Zur Aufstellung Moderner Verbande der Landstreitkräfte der NVA im Jahre 1956." *Militärge-schichte*, 4 (1967).

Greese, Karl, Voerster, Alfred. "Waffenbrüderschaftsbeziehungen mit Truppen und Stäben der GSSD-Hilfe und Kraftquell beim Aufbau der NVA." *Militärgeschichte*, 4 (1974).

"Probleme der Auswahl und Förderung der Offizierkader in der NVA.", *Militärgeschichte*, 1 (1966).

Greese, Karl, Schramm, Peter, Voerster, Alfred. "Herausbildung und Ent-wicklung der Waffenbrüderschaftsbeziehungen der NVA zur Polnischen Armee bis Ende der sechziger Jahre." *Militärgeschichte*, 4 (1979). "Die Waffenbrüderzwischen der NVA der DDR zur Polnischen Armee in den siebziger fahren." *Militärgeschichte*, 1 (1978).

"Die Waffenbrüderschaftsbeziehungen der NVA zur Polnischen Armee in den siebziger Jahren." *Militärgeschichte*, 3 (1980).

Gruemmert, J., "Die Waffenbrüderschaftsbeziehungen eines Panzerverban-des der NVA zu seinem Partnerverband der GSSD 1970–1976." *Militärge-schichte*, 2 (1980).

Gustafson, Thane, Mann, Dawn. "Gorbachev at the Helm: Building Power and Authority." *Problems of Communism*, May–June 1986.

Hampf, Ernst. "30 Jahre DDR and ihr zuverlässiger bewaffneter Schutz. Geschichtliche Entwicklung und Auftrage der Nationalen Volksarmee." *Militärgeschichte*, 4 (1979).

Hanhardt, Arthur. *The German Democratic Republic*. Baltimore, Md.: Johns Hopkins Press, 1968.

Hentschel, Volcker. *Preussens streitbare Geschichte*. Düsseldorf: Droste, 1980.

Herspring, Dale R. *Civil–Military Relations in Communist Systems*. Boulder, Col.: Westview Press, 1978.

Herspring, Dale, and Volyges, Ivan. "The Military as an Agent of Sociali-zation in Eastern Europe." *Armed Forces and Society*. 3, 2, Feb. 1977.

Hines, John and Petersen, Phillip. "Changing the Soviet System of Control: Focus on Theater Warfare." *International Defense Review*, 3 (1986).

"Is NATO Thinking too Small? A Comparison of Command Structures." *International Defense Review*, 5 (1986).

Hirschman, O. Albert. *National Power and the Structure of Foreign Trade*. Berkeley, Cal.: University of California Press, 1980.

Hoehn, Hans. "Einige Probleme der Landstreitkräfte der NVA in den sech-ziger Jahren." *Militärgeschichte*, 4 (1978).

"Zur Aneigung und Anwendung von Principien des Einsatzes der Land-streitkräfte in der Nationalen Volksarmee." *Militärgeschichte*, 5 (1980).

Hoern, Karl and Markowsky, Gerhard and Sternkopf, Horst. "Einige Entwick-lungsprobleme der Grenztruppen der DDR in den sechziger und sieb-ziger Jahren." *Militärgeschichte*, 4 (1979).

Hoffman, Erik, Fleron, Frederic, eds. *The Conduct of Soviet Foreign Policy.* Hawthorne, NY: Aldine, 1980.

Holzweissig, Gunter, "DDR – Zivilverteidigung reorganisiert." *Deutschland Archiv,* 11, 2 (Feb. 1978).

Honecker, Erich. *From My Life.* London: Pergamon Press, 1980.

Huntington, Samuel. *Political Order in Changing Societies.* New Haven, Conn.: Yale University Press, 1968.

Ingle, Harold. *Nesselrode and the Russian Rapprochement with Britain, 1836–1844.* Berkeley, Cal.: University of California Press, 1976.

Jacobsen, Hanns-Dieter. "Strategy and Focal Points of GDR Foreign Trade Relations." in Eberhard Schulz, *et al.,* eds., *GDR Foreign Policy.*

Johnson, A. Ross, Alexiev, Alex. "East European Military Reliability: An Émigré-based Assessment," *R-3480.* Santa Monica, Cal.: Rand Corporation, Oct. 1986.

Johnson, A. Ross, Dean, Robert W., Alexiev, Alexander. *East European Military Establishments: The Warsaw Pact Northern Tier.* New York: Crane, Russak, 1982.

Johnson, Chalmers, ed. *Change in Communist Systems.* Stanford, Cal.: Stanford University Press, 1970.

Joint Economic Committee, Congress of the United States. *Soviet Economy in the 1980s: Problems and Prospects.* Washington, DC: US Govt. Printing Office, 1983.

Jones, Christopher D. *Soviet Influence in Eastern Europe: Political Autonomy and the Warsaw Pact.* New York: Praeger, 1981.

Jones, Christopher and Rakowska-Harmstone, Teresa. *The Warsaw Pact: Question of Cohesion.* Ottawa: Department of National Defense, 1986, vols. 1–111.

Kahn, Helmuth Wolfgang. *Die Deutschen und die Russen: Geschichte ihrer Beziehungen.* Cologne: Pahl Rugenstein, 1984.

Kater, Michael H. *The Nazi Party: A Social Profile of Members and Leaders, 1919–1945.* Cambridge, Mass. Harvard University Press, 1983.

Keefe, Eugene K. *East Germany: A Country Study.* 2nd edn. Washington, DC, GPO, 1982.

Keegan, John. *World Armies.* New York: Facts on File, 1979.

Keren, Michael. "The Return of the Ancien Regime: The GDR in the 1970s." *East European Economies Post-Helsinki.* Washington, DC: US Congress Joint Economic Committee, 1977.

Kessler, Heinz. "Der Warschauer Vertrag und die Nationale Volksarmee der DDR." *Militärgeschichte,* 3 (1969).

Kimerling, Elise. "Soldier's Children, 1719–1856: A Study of Social Engineering in Imperial Russia." *Forschungen zur Osteuropäischen Geschichte.* Wiesbaden: Otto Harrassowitz, 1982.

Kiser, John W., III. "Tapping Eastern Bloc Technology." *Harvard Business Review,* Mar.–Apr., 1982.

An Examination of Technology Transfer from Eastern Europe to the US and Selected Western European Countries. Washington, DC: US Department of State, 1980.

Klemperer, Klemens von. *Germany's New Conservatism: Its History and Dilemma in the Twentieth Century*. Princeton, NJ: Princeton University Press, 1968.

Knoll, Werner. "Eine Rüstungskonzeption des deutschen Generalstabes aus dem Jahre 1934." *Militärgeschichte*, 2 (1978).

"Zur Entwicklung von Offiziersschulen und Militärakademien in Deutschland Anfang des 19 Jahrhunderts." *Militärgeschichte*, 4 (1978).

Koehler, Heinz. *Economic Integration in the Soviet Bloc; With An East German Case Study*. New York: Praeger, 1965.

Koestring, General Ernst. *General Ernst Koestring, Der militärische Mittler zwischen dem deutschen Reich und der Sowjetunion 1921–1941*, ed. Hermann Taske. Frankfurt: E. S. Mittler und Sohn, 1965.

Kolkowicz, Roman, Korbonski, Andrej, eds. *Soldiers, Peasants and Bureaucrats*. London: George Allen and Unwin, 1982.

Korbel, Josef. *Poland Between East and West: Diplomacy Toward Poland 1919–1933*. Princeton, NJ: Princeton University Press, 1963.

Kreusel, Dietmar. *Nation und Vaterland in der Militärpresse der DDR*. Stuttgart: Seewald Verlag, 1971.

Krisch, Henry. *German Politics Under Soviet Occupation*. New York: Columbia University Press, 1974.

The German Democratic Republic: The Search for Identity. Boulder: Westview Press, 1985.

Kuhns, Woodrow J. "The German Democratic Republic in the Soviet Foreign Policy Scheme." *Soviet Union*, 12, 1 (1985).

Kuklinski, Ryszard. "Wojna z Narodem Widziana od Srodka." *Kultura*, 4, 475 (1987).

Larrabee, Stephen. *The Challenge to Soviet Interests in Eastern Europe: Hungary, Romania, and East Germany. R-3190-AF*. Santa Monica, Cal.: Rand Corporation, 1984.

Leggett, George, "Lenin, Terror and Political Police." *Survey*, Fall 1975.

Legters, Lyman H., ed. *The German Democratic Republic: A Developed Socialist Society*. Boulder, Col.: Westview Press, 1978.

Leptin, Gert. *Economic Reform in East German Industry*. Translated from the German by Roger A. Clarke. Oxford: Oxford University Press, 1978.

Lieven, D. C. B. *Russia and the Origins of the First World War*. New York: St Martin's Press, 1983.

Linke, Horst Günther. "Russlands Weg in den Ersten Weltkrieg und seine Kriegsziele 1914–1917." *Militärgeschichtliche Mitteilungen*, 2 (1982).

Lippert, Guenter. "Warschauer Pakt: Die NVA der DDR." *Wehrtechnik*, 10 (Oct. 1980).

"Die GSTD – Vier Jahrzehnte Sowjettruppen in Deutschland." *Soldat und Technik*, 11 (Nov. 1986).

Loesche, Peter. *Der Bolschewismus im Urteil der Deutschen Sozialdemokratie 1903–1920*. Berlin: Colloquium, 1967.

Lolland, Joerg. *Zu Befehl, Genosse Unterleutnant: Authentische Berichte aus dem Alltag der Nationalen Volksarmee.* Stuttgart: Seewald, 1971.

Ludz, Peter C. *The Changing Party Elite in East Germany.* Cambridge, Mass.: MIT Press, 1972.

Lukacs, John. "The Soviet State at 65." *Foreign Affairs,* 65 1 (Fall 1986).

Lux, Gerhard. "Die Entwicklung der motorisierten Schützentruppen der NVA in der ersten Hälfte der sechziger Jahre." *Militärgeschichte,* 2 (1978).

"Die Entwicklung der motorisierten Schützentruppen der NVA in der ersten Hälfte der sechziger Jahre." *Militärgeschichte,* 4 (1978).

de Madariaga, Isabel. *Russia in the Age of Catherine the Great.* New Haven, Conn.: Yale University Press, 1981.

Marks, Heinz. *Die Kampfgruppen der Arbeiterklasse.* Cologne: Markus, 1970.

Marrese, Michael and Jan Vanous. *Soviet Subsidization of Trade with Eastern Europe: A Soviet Perspective.* Berkeley, Cal.: University of California, 1983.

Marsh, Peter. "Foreign Policy Making in the GDR; The Interplay of Internal Pressures and External Dependence," in Hannes Adomeit and Robert Boardman, eds. *Foreign Policy Making in Communist Countries.* New York: Praeger, 1979.

Marwege, Ulf. *Neuorientierung im Westhandel der DDR? Die Wirtschaftsbeziehungen mit der Bundesrepublik Deutschland, Frankreich, Japan and Österreich.* Bonn: Europa Union, 1984.

Massie, Robert K. *Peter the Great: His Life and World.* New York: St Martin's Press, 1983.

Mastny, Vojtech. *Russia's Road to the Cold War.* New York: Columbia University Press, 1979.

Mastny, Vojtech. "Stalin and the Militarization of the Cold War." *International Security* 9, 3 (Winter 1984–85).

ed. *Soviet–East European Survey 1983–1984.* Durham, NC: Duke University Press, 1985.

McAdams, A. James. *East Germany and the West: Surviving Detente.* New York: Cambridge University Press, 1985.

"Surviving the Missiles: The GDR and the Future of Inter-German Relations." *ORBIS,* Summer 1983.

McCauley, Martin. *The German Democratic Republic Since 1945.* New York: St Martin's Press, 1983.

Mieroszewski, Juliusz. *Kehrt Deutschland in den Osten zurück?* Berlin: Colloquium, 1961.

Mills, Richard. "The Soviet Leadership Problem." *World Politics,* 32 (July 1981).

Monks, Alfred. *Soviet Military Doctrine: 1960 to the Present.* New York: Irvington, 1984.

Moreton, Edwina. *East Germany and the Warsaw Alliance: The Politics of Detente.* Boulder, Col.: Westview Press, 1978.

Moskow, Dietrich. "German Democratic Republic," in Dennis Campbell, ed., *Legal Aspects of Joint Ventures in Eastern Europe.* Boston: Kluwer, 1981.

Mosse, Werner. *Alexander II and the Modernization of Russia.* New York: Collier, 1962.

Mueller, Schulz, Wollina. *Warschauer Vertrag Schild des Sozialismus.* East Berlin: DDR Militärverlag, 1975.

Myagkov, Aleksei. *Inside the KGB.* London: New Goswell Printing, 1976.

"Nach 40 Jahren in Deutschland." *Soldat und Technik,* 6 (June 1985).

Naimark, Norman. "Review Essay." *Problems of Communism.* July–Aug., 1983.

Nelson, Daniel, ed. *Soviet Allies: The Warsaw Pact and the Issue of Reliability,* Boulder, Col.: Westview Press, 1984.

Nettl, J. Peter. *The Eastern Zone and Soviet Policy in Germany, 1945–1950.* London: Oxford University Press, 1951.

Neugebauer, Gero. *Partei und Staatsapparat in der DDR.* Opladen: Westdeutscher Verlag, 1978.

Odom, William E. "Soviet Force Posture: Dilemmas and Directions." *Problems of Communism,* July–Aug. 1985.

"The Militarization of Soviet Society." *Problems of Communism,* Sept.–Oct. 1976.

"The Soviet Approach to Nuclear Weapons." *Annals,* AAPSS, No. 469, Sept. 1983.

Oldenburg, Fred. "Die DDR und die polnische Krise." *Osteuropa,* 12 (1982).

Oschlies, Wolf. "Ich fürchtete Unmutsäusserungen ... Polen und die DDR 1981." *Deutschland Archiv: Kommentare und aktuelle Beiträge,* Oct. 1981.

Postier, Dieter. "Die Entwicklung der Panzertruppen der NVA in den sechziger Jahren." *Militärgeschichte,* 1 (1981).

Radio Free Europe and Radio Liberty Research Reports, 1970–1982.

Rahn, Guenter. "Das Feindbild der NVA in der sozialistischen Wehrerziehung." *Deutschland Archiv,* 10, 5 (May 1977).

Raina, Peter. *Political Opposition in Poland: 1954–1977.* London: Poets and Painters Press, 1978.

Revesz, Laszlo. *Militärische Ausbildung in Osteuropa.* Bern: W. Steiger, 1975.

Ribbentrop, Joachim. *The Ribbentrop Memoirs,* translated by Oliver Watson. London: Weidenfeld and Nicholson, 1954.

Rice, Condoleeza. "The Soviet Military Under Gorbachev." *Current History,* Oct. 1986.

The Soviet Union and the Czechoslovak Army 1948–1983: Uncertain Allegiance. Princeton, NJ: Princeton University Press, 1984.

Roger, Hans. *Russia in the Age of Modernization and Revolution, 1881–1917.* London: Longman, 1983.

Rosenberg, Hans. *Bureaucracy, Aristocracy and Autocracy: The Prussian Experience 1660–1815.* Boston: Beacon Press, 1966.

Ruehmhand, Ulrich. *Die DDR in Stichworten,* Bonn-Röttgen: Bonner Druck- und Verlagsgesellschaft, 1978.

Sanderson, Paul. "East German Economists and the Path to the New Economic System in the GDR." *Canadian Slavonic Papers*, 23, 2 (June) 1981.

Sanderson, Paul W. "Scientific–Technical Innovation in East Germany." *Political Science Quarterly*, 96 (1981–82).

Sandford, Gregory W. *From Hitler to Ulbricht*. Princeton, NJ: Princeton University Press, 1983.

Scharf, C. Bradley. *Politics and Change in East Germany: An Evaluation of Socialist Democracy*. Boulder, Col.: Westview Press, 1984.

Schulz, Eberhard. "Verständigung mit Polen." *Europa Archiv*, 4 (1986).

Schulz, Eberhard, Jacobsen, Hans-Adolf, Leptin, Gert, Scheuner, Ulrich. *GDR Foreign Policy*. Armonk, NY: M. E. Sharpe, 1982.

Schulz, Gunter. "Erziehungs und Ausbildungsprobleme an den Offiziers-schulen der Landstreitkräfte nach der Schaffung der NVA." *Militärge-schichte*, 3 (1970).

Schweigler, Gebhard. *National Consciousness in a Divided Germany*. London: Sage, 1975.

Sievers, Leo. *Tausend Jahre gemeinsame Geschichte: Deutsche und Russen*. Augsburg–Munich: Wilhelm Goldman, 1983.

Simon, Jeffrey. *Warsaw Pact Forces: Problems of Command and Control*, Boulder, Col.: Westview Press, 1985.

Simon, Jeffrey, Gilberg, Trond, eds. *Security Implications of Nationalism in Eastern Europe*. Boulder, Col.: Westview Press, 1985.

Snydor, Charles. *Soldiers of Destruction: The SS Death's Head Division*. Princeton, NJ: Princeton University Press, 1977.

Sodaro, Michael. "Limits to dissent in the GDR: Fragmentation, Cooptation, and Repression," in Jane Leftwich Curry, ed., *Dissent in Eastern Europe*. New York: Praeger, 1983.

Sommer, Theo. "Trip to the Other Germany: Visit to the People's Army; Would Germans Shoot Germans?" *Die Zeit*, 27 June 1986.

Soviet Analyst, 1978–83.

Spalcke, K., "Begegnungen zwischen Reichswehr und Roter Armee: 1924–1933, ein Rückblick," *Aussenpolitik*, 9 (1958).

Speidel, H. "Reichswehr und Rote Armee," *Vierteljahreshefte der Zeitge-schichte*, Jan. 1953.

Stahnke, Arthur A. "The Economic Dimensions and Political Context of FRG–GDR Trade," in *East European Economic Assessment*, US Congress, Joint Economic Committee, 1981.

"GDR Economic Strategy in the 1980s." *Studies in GDR Culture and Society*, 3 (1983).

Steele, Jonathan. *Socialism With a German Face*. New York: Urizen Books, 1977 (revised edition forthcoming).

Stegemann, Bernd, "Geschichte und Politik: Zur Diskussion über den deutschen Angriff auf die Sowjetunion 1941." *Beiträge zur Konfliktfor-schung*, 1 (1987).

Stern, Carola. *Ulbricht: A Political Biography.* New York: Praeger, 1965.

Statistisches Jahrbuch der Deutschen Demokratischen Republik. Leipzig. Annual.

Strode, Rebecca. "The Soviet Armed Forces: Adaptation to Resource Scarcity." *The Washington Quarterly,* Spring 1986.

Suvorov, Viktor. *Inside the Soviet Army.* New York: Macmillan, 1982.

Tarschys, Daniel. "The Soviet Political System: Three Models." *European Journal of Political Research,* 5 (1977).

Taylor, Telford. *Sword and Swastika: Generals and Nazis in the Third Reich.* Chicago, Ill.: Quadrangle Books, 1952.

Thaden, Edward C. *Russia Since 1801: The Making of a New Society.* New York: John Wiley and Sons, 1971.

The Military Balance. London, International Institute of Strategic Studies, Annual.

Thomas, John R. "Soviet Foreign Policy and Conflict Within Political and Military Leadership." Paper for the US Department of Defense, RAC-P-61, Sept. 1970.

Tucker, Robert C. "The Emergence of Stalin's Foreign Policy," *Slavic Review,* Dec. 1977.

Tucker, Robert. *The Lenin Anthology.* New York: W. W. Norton and Co., 1975.

Turantajew, W. W. "Die Gruppe der sowjetischen Streitkräfte in Deutschland beim Schutz der Westgrenze des sozialistischen Lagers." *Militärgeschichte,* 1 (1969).

Tyushkevich, S. A. *The Soviet Armed Forces: A History of Their Organizational Development,* translated by CSIS Multilingual Section, Secretary of State, Canada. Washington, DC: US Govt. Printing Office, 1978.

Ulrich, R. P., "Die deutsch–sowjetischen Beziehungen 1917–1932 im Spiegel sowjetischer Dissertationen." *Ostbrief,* Lüneburg, 6.

Urban, Mark. "Red Flag Over Germany." *Armed Forces,* Mar. 1985.

Vale, Michel and Steinke, Rudolf, eds. *Germany Debates Defense: NATO at the Crossroads.* Armonk, NY: M. E. Sharpe, 1983.

Valenta, Butler, Shannon, "East German Security Policies in Africa." *Eastern Europe and the Third World.* New York: Praeger, 1981.

Venohr, Wolfgang. *Preussische Portraits.* Hamburg: Christian Wegner, 1969.

Vigor, P. H. *Soviet Blitzkrieg Theory.* New York: St Martin's Press, 1977.

Viktoria Louise, Herzogin. *Im Strom der Zeit.* Göttingen-Hannover: Göttinger Verlaganstalt, 1974.

Volgyes, Ivan. "Troubled Friendship or Mutual Dependence? Eastern Europe and the USSR in the Gorbachev Era." *ORBIS,* Summer 1986.

Wagner, D. "Organisation, Auftrag und militärischer Stellenwert der Kampfgruppen der Arbeiterklasse in der DDR." *Europäische Wehrkunde,* July 1981.

Waldman, E. "The Other Side of the Hill II: The Military Policy of an Archetypal Soviet Satellite, the German Democratic Republic." *Canadian Defence Quarterly,* 5, 4 (Spring 1976).

Walter, Christian. "Warum östliche Armeen ein westliches Feindbild brauchen." *Europäische Wehrkunde*, Sept. 1984.

Weidenfeld, Werner, ed. *Die Identität der Deutschen*. Darmstadt: Carl Hanser, 1983.

Weinreich, Paul. "Solidarnosc provoziert Chaos und Anarchie." *Neues Deutschland*, 3 Feb. 1981.

Wettig, Gerhard. *Community and Conflict in the Socialist Camp: The Soviet Union, East Germany and the German Problem 1965–1972*. New York: St Martin's Press, 1975.

Whaley, Barton, *Covert German Rearmament, 1919–1939: Deception and Misperception*. Frederick, Md.: University Publications of America, 1984.

Willerding, Klaus. "Zur Afrikapolitik der DDR." *Aussenpolitische Korrespondenz*, 38 (1978).

Winter, P. J. "Angst vor dem Polnischen Bazillus." *Deutschland Archiv*, Oct. 1981.

Wolf, Horst. "Zur Hilfe der Sowjetarmee bei der Entwicklung der Gefechtsausbildung der Landstreitkräfte der NVA." *Militärgeschichte*, 6 (1973).

Wolfe, Thomas. *Soviet Power and Europe, 1945–1970*. Baltimore, Md.: Johns Hopkins Press, 1970.

Wollstein, Guenther. "Preussen–Literatur zur Geschichte des Aufgehobenen Staates in 'Preussenjahr und in dessen Umfeld.' " *Militärgeschichtliche Mitteilungen*, 1 (1983).

Wozniuk, Vladimir, PhD dissertation, University of Virginia, May 1984.

Wright, Quincy. *A Study of War*. Chicago, Ill.: University of Chicago Press, 3rd edn, 1971.

Yearbook on International Communist Affairs. Stanford, Cal.: Hoover Institution. Annual.

Yurechko, John. "Command and Control for Coalitional Warfare: The Soviet Approach." *Signal*, Dec. 1985.

Ziemke, Earl F. "The Soviet Theory of Deep Operations." *Parameters*, 13, 2.

Zimmerman, Hartmut. "The GDR in the 1970s." *Problems of Communism*, Mar.–Apr. 1978.

Index

178 **Index**